The Political Economy of Interwar Foreign Investment

France was interwar Poland's main ally, and the biggest source of the country's foreign investment. The two roles were closely connected: Paris used its position in Warsaw to win preferential treatment for its firms, while Polish authorities depended on France to finance their modernization policies and military spending. The relationship's asymmetric character bred conflict, and in the 1930s dissenting voices compared French actions in Poland to imperialism and colonial expansion. This book untangles the complex mix of economics, policy, and politics in Franco–Polish relations. Based on government and company-level sources, it evaluates the part played by French capital in Poland and discovers the mechanisms ruling French FDI and public loans. Exploring case studies of specific sectors and themes, it asks questions about the modernizing potential of FDI, interwar economic imperialism, the workings of asymmetric investment, and the interactions between investments and politics. Understanding the unequal footing of Warsaw and Paris, it goes beyond imperialistic interpretations, and examines the leeway available to the weaker partner of the relationship. The book contributes to economic history of Central and Eastern Europe, and, more generally, to our understanding of the position of peripheral countries in the interwar global system.

Jerzy Łazor, PhD is an Assistant Professor at the Warsaw School of Economics, Poland, and a former research fellow at the Imre Kertész Kolleg in Jena, Germany. He writes on 20th-century economic and business history in Central and Eastern Europe, concentrating on capital flows and centre-periphery relations.

Routledge Explorations in Economic History
Edited by Lars Magnusson
Uppsala University, Sweden

The Real Estate Market in the Roman World
Edited by Marta García Morcillo and Cristina Rosillo-López

An Economic History of the First German Unification
State Formation and Economic Development in a European Perspective
Edited by Ulrich Pfister and Nikolaus Wolf

Inequality and Nutritional Transition in Economic History
Spain in the 19th–21st Centuries
Edited by Francisco J. Medina Albaladejo, José Miguel Martínez Carrión and Salvador Calatayud Giner

Property, Power and the Growth of Towns
Enterprise and Urban Development, 1100–1500
Catherine Casson and Mark Casson

The Age of Global Economic Crises
(1929–2022)
Edited by Juan Manuel Matés-Barco and María Vázquez-Fariñas

The Sustainability and Development of Ancient Economies
Analysis and Examples
Clement A. Tisdell and Serge Svizzero

The Economy of Classical Athens
Organization, Institutions and Society
Emmanouil M. L. Economou

The Political Economy of Interwar Foreign Investment
Economic Nationalism and French Capital in Poland, 1918–1939
Jerzy Łazor

For more information about this series, please visit: www.routledge.com/Routledge-Explorations-in-Economic-History/book-series/SE0347

The Political Economy of Interwar Foreign Investment

Economic Nationalism and French Capital in Poland, 1918–1939

Jerzy Łazor

Routledge
Taylor & Francis Group
LONDON AND NEW YORK

First published 2024
by Routledge
4 Park Square, Milton Park, Abingdon, Oxon OX14 4RN

and by Routledge
605 Third Avenue, New York, NY 10158

Routledge is an imprint of the Taylor & Francis Group, an informa business

British Library Cataloguing-in-Publication Data
A catalogue record for this book is available from the British Library

This work was supported by the National Science Centre, Poland grant no. 2018/31/D/HS3/00405.

ISBN: 978-1-032-45141-1 (hbk)
ISBN: 978-1-032-45143-5 (pbk)
ISBN: 978-1-003-37558-6 (ebk)

DOI: 10.4324/9781003375586

Typeset in Times New Roman
by SPi Technologies India Pvt Ltd (Straive)

To Ola and Helena

Contents

Illustration

Figures

Tables

Maps

Acknowledgements

Books and children seem to have one thing in common. They both take a village. Over the years, I discussed my work with dozens of people. The first push towards Central and Eastern European history came from the many stimulating conversations with Bogdan Murgescu and Stanislav Holubec during my stay at the Imre Kertész Kolleg in Jena. As I moved to early conceptualizations of the project, I received great comments from Bartosz Dziewanowski-Stefańczyk, Magdalena Góralska, Antoni Grabowski, and Kirył Zach. Later on, Antoni Grześczyk provided great research assistance, Bernard Bartet, Wojciech Chudzik, Jakub Jastrzębski, and Juliusz Zieliński helped me access archives and other documents, while Tomasz Panecki prepared the wonderful maps used in Chapters 3 and 4. I was also fortunate to get great feedback from participants of many conferences. Two stand out: the *4th Workshop on Business History in Central and Eastern Europe* in Venice, and *Anno 1922: Central Europe Between Old and New Order* in Jerusalem and Beer Sheva (both in 2022), as the discussions helped me rethink some theoretical problems.

I am also grateful to everyone who read parts of my research and offered comments: Anna Bąk, Maciej Jaworski, Dawid Keller, Cecylia Leszczyńska, Jacek Luszniewicz, Piotr Puchalski, Wojciech Morawski, colleagues from the Department of Economic and Social History at SGH Warsaw School of Economics, and the anonymous reviewers of the book proposal and articles I published along the way. A special thank you goes to Adam Rogoda, who not only helped me with most of the papers and grant proposals that went into this project, but also read the entire book. I am grateful for his ongoing support, stimulating discussions, and great comments. Any mistakes and problems with this work obviously are on me.

Much of the book was researched and written in archives and libraries: in Paris, Nantes, Warsaw, Łódź, Katowice, London, and Oxford. As always, I am grateful to the archivists and librarians whose work allows and facilitates my own. Sometimes, as in the Archives Diplomatiques in La Courneuve and in the Archives Departamentales in Nantes, it even included first aid necessitated by my clumsiness.

This project was made possible by financial support of the National Science Centre, Poland grant no. 2018/31/D/HS3/00405.

Last but not least, no-one helped me more than my family: my wife Ola, and, in her way, our daughter Helena, who was born in the closing years of work on this project. They brought joy and love into my life. Ola not only kept me sane, but also read crucial parts of the book and earlier articles, offering great comments. I dedicate the book to them both. And without Ola, as well as my mother, mother-in-law, and brother-in-law Kamil, I would not have been able to finish the manuscript on time. Thank you.

A note on language

This book uses one language to describe events at the junction of two others, and concerns an area where frequent border changes continue to confuse outside observers. For instance, during the interwar period, the city where most French oil companies were headquartered was known under the Polish name Lwów. Today, it is Ukrainian Lviv, yet when the French first invested in the region before World War I, it was Austrian Lemberg. And between Lwów and Lviv came Russian Lvov. To lessen the confusion, the book uses period names – all places in interwar Poland are named in Polish, as they were during the studied years, unless there is a widely-used English toponym. Unless otherwise noted, all translations in the book were done by the author.

List of acronyms and abbreviations

AAN	Archiwum Akt Nowych, Warsaw
AdN	Archives diplomatiques, Nantes
AdC	Archives diplomatiques, La Courneuve
APK	Archiwum Państwowe, Katowice
APŁ	Archiwum Państwowe, Łódź
BGK	Bank Gospodarstwa Krajowego
CAÉF	Centre des archives économiques et financières, Savigny-Le-Temple
CAW	Centralne Archiwum Wojskowe, Rembertów
CPC PL	Correspondance politique et commercial, 1918–1940, Pologne
DzU RP	Dziennik Ustaw Rzeczypospolitej Polskiej
FCK	French Consulate in Katowice
FEB	French Embassy in Berlin
FEW	French Embassy in Warsaw
FLW	French Legation in Warsaw
FO	Foreign Office
MAÉ	Ministère des Affaires étrangeres, the French Ministry of Foreign Affairs
MPiH	Ministerstwo Przemysłu i Handlu, the Polish Ministry of Industry and Trade
MRS	*Mały Rocznik Statystyczny*
MS	Ministerstwo Skarbu, the Polish Ministry of Treasury
MSZ	Ministerstwo Spraw Zagranicznych, the Polish Ministry of Foreign Affairs
PEP	Polish Embassy in Paris
PLP	Polish Legation in Paris
RISA	*Rocznik Informacyjny o Spółkach Akcyjnych*
RPPiH	*Rocznik Polskiego Przemysłu i Handlu*
RSRP	*Rocznik Statystyczny Rzeczypospolitej Polskiej*
TNA	The National Archives, Kew

1 Interwar Poland and French capital

Economic development in a hierarchical world

This book is about the failure of a semi-peripheral country to import foreign capital for development at a time of global economic disintegration. Poland – the country in question – tried to attract investment to stabilize its currency, rebuild its economy, and later bolster its industry. For much of the interwar period, it used the pre-war handbook of adopting the gold standard, importing capital, and protecting its market.[1] However, like other emerging economies in Central and Eastern Europe, it had to cope with a "hostile economic climate," limited export opportunities, and expensive capital imports.[2] Foreign investors became more risk-averse after the war, which saw many of their factories taken over, plundered, or (in the case of Soviet Russia) lost. This is why Warsaw tried to leverage its political connections with Paris to get money and attract private investors. Faced with reluctance in France and the collapse of the global economic order during the Great Depression, Poland found itself moving away from liberal economic tenets towards economic nationalism, with the introduction of exchange control and high import tariffs, and the expansion of state enterprise.

This is also a book about how French investment in interwar Poland – like all foreign investment – was at once an economic and a political phenomenon. France was Poland's most important ally and the biggest source of its foreign capital, and Paris used its dominant political position to win preferential treatment for French companies, secure access to Polish oil, exert control over the economy of its eastern ally, and pursue projects aimed at strengthening its security. This was part of Paris's wider economic and political push into Central and Eastern Europe. The Poles got loans to bolster their military and build the infrastructure central to the authorities' modernization programme, which also relied on attracting friendly foreign capital. The asymmetric relationship and the sometimes-ruthless actions of French factory owners bred Polish resentment, which the authorities used in domestic politics.

Finally, this is a book about the mechanisms of such asymmetric economic relationships. Both French and communist-era Polish researchers viewed their countries' relations through the lens of imperialism. However, this way of thinking focuses attention on France as the active side, transforming Poland into a passive object of policy. A competing interpretation revolves around the

DOI: 10.4324/9781003375586-1

emergence of economic nationalism in 1930s Poland, and its influence on foreign investment. While it appreciates the role of Warsaw, it loses explanatory power when dealing with French actions. Instead, in this book, I argue that we should view such cases as relationships between unequal partners in a hierarchical global economic order. Both sides pursued their own policies, with decisionmakers understanding the limitations brought by the other sides' attitudes. The outcomes of their contacts were to some degree determined by the asymmetric character of the relationship, but the scale of asymmetry changed in step with the political and economic context. Moreover, the two states were not monolithic. Both French and Polish actions were the result of networks of and entanglements between various state officials, political actors, and the owners of private companies. As Pieter Judson writes, "Region, locality, even the globe are all ultimately defined situationally by the actions, and potential for actions, of real people."[3]

This book represents economic history rooted in heterodox economic theory and based on the detailed study of sources, rather than on cliometric model building and regressions. This choice of "reasoned history" owes both to the studied topic, and to the author's convictions.[4] It fits the study of interwar investment, as the questions I ask do not easily yield to numbers and statistics, and interwar data for Poland are often questionable. Even believers in cliometrics end up admitting the existence of "black boxes" of politics, with bearing on economic decisions and outcomes.[5] Understanding capital flows, the decision process behind them, and the influence of such asymmetric relationships on qualitative industrial development requires looking into the story of specific investments and analyzing specific negotiations.[6] I am thus happy to build on quantitative results – but I prefer working with primary sources, and studying the interrelatedness of economic and political phenomena.

In my research of French investment in Poland as part of Central and Eastern Europe, I am inspired by recent works on Polish history, which interpret it through a global lens, and thus help escape "methodological nationality."[7] This literature underlines the country's semi-peripheral, "in-between" position. Neither a great power, nor a colony, it functioned as an intermediate space.[8] As Kathryn Ciancia recently showed, the Poles were well aware of their place in the world, and were consciously pursuing policies "that reflected an ongoing repositioning on global civilizational scales."[9] In this book, I argue that such attempts at repositioning also extended to the economic sphere. Poland's elites had ambitions to move up the global economic, political, and prestige hierarchies, yet were afraid of succumbing to more powerful players.[10] Warsaw's failure to leverage foreign capital for development was also a failure to change the country's place in the global hierarchy.

1.1 The political and economic ties between Poland and France

Poland, returned to the political map in 1918 after over a century of foreign rule, was one of the poorest states in Europe, and among those most affected by World War I, with "some 90 per cent of Polish territory […] the scene of war operations at one point or another".[11] Estimates of Gross Domestic Product per capita for its territories before the war place the future country ahead of only Albania, Bulgaria, Romania, and Serbia, and behind both Czechoslovakia and Hungary. The Historic Index of Human Development shows similar results. The country was predominantly agricultural, even in its most industrialized parts.[12]

The new country had no settled borders, yet as its territories grew, authorities in Warsaw had to contend with five systems of commercial law and currencies (more if you include money from Ukrainian East Galicia and various notes printed by local administrations) and stocks of weapons made by opposing sides of the Great War.[13] Austria-Hungary, Germany, and Russia, which had ruled over its territories since the late 18th century, fostered little connections between themselves.[14] The three parts of Poland were disjointed, with their economies and communications oriented towards St Petersburg, Berlin, and Vienna. As these connections collapsed, the country had to consolidate its economy into a new whole, and reintegrate it with the world. Dealing with the destruction caused by the war was another immediate problem, with a severe fall in agricultural and industrial production, food shortages, and widespread disease.

Faced with such challenges, the Poles needed money. The domestic banking sector, which had been the strongest in Russian Poland, had become greatly decapitalized, and remained weak until the end of the interwar period. Private investors likewise lacked the needed funds, and revival of economic activity was sluggish.[15] As a result, virtually all Polish governments viewed attracting foreign capital as a "fundamental condition of the country's reconstruction and development."[16] This was a continuation of pre-war policy, followed throughout Central and Eastern Europe. The region saw "marked presence of foreign capital in modern joint-stock companies," sometimes leading to "foreign dominated enclaves" with few connections to the rest of the economy.[17] Now, again, their governments strove to import capital.

Despite the risk involved in investing in new, often politically unstable countries, Central and Eastern Europe presented opportunities. Its political and economic weakness meant that Western investors could hope to win special treatment. As an American expert said in 1919, commenting on the position of the Baltics, "no use blinking the fact that these [...] countries must be exploited by someone."[18] Soon capital from the Entente powers moved in, making Central and Eastern Europe the third principal area of investment for the West, which continued to bring returns even during the Great Depression, when international trade collapsed.[19] As Derek Aldcroft argues,

> one must question whether the large capital inflow was in the best interests of the debtor countries. Borrowing from abroad was expensive, the proceeds were often used unproductively, and the rising servicing costs proved fatal once the flow of foreign capital ceased and economic conditions globally turned sour.[20]

As Polish representatives looked for sources of money, they counted on France, a major investor country, and Warsaw's close ally. With the revolution in Moscow, Paris had been looking for partners to replace Russia in the French geopolitical struggle against Germany. While they found welcome ears in Prague, Bucharest, and Belgrade, ultimately no relationship was more important than that with Warsaw.

Based on this relationship, the French afforded Warsaw significant loans and credits, from the 400 million francs promised in the alliance of 1921, to the 2.6 billion envisaged in the 1936 treaty of Rambouillet. While this was less than the Poles expected, and often came with arduous payback schemes, no comparable source of military funding was available.[21] French authorities also supported and facilitated the financing of the two largest infrastructural investments undertaken by Warsaw, and built by Franco–Polish consortia. The new commercial harbour in Gdynia soon overtook the Free City of Danzig as a major shipping hub, and the Coal Trunk Railway linked the port with Polish Upper Silesia. These works made Poland the most important foreign market for the beleaguered French civil engineering sector.[22]

Turning to FDI, the French likewise engaged a lot of capital in Poland. By 1930, its value amounted to about 1 billion Polish zloty or c. 109 million dollars, which made the French the largest foreign shareholder in the Polish economy. Including other forms of long-term investment, French holdings in Poland in 1930 amounted to some 1.4 billion francs germinal, or ten per cent of all such French investment abroad (17.5 per cent of holdings in Europe). For comparison, the more developed Czechoslovakia received less than half the amount of French FDI per head, despite also being Paris's ally.[23]

The two sides had different expectations for the relationship. For Warsaw, Paris was a traditional friend in Europe, with Polish memories shaped by the romanticized tales of the Poles' fight alongside Napoleon. The Poles assumed that political friendship would translate into significant economic help. The French remembered these events as well, but were more pragmatic. In one of the first documents concerning the new Poland's finances in December 1918, officials in Paris wondered whether they could get back some of Napoleon's loans to the short-lived Duchy of Warsaw.[24] The Poles were summarily disappointed by the relatively small scale of French investment, the difficulty of getting loans and credits from Paris, the high price Warsaw had to pay for what it did receive, and by what they saw as exploitative or illegal actions of French companies. Authorities in Paris used the political position in Poland, and the dearth of other sources of money in interwar Europe, to force the Poles to allot privileges to French firms and owners and to protect the latter from Polish authorities. As I explore in more detail in Chapter 2, they also interfered with the Polish legislative process, and used conditionality to continuously link outstanding issues in Franco–Polish relations with economic outcomes. Treasury Minister Leon Biliński observed that while "only France in all Europe truly loves us in the political sphere; in the economic field it loves itself more, and is nothing more than a merchant"[25] – hardly a praise considering the low prestige of commercial activity among Poland's interwar elites. As the Polish historian Maria Pasztor meticulously showed, the French were likewise quick to criticize the Poles and describe their attitudes as "childlike," or the result of the Polish "national character."[26] Behind these disagreements and judgements lay a deeper asymmetry. The Polish historian Józef Kukułka wrote: "French authorities repeatedly suggested that true equality in the Franco–Polish alliance was impossible. Poland was, after all, too weak, and needed constant advice and help from the stronger partner."[27]

The Franco–Polish relationship evolved. As relations cooled after the Locarno treaties in 1925, and the Polish May coup in 1926, which brought Józef Piłsudski and his Sanacja movement to power, the decision makers in Warsaw were less likely to romanticize Paris. Moreover, French diplomats now pondered how to disassociate themselves from the alliance. By the early 1930s the relationship was reaching its nadir, and Warsaw pursued two major French-owned companies: a textile plant in Żyrardów, and the Warsaw power plant, leading to forced takeovers of both. Piłsudski's death in 1935, and the remilitarization of the Rhineland in the following year, resulted in rapprochement, which culminated in 1936 with the signing of the Rambouillet treaty, and another wave of French investment.

1.2 Conceptualizing the Franco–Polish relationship

Jonathan A. Grant in his recent book on the arms sector in the interwar period studied how the French giant Schneider took over Škoda in Czechoslovakia.[28] As he argued, neither the French banking and corporate perspective, adopted by Alice Teichova, nor the Czech point of view, seen in the research of Aleš Skřivan, fully explain the company's story. The first focused on how all the main decisions concerning the Plzeň company had been taken in Paris, the latter argued that since the Prague government was Škoda's main customer, it had a preponderant influence on the company's strategy. According to Grant, rather than a takeover, the relationship between Škoda and Schneider can more rightfully be seen as a corporate alliance, where multiple parties – including different factions within Škoda itself – influenced the outcome. "The combination of French and Czech control required a balancing of respective interests," even if the French government did not always appreciate the need for such a balancing.[29]

In this book, I argue that a similar rethinking is needed for French investment in Poland. Historians from the two countries – even if they sometimes spoke in unison – mostly posed different questions and framed their answers in different narratives.[30] The French saw their country's expansion in Poland as a lone case of economic and diplomatic vitality during the age of Paris's relative interwar decline. For many Poles, it was a story of foreign control over their economy, and the high cost of Warsaw's economic and security policy. Members of both groups defined French expansion in Poland as imperialism, and most would likely agree with Cain's and Hopkins's definition of the term as "an incursion or attempted incursion, into the sovereignty of another state," no matter the form taken.[31] However, for one group the term described a mechanism of dominating others; for the other that of being dominated.

Looking at the Franco–Polish relationship through this lens means assigning roles to the two countries. France becomes the expansionist acting party, and Poland the victim, with its activities focused on resisting the stronger partner. Even the ultimate failure of Paris to dominate Central and Eastern Europe is explained by French factors. However, new detailed studies show that the story is not always true.[32] We see Polish authorities initiating and sometime leading the talks, or deftly ignoring agreements which they had signed, prosecuting French owners, or carefully controlling the role of foreign investors. Evidently, therefore, if Paris attempted to build an informal empire in Central and Eastern Europe, Warsaw was hardly a passive receiver of French actions, and pursued its own policy.[33]

The 1920s, when French policy appears more obviously imperialistic, were quite different than the next decade, which saw more forceful Polish reactions, with Warsaw less likely to listen to its Western ally. Historians have conceptualized Poland's approach in the 1930s as a form of economic nationalism. However, adopting this perspective – which explains the state of the Franco–Polish relationship with changes in Warsaw – allows little understanding of French policy at the time, or of the way in which the two countries' actions influenced each other.

What emerges from these discussions is a story of interrelatedness between investment and policy, irreducible to either French imperialism, or Polish economic policies and national politics. Like Grant in his story of Škoda, we need to consider both perspectives. In doing so, we will see governments in the two capitals engaging in a struggle with private capital, mediated through diplomatic agreements, legal systems, and the financial market. Intergovernmental relations, further complicated by a plurality of views within each country, and by industrialists competing with each other for foreign investment, are just an element in an asymmetric relationship between a core nation and a peripheral partner.[34]

A focus on complexity and interrelatedness protects from simple answers, but makes operationalization difficult. To counter this, I propose recasting the Franco–Polish relationship in terms of goals, tools, and results. Inspired by Jeffry A. Frieden's theoretical work on colonialism, I argue that relations between Paris and Warsaw were a particular case in the much wider issue of "the role of foreign investment in conflict between investing and receiving societies," which remained contentious both before and after World War I.[35]

In the economic sphere, Frieden suggests looking at property rights of investors, and the associated rents. From this point of view, as we will discuss in Chapters 2 and 3, French goals in Poland were indeed focused on protecting, guaranteeing or (if possible) increasing the profits of French companies, and on their ability to transfer money back home. At first, this was done through unequal treaties, yet as Warsaw's position hardened, French tools chiefly took the form of diplomatic interventions concerning specific cases. The Poles, on the other hand, had to choose between two goals which where opposed to each other: increasing foreign investment, and limiting the transfer of profits of foreign-owned companies. By the 1930s, this led Warsaw to conflict with French firms, including the linen factory in Żyrardów (which will be discussed in Chapter 7), and to regulating the two principal sectors with French investment (Chapter 5).

Nonetheless, a look at older interpretations is still worthwhile, as they suggest questions and contexts to pursue. Let us start with imperialism. Here, George-Henri Soutou proposed the principal French narrative, in which his country's economic expansion in Central and Eastern Europe was an untypical form of imperialism – one based not on private initiative, but on state policy. The latter included government pressure on private companies to engage in the east, and strong-arming the Poles into granting the French economic concessions, accepting asymmetric treaties, and giving privileged treatment to French companies. Soutou called it "imperialism of the poor," since without capital, drained by the Great War, post-war reconstruction, and inflation, the French resorted to politics rather than economic might to foster expansion.[36] Mylène Mihout-Natar confirmed this interpretation in her work on investment in Poland, adding that such policy, which she called simply "economic imperialism," mostly affected sectors important to French security (oil extraction, military production, or Polish infrastructure).[37]

Challenging Soutou's interpretation, Philippe Marguerat proposed a new reading of French policy in the Danubian states.[38] Looking beyond a few government-sponsored projects, he showed that while the French state had an interest in supporting the expansion of French capital, much of it occurred due to private initiative, sometimes without the knowledge of the authorities. The large scale of takeovers in the Danubian Basin, he argued, also undermined the "poor" component of Soutou's interpretation. Moreover, these investments were aimed at the long-term rather than at short-term profits we might otherwise expect from investors strapped on cash. Marguerat explained this development with a change in the functioning of Paris's financial markets. Before the war, the system was with the purchasing of foreign rents with private savings mediated by banks. After 1918 this mechanism stopped due to the scarcity of funds, a crucial component of Soutou's thesis. In a new development, however, now the banks cooperated with industrial companies to pursue takeovers abroad, especially in the first years after the war. Marguerat argued that these banks were hardly weak, nor were they excessively burdened by capital export controls.

Extending Marguerat's argument to Poland would mean rejecting Soutou's thesis, and thus the special character of French expansion in Central and Eastern Europe in the interwar period. I would not commit to such an argument: as we will see, there are ample examples of the French authorities' direct activities in Poland. Nonetheless, even accepting Marguerat's position would not entail removing political factors from French expansion – but merely removing some of the focus from them. Both interpretations push us to consider the changing relationship between the political and economic spheres, as well as the differences in interests of the French government and firms. Moreover, it is important to underline that both French policy, and the dynamic between public and private forces changed throughout the 1920s.[39]

For Polish researchers, the word imperialistic was (and continues to be) politically loaded, as it had been extensively used during the Stalinist period, when history was a tool of forceful propaganda. Authors from these years, such as Franciszek Ryszka, saw the French as imperialistic in the Leninist sense, with great financial capital monopolizing the world economy. In this vision, the Polish authorities and owners were traitors, as they allowed foreigners into the country, and the French government was subservient to big capital.[40]

After the thaw in 1956, a new generation of researchers led by Zbigniew Landau and Jerzy Tomaszewski distanced themselves from the language used in the previous period, even if their interpretations were not drastically different. The authors were still critical of foreign "anonymous masters" (as they titled one of their books on the topic), exploiting Poland and acting against the country's interests. They considered foreign capital to be among the principal factors influencing interwar Poland's poor economic results.[41] Talking specifically about France and Poland, Landau and Tomaszewski pointed to exceptional levels of exploitation and control, for which they blamed both Warsaw and Paris. The former was guilty of policy mistakes or corruption, the latter of predatory actions. Their theses were generally confirmed by researchers working on Franco–Polish relations, such as Jan Ciałowicz and Józef Kukułka, who seemed to channel much of the interwar anger at France.[42] Recently, Anna Ambrochowicz-Gajownik (admittedly without any theoretical reflection) suggested that France had treated Poland as a "semi-colony."[43]

Differently to Soutou, Landau and Tomaszewski emphasized the dominant role of private initiative in French expansion. However, unlike Marguerat, they argued that financial capital dictated political decisions in Paris. This brought them close to Hobson's definition of imperialism as "the use of the machinery of government by private interests…to secure for them economic gains outside their country."[44] Such views, sometimes not stated explicitly, continued to influence interpretations of international scholars, who sought sources from both countries. Neither Piotr Wandycz nor Alice Teichova used the term imperialism, but their way of framing French investment in Poland was close to Landau's and Tomaszewski's.[45] This interpretation remains current today. When Máté Rigó recently wrote about French expansion in Central and Eastern Europe, he focused on the influence of private capital on the French government, calling the result a French "Empire," with the word in quotation marks.[46]

The Polish interpretation was part of a wider discussion on the origins of the country's, and much of Eastern Europe's, economic backwardness. Leading Polish historians after 1945, such as Marian Małowist and Witold Kula, argued that the region's woes had been directly caused by its relationship with the developing West, with Poland evolving into a quasi-colony of its more dynamic neighbours. This approach, which finds parallels in the works of researchers dealing with other countries of the region, inspired Immanuel Wallerstein's monumental reinterpretation of global economic history, to which I will return later in this chapter.[47]

Let us now turn to economic nationalism, a political and economic ideology based on the rejection of free exchange between poorer and richer countries, a "structurally determined response of the underdeveloped economies and societies to crisis and to the very fact of their underdevelopment," generally of a defensive nature.[48] It was a variation on Friedrich List's work, interpreted through a nationalist lens. List, a leading member of the early German historical school, argued against the use of economic liberalism by poor countries. According to him, liberalism had worked for Great Britain, and was a good fit for other rich states, but developmental latecomers had to protect their markets and support budding industries or risk losing them. Before World War I, some Central and Eastern European countries, such as Romania, Serbia, or Hungary, adopted an early, "liberal" variant of economic nationalism. It combined protectionism, and using the proceeds from agricultural exports and foreign loans for modernization. Long-term, these policies were fairly successful, as the region managed to grow faster than the Western core, yet they did not produce an economic take-off.[49]

Polish economic policy in the 1920s roughly corresponded with this "liberal" version of economic nationalism, although much of the authorities' focus was on reconstruction and economic integration of the state, rather than on industrialization. Nonetheless, high tariffs protected the market, the government hoped to attract foreign capital, and took part in setting up factories (almost exclusively in the defence sector). Its share in the economy also continued to grow, even in the periods of ostensibly liberal policy.[50] It was also obvious to the subsequent ministers and economic commentators that a country's wealth depended on engaging with the world market.[51]

However, as I mentioned, the post-war economic landscape had little in common with that of the Belle Époque. Central and Eastern Europe had to cope with the consequences of imperial collapse, and the disappearance of the Russian market. Its governments had to tackle rising protectionism, the shrinking of global trade, and the collapse of the gold standard during the Great Depression.[52] In the realm of politics, new countries emerged with robust nationalist ideologies, strengthened by long conflicts concerning post-war borders. Authoritarian regimes, which increasingly controlled the states of the region, used these exclusionary doctrines to buttress their power.

By the end of the 1930s, the new context resulted in the emergence of a more comprehensive economic nationalism promoted by a new state technostructure, in Poland taking the form of the rising economic-military complex. Its chief theoretician in the region was the widely translated Romanian engineer-turned economist Mihail Manoilescu, often quoted in Polish discourse. His writings anticipated the post-war dependency theory in Latin America in understanding that trade between industrialized and agricultural countries was unequal. The resulting ideology broadly translated into a rejection of free trade and liberalism, and placed the nation state at the centre of the economy. In practice, this meant protectionism, strengthened by the wide adoption of exchange control, and interventionism, with Poland's Central Industrial Basin and government development plans as the most radical examples of the trend. Increasingly, this ideology pushed countries towards "independent industrialization," with exports treated as a means to finance critical imports, rather than as a vehicle for development. The goal was economic independence, with economic nationalism an "essential element" for the region's authoritarian regimes.[53]

The consequences of economic nationalism for foreign investment were nuanced. There was little theory to influence policy in the interwar period. Polish attitudes, especially regarding foreign capital, were shaped by reactions to successive problems, rather than by a premeditated programme. As in other countries, economic nationalism never took a "clearly defined and logical shape forming a coherent whole."[54] Underdeveloped states still needed capital to finance their policies, especially if they embarked on ambitious programmes of state-led modernization. While proponents of economic nationalism in interwar Poland aimed to limit imports of goods, they were willing to accept capital imports. However, they showed a dislike for foreign capitalists, and often did not appreciate the "contradiction between the desire to industrialize, build up an industry, for which you often need to attract foreign investors, and the desire to nationalize industry, enlarging the share of local capitalists at the expense of foreign investors."[55] More generally, the "ideology of nationalism subordinated economic interests to the prestige of national strength" – which we can easily see in Franco–Polish conflicts in the mid-to-late 1930s – pushing the "public mood to the right."[56]

Was there a direct connection between French imperialism and the emergence of economic nationalism in Poland? Not really. This nationalism was an outgrowth of its political analogue, and emerged in reaction to Poland's economic and international position, of which its relationship with France was but one facet. Nonetheless, as I mentioned, Warsaw's policy grew organically rather than deliberately. As major conflicts surrounding French companies like the Żyrardów textile factory, or the Warsaw power plant, festered for years, their owners found themselves at the locus of policy change in 1934. Warsaw took radical steps, ending in the nationalization of the two companies. In this context, new Polish attitudes towards foreign capital finally coalesced.

1.3 Development, foreign capital, and policy

International economic relations are hierarchical, and "worrying about development means worrying about your place in the hierarchy," with a country's situation both determined by the past strength of its economy, and influencing its future strength.[57] At the top are rich countries forming the core, which dominate over poorer peripheries. The concepts of core and periphery – originating in the dependency theory from Latin America – were used most influentially by the sociologist and historian Immanuel Wallerstein. He argued that the disparity between the two groups came from differences in production. The most developed states have a monopoly on the production of successive leading products, which give extraordinary profits. These profits in turn allow the accumulation of capital, translating into riches and power. Poor countries import such products while exporting resources and other, less profitable goods.[58] However, Wallerstein did not adequately explain the economic mechanism of the core's monopoly on leading products. To this, we need to turn to the effects of scale, technology, and their relationship with different types of goods.

Markets tend towards concentration.[59] One of the principal reasons behind this are the effects of scale, which appear when production requires significant initial investment, such as the development of new technologies or the construction of new factories. Producing the first lathe or computer graphics card is expensive, but with each subsequent unit the average cost of production goes down. As a result, the more units produced, the lower their cost. Smaller players are thus unable to compete with bigger firms.[60] A few producers dictate prices, and profit handsomely.

The greatest profits occur in the production of technologically advanced products, historically manufactured in core countries. These are Wallerstein's leading products. Successful innovation requires significant spending on R&D, a skilled workforce, and a deep market. Core countries possess these three factors, and so in the 20th century they have produced cars, planes, or computers when these were leading products. Occupying these niches and earning extraordinary profits promoted a wider environment supporting development.[61]

Products do not always stay new. While changes in the textile industry kick-started the Industrial Revolution, today such production has been relocated to countries of the Global South. To explain these changes, Raymond Vernon and Louis T. Wells proposed the product life cycle theory.[62] They argued that with time a product matures, and its design and features stabilize. Production becomes more efficient, and no longer requires highly skilled specialists. The price drops, allowing consumers from poorer countries to purchase the product. Manufacturing also partially moves to these countries. The next phase comes with full standardization. No new improvement of the product is likely at the existing technological level. Competing products become similar, and the main difference is price. As a result, their production moves to the peripheries, where labour is cheap and capital scarce. Despite the effects of scale, ample competition translates into a lack of extraordinary profits. This phase thus has limited impact on economic development. The same is true for sectors based on natural resources (such as mining or agriculture), which suffer from diminishing returns. This does not mean that countries exporting resources necessarily stay poor – history shows that the opposite is true – but rather than such states should at some point turn to industrialization, allowing extraordinary profits.[63]

How does the product life cycle work with history? Since the 18th century, economic processes have changed through a series of revolutions bringing new techno-economic paradigms.[64] The Venezuelan economist Carlota Perez argued that certain key technologies make existing production methods obsolete and create markets for new products. For instance, electricity brought communication technologies, electro-chemistry, and electric engines, paving the way for a plethora of new products, from wireless telegraphs, to lightbulbs, power tools, or aluminium foil. These goods did not come about through the gradual improvement of production lines, but from entirely new ones. The same wave of technological change also brought giant cartels and vertical integration–a new "common sense" approach to business. New technologies were dangerous to established companies, shifting the life cycle of entire product bundles. Within the "fast growth constellation" of a new paradigm, new opportunities rose to make extraordinary profits, incentivizing financial capital to invest. The transition between techno-economic paradigms is gradual, even if it results in revolutionary change. It starts with the discovery of new technologies which slowly appear in the economy, at first in the most innovative industries. As old production stagnates, new industrial processes grow fast, and take its place.[65] By the time the revolution is in full swing, new technologies dominate the leading industries in advanced nations.

The theory of techno-economic paradigms, along with its descriptive elaboration presented in Table 1.1, provides a set of stylized facts on the interwar period. It was a time of transition. The steel mills of the late 19th century still blazed, and early power plants churned out electricity, carried on power lines which reached ever more homes, as an increasing number of cars, many of them mass-produced, drove along another new invention: the highway. From the first civilian airports small planes took off, shortening the travel of letters and the rich. In a growing number of houses families congregated around the radio, while in universities and labs the foundations for early computers took shape.

These stylized facts afford a powerful way to analyze the structure of French investment, and understand its role in Poland's economy in the period. Development–a qualitative change in a country's production structure resulting in a better position in the global division of labour–must entail shifting towards leading products. Thus an increase in French activities in the textile industry will have little impact on Polish development. On the other hand, attempts to build automobiles, aeroplanes, or synthetic materials – the fast growth products of the era – will signify a more positive impact of French investment.

Using these tools to analyze French investment in Poland leaves us with little positive to say, as we will discuss more broadly in Chapter 3. Most of the capital engaged in Poland belonged squarely in the previous economic paradigms, dating to before World War I, and much of the new money put into the country after the war represented brownfield investment. The few rare modern investments were often not successful, and French engagement in the automobile industry was clearly detrimental to Polish interests (Chapter 4). These

Table 1.1 Technological revolutions and techno-economic paradigms (Carlota Perez)

Technological revolution	*New technologies and new or redefined industries*	*New or redefined infrastructures*	*Techno-economic paradigm. "Common sense" innovation principles*
Second Industrial Revolution, 1880–1940	Cheap steel Full development of steam engine for steel ships Heavy chemistry and civil engineering Electrical equipment industry Copper and cables Canned and bottled food Paper and packaging	Worldwide shipping in rapid steel steamships Worldwide railways Great bridges and tunnels Worldwide telegraph Telephone Electrical networks	Giant structures Economies of scale of plant/vertical integration Distributed power for industry Science as a productive force Worldwide networks and empires Universal standardization Cost accounting for control and efficiency Great scale for world market power/"small" is successful if local
Mass production, 1930–1990	Mass-produced automobiles Cheap oil and oil fuels Petrochemicals Internal combustion engine for automobiles, transport, tractors, aeroplanes, war tanks, and electricity Home electrical appliances Refrigerated and frozen foods	Networks of roads, highways, ports, and airports Networks of oil ducts Universal electricity Worldwide analogue telecommunications	Mass production/mass markets Economies of scale/horizontal integration Standardization of products Energy intensity Synthetic materials Functional specialization/hierarchical pyramids Centralization/metropolitan centres–suburbanization National powers, world agreements and confrontations

Sources: Perez, *Technological Revolutions*, 11, 14, 18.

results confirm the theses of Landau and Tomaszewski about the impact of French capital on Poland, and undermine the more positive French interpretations, such as that of Christophe Laforest, who argued that his country's imperialism was relatively benevolent and brought development to Warsaw.[66]

Turning to Polish policy, let us start by looking at the country's place in the global economic hierarchy. Within Europe, it belonged to peripheral states – to "Europe's Third World" – selling mainly resources, with GDP per capita at about half the level of Western Europe, significant surplus population in agriculture, and fast population growth.[67] In 1928, coal and wood accounted for 40 per cent of Polish exports, the majority of the population worked in agriculture, lived in the countryside, and took little part in commercial activity.[68] Even in its best year (1929), Polish expenses on capital formation amounted to some

8 per cent of the national income, and throughout the period averaged 5–6 per cent. These were typical results for Central and Eastern Europe, and lower than in the Western part of the continent.[69] The situation became even worse during the Great Depression. It hit Poland particularly hard, with one of the greatest global falls of industrial production, and slow recovery. The national market was shallow, which limited the demand for new products, and thus the chance of competition with other countries. The lack of an extensive agrarian reform to counter Poland's antiquated economic structure was another problem.[70] Moreover, the country did not undergo a meaningful industrial transformation in the interwar period. If in 1910 the future state's industrial potential per capita reached a third of Great Britain's result, by 1937 the ratio decreased to one-seventh.[71] As in the rest of the region, "Industrial progress did not lead to any great structural transformation."[72]

The picture becomes less obvious if we zoom out and look at Poland in a global context. Now its archipelagic modernity stands out more: the islands of industry in Warsaw, Łódź, Upper Silesia, the Central Industrial Basin, its millions of radio listeners, experimental TV, and award-winning planes.[73] These results are far from the scale of development in core countries, but they are also different from what was happening in resource-producing colonies. From the point of view of the latter, Poland with its industry, functioning railways, modern ports, and decent universities, could be Western Europe's poorer cousin.

Immanuel Wallerstein called such states part of the semi-peripheries, with production combining features of both the core, and the periphery. They were under constant economic pressure from richer countries, while at the same time trying to exert such pressure on poorer ones. When we consider the product life cycle theory, semi-peripheral countries produce standardized and mature products, the latter readily taken up by such states in their pursuit of the core. We should also expect attempts to develop new technologies, especially led by the state. Wallerstein argued that the important role played by authorities in the economies of such countries is a typical element of their development.[74]

If a country's position in the global hierarchy depends on production, itself a function and cause of wealth, then improving it must necessarily be difficult, and "does not happen 'naturally'".[75] It is not enough to increase a country's output. A move up the global division of labour is needed, based on a profound change in the technological and economic capacity. Such a move is possible, as evidenced by the rise of Germany or Western offshoots in the 19th century, or Japan, Korea, Taiwan, and China in the 20th. It requires careful state policies and a well-functioning bureaucracy guiding industrial transformation.[76] Industrialization is not a one-size-fits-all process, with the required policy depending on both the country's endowments and on the moment when it is undertaken. Latecomers need to take a different approach than early industrialized states.[77] Nonetheless, some elements remain constant, namely "interventionist industrial, trade, and technology policies,"[78] aimed at "ways to participate in 'leading' sectors and shed 'lagging' ones."[79]

Such policy translates into attempts to foster domestic entrepreneurs, steer them into the authorities' sectors of choice, then gradually expose them to the world market. Steering means such targeted policies as government orders, facilitating access to capital, a "greenhouse" of protective tariffs (infant industry protection), and export subsidies.[80] Domestic firms also need to "learn how to learn," to allow the adoption and integration of new technologies, also through spillovers.[81] Peter Evans conceptualized these actions as the state taking on the roles he called "midwifery" and "husbandry"–bringing new entrepreneurship into the economy and fostering its development.[82]

To develop, poorer countries need capital and expensive technology. The state needs to become "implicated in the process of capital accumulation," moulding the shape it ultimately takes.[83] One possibility available to authorities is the use of foreign capital in the process.

Mainstream economics points to multi-layered positive consequences of foreign investment, ranging from the most direct increase in productive capacity, to more indirect spillover effects (through technology and know-how sharing and the spread of novel managerial techniques). Moreover, investors' choice of particularly promising acquisitions might increase the competitiveness of the economy, while their threat to pull out might affect a country's institutional make-up. Such benefits are more likely to come from foreign direct investments or FDI (the purchase of stakes over ten per cent), while loans and equity investments (up to ten per cent) are more volatile and pro-cyclical.

These arguments are difficult to reconcile with the production-based global economic hierarchy which we discussed. Foreign investors are unlikely to export frontier technologies and move cutting-edge production to undeveloped countries, which lack adequate infrastructure and a highly skilled workforce. It is likely that investors in poorer countries might use old technologies, focus on the domestic market, and transfer profits abroad (through transfer prices and other forms of window dressing), with little further reinvestment into the host economy.[84] This is particularly true if FDI takes the form of brownfield investment, merely transferring the ownership of a company to foreign owners. Moreover, spillover effects remain difficult to quantify, while institutional arguments are dubious. Between the profit motive of companies, and the underdeveloped institutions in poorer states, investment might lead to institutional capture. When it comes to loans, countries of the periphery pay higher interest than the core, and are less likely to service their debt easily.

With potential benefits and dangers, the way foreign capital impacts each economy depends on domestic economic policy. Today, mainstream economics argues for a permissive approach to foreign investment, and little intervention in the investment process. However, heterodox approaches and historical experience of countries which are rich today (such as the US, Japan, or Finland), suggest more active policy.

Specifically, regulations need to "maximize technology spillover,"[85] and induce, "transnational capital to make deeper commitment to local development."[86] In practice, this might mean

> requirements of joint-ventures, which increases the chance of technology transfer to the local partner; explicit conditions concerning technology transfer; local contents requirements, which forces the TNC [transnational corporation] to transfer some technology to the supplier; and exports requirements which force the TNC to use up to date technology in order to be competitive in the world market.[87]

We can also imagine policy aiming to increase the number of local specialists working for foreign-owned companies.

On the other hand, Ha-Joon Chang argues that "foreign investment is not going to be the key element in most countries' growth mechanisms." Institutions need to stimulate domestic entrepreneurial forces instead of inducing foreign investment, which is likely to follow development, rather than the other way around.[88] This put interwar Poland, with its attempts to attract foreign investors as a crucial part of its development strategy, in a difficult position. As we will see in the following chapters, Warsaw tried to mitigate the dangers, not always unsuccessfully, by resorting to its limited political and diplomatic resources, and by building domestic support for economic nationalism.

1.4 The structure and outline of this book

The rest of the book is divided into six chapters. Chapters 2 and 3 offer a bird's-eye view of French capital in Poland, while Chapters 4–7 focus on detailed studies of key sectors or companies.

In Chapter 2, I explore French investments in Poland from the point of view of the two governments. This means looking at the goals and the instruments used to pursue them by Paris and Warsaw, and the mechanisms of their interactions. I argue that security considerations were the most important factor for both partners, affecting what projects they supported, and how they interacted with private companies. The focus on security in Paris meant that the Poles could count on limited help in purely economic matters. Nonetheless, the little help the French did offer, allowed Paris to pressure Warsaw into significant concessions. This was done primarily through the relentless use of conditionality. As a result, Paris's actions were the most effective when Poland was at its weakest in the early 1920s, and increasingly lost their edge. Beyond corralling French companies, the government in Paris most commonly worked through loans and credits. These, however, were mostly earmarked for military purposes, and their impact on Polish development was detrimental due to high servicing costs.

In Chapter 3, I look at the position of French-owned private companies in Poland. I argue that despite seemingly major investment in the early 1920s, the value of French holdings changed relatively little between 1914 and 1930, as much of the money went into post-war reconstruction, or overvalued projects in the oil sector. Moreover, these investments had a limited influence on Poland's development, with few greenfield projects, and most of the capital placed in 19th-century technology. Turning to financial results, I show that French companies performed better than their competitors when the economy was doing well, and significantly worse during the Great Depression. I explain this with their sectoral structure, as the sectors with important French presence were hit particularly hard by the Depression. I end this chapter by turning to the political economy of these companies. I argue that the extensive privileges which the French obtained ultimately had little influence on their results, as the economic reality of most of the interwar period made these benefits of limited practical importance. Nonetheless, the political backing of Paris served as a powerful deterrent to government takeovers (with few companies ending under the growing umbrella of the Polish state sector), and helped firms in their conflicts with the authorities.

With Chapter 4 I begin my closer inspection of specific investments, starting with the role of French capital in the Polish state's development projects. I focus on sectors with significant modernization potential: infrastructure crucial for Polish exports, and interwar high-tech – cars and aviation. I argue that the Franco–Polish asymmetric relationship had a significant if mixed influence on the studied projects. In the case of infrastructure, France's role was mostly positive, as Paris authorities considered such projects important to French security. Nonetheless, the direct engagement of the Quai d'Orsay and the French army meant that the projects remained under close scrutiny, and proved relatively expensive to the Poles. The impact of French investment in high-tech production was largely negative. The Poles attempted to use foreign capital to quickly create automobile and aviation manufacturing, using well-chosen tools of industrial policy. The French were able to torpedo competing offers coming from other countries, delay the process of choosing contractors, and later failed to start production. The one exception in the form of Škoda's successful investment was cut short by rising Polish economic nationalism, resulting in a government takeover of the factory.

Chapter 5 discusses the performance of the Polish state as a regulator in two sectors with a large presence of French capital: oil and coal. I show that the significant support these producers enjoyed from the French state, which took the most visible form in the oil treaty from 1922, proved of little importance due to the difficult position of Polish coal and oil production. In both sectors, producers were forced to export due to limited domestic demand. In both sectors, they resorted to dumping. In coal production, because of its importance to Poland's balance of payments, producers could count on significant government help, but in the oil sector no comparable aid was forthcoming. The need to export at low prices resulted in conflicts among producers, causing the Polish state to regulate the sectors through mandated, ministry-controlled cartels. Ultimately, these major French investments held little practical value for development, but Poland was able to mitigate some of their negative impact in the 1930s.

Chapter 6 is about the influence of politics on the functioning of private-public enterprises. It focuses on mixed companies in Upper Silesia combining French private capital and Polish government control. I argue that their story does not easily conform to imperialistic interpretations of French actions in Poland. Instead, we see the Poles initiating negotiations, winning some of them, and ignoring the results of others. I then move to a systematic analysis of the functioning of mixed companies, showing how their political structure undermined their economic performance. Moreover, the private-public ownership of the companies presented corruption opportunities, and facilitated excessive lobbying and rent-seeking by political actors.

In Chapter 7 I explore how foreign capital can function in and affect domestic politics. I also analyze the limits of governmental intervention in an asymmetric relationship within a global hierarchical economy. I do so by studying the Żyrardów Affair, the biggest economic conflict between France and Poland. It concerned a large linen plant near Warsaw, bought by the French after World War I. The Poles accused the new owners of labour exploitation and tax fraud. I show that the position of the company depended on the state of Franco–Polish relations, and its financial results cannot be read without considering politics. Moreover, while Paris consistently focused on protecting the French owners' property rights and the ability to transfer profits home, Warsaw used the company within changing domestic conflicts. In particular, in 1934 the authorities hoped to profit from the affair to unify the reading public behind an economic nationalist message. Within the scope of the conflict, which culminated in a forced takeover, officials in Warsaw redefined the rights and obligations of foreign investors in moral terms.

Notes

1 Thomas David, *Nationalisme économique et industrialisation: l'expérience des pays d'Europe de l'Est (1789–1939)* (Genève: Librairie Droz, 2009).

2 Derek H. Aldcroft, *Europe's Third World: The European Periphery in the Interwar Years*, (Aldershot and Burlington: Ashgate Publishing, 2006), 16; Harold James, *The End of Globalization: Lessons from the Great Depression* (Cambridge, MA and London: Harvard University Press, 2002).

3 Pieter M. Judson, "Seeing the Habsburg Monarchy as a Global Empire in an Age of Self-Styled Nation-States," *Geschichte Und Region/Storia e Regione* 30, no. 1 (2021): 223–29; 225. Cf. Robert D. Putnam, "Diplomacy and Domestic Politics: The Logic of Two-Level Games," *International Organization* 42, no. 3 (1988): 427–60; Mark S. Granovetter, *Society and Economy: Framework and Principles* (Cambridge, MA and London: The Belknap Press of Harvard University Press, 2017).

4 Cf. Chris Freeman and Francisco Louçã, *As Time Goes By: From the Industrial Revolutions to the Information Revolution* (Oxford: Oxford University Press, 2001), 123–30.

5 Nikolaus Wolf, "Should I Stay or Should I Go? Understanding Poland's Adherence to Gold, 1928–1936," *Historical Social Research* 32, no. 4 (2007): 351–68.

6 Francesco Boldizzoni, *The Poverty of Clio: Resurrecting Economic History* (Princeton: Princeton University Press, 2011).

7 Judson, "Seeing the Habsburg Monarchy."
8 Brian Porter-Szűcs, *Poland in the Modern World: Beyond Martyrdom* (Chichester: Wiley-Blackwell, 2014), 3. See also: Piotr Puchalski, *Poland in a Colonial World Order: Adjustments and Aspirations, 1918–1939* (London and New York: Routledge, 2022); Jerzy Łazor, "'A Colony of Alien Capital.' French Investments, Polish Identity, and a Story of Murder in 1930s Warsaw," *Slavic Review* 81, no. 1 (2022): 122–41, https://doi.org/10.1017/slr.2022.79.
9 Kathryn Ciancia, *On Civilization's Edge. A Polish Borderland in the Interwar World* (Oxford: Oxford University Press, 2020), 4.
10 See also: Tomasz Zarycki, *Ideologies of Eastness in Central and Eastern Europe* (London and New York: Routledge, 2014), Ch. 1.
11 Aldcroft, *Europe's Third World*, 108.
12 *Maddison Project Database, version 2020*. Jutta Bolt, and Jan Luiten van Zanden, "Maddison Style Estimates of the Evolution of the World Economy. A New 2020 Update," *Maddison-Project Working Paper* WP-15, 2020; Cf. Jerzy Łazor and Bogdan Murgescu, "Economic Development," in *The Routledge History Handbook of Central and Eastern Europe in the Twentieth Century: Challenges of Modernity*, ed. Stanislav Holubec, Władysław Borodziej, and Joachim von Puttkamer (London–New York: Routledge, 2020), 313–84, 321–26; Leandro Prados de la Escosura, "World Human Development: 1870–2007," *Review of Income and Wealth* 61, no. 2 (2015): 220–47. https://doi.org/10.1111/roiw.12104; Iván T. Berend, *History Derailed: Central and Eastern Europe in the Long Nineteenth Century* (Berkeley, CA: University of California Press, 2003), 179.
13 Robert Jastrzębski, "Prawo handlowe i gospodarcze," in *Prawo handlowe i gospodarcze II Rzeczypospolitej*, ed. Robert Jastrzębski (Warszawa: Wolters Kluwer Polska, 2019), 31; Wojciech Morawski, *Od marki do złotego. Historia finansów Drugiej Rzeczypospolitej* (Warszawa: Wydawnictwo Naukowe PWN, 2008), 53; Aldcroft, *Europe's Third World*, 109. Cf. Jochen Böhler, *Civil War in Central Europe, 1918–1921. Reconstruction of Poland* (Oxford: Oxford University Press, 2018).
14 Cf. Jawad Daheur, "Productive or Extractive Periphery? Russian Poland and Timber Exports to Germany in the Late Nineteenth and Early Twentieth Centuries," *Global Environment* 15, no. 1 (2022): 107–47, https://doi.org/10.3197/ge.2022.150105.
15 Bogdan Murgescu, "Economic Revival in East Central Europe after the Great War," in *A New Europe, 1918–1923: Instability, Innovation, Recovery*, ed. Bartosz Dziewanowski-Stefańczyk and Jay M. Winter (London and New York: Routledge, 2022), 69–81, 69–73.
16 Zbigniew Landau, "Foreign Capital in Poland 1918–1939," *Acta Poloniae Historica* 59 (1989): 58.
17 Aldcroft, *Europe's Third World*, 11–24.
18 Merja-Liisa Hinkkanen-Lievonen, "Exploited by Britain? The Problems of British Financial Presence in the Baltic States after the First World War," *Journal of Baltic Studies* 14, no. 4 (1983): 328–39, 328, https://doi.org/10.1080/01629778300000341.
19 Teichova, *An Economic Background*, 12–14.
20 Aldcroft, *Europe's Third World*, 53.
21 The total value of loans extended by the US in the interwar period was greater, mostly due to the 1927 stabilization loan, but they had no impact on the military and little to do with investment programmes (Landau and Tomaszewski, *Kapitały obce*).
22 Dominique Barjot, *La grande entreprise française de travaux publics (1883–1974)* (Paris: Economica, 2006).
23 Teichova, *An Economic Background*, 2; Jean-Claude Debeir, "Le problème des exportations de capitaux français de 1919 á 1930. Subsitutions et concurrences," *Relations internationales* 6 (1976): 171–82; Jean Baptiste Duroselle, *Politique*

étrangère de la France: la décadence, 1932–1939 (Paris: Éditions du Seuil, 1983), 224–28.

24 Archives Diplomatiques, La Courneuve [henceforth: AdC], Correspondance politique et commercial, 1918–1940, Pologne [henceforth: CPC PL], 234, Note pour les service des archives, 23 December 1918, 8.

25 Leon Biliński, *Wspomnienia i Dokumenty. Tom II, 1915–1922* (Warszawa: Księgarnia F. Hoesicka, 1925), 262.

26 Maria Pasztor, *Polska w oczach francuskich kół rządowych w latach 1924–1939* (Warszawa: Wydawnictwo Akademickie Dialog, 1999).

27 Józef Kukułka, *Francja a Polska po Traktacie Wersalskim: 1919–1922* (Warszawa: Książka i Wiedza, 1970), 576.

28 Jonathan A. Grant, *Between Depression and Disarmament: The International Armaments Business, 1919–1939* (Cambridge University Press, 2018), 24–51, https://doi.org/10.1017/9781108552721.

29 Ibid., 29, 51.

30 Cf. Jerzy Łazor, "Kapitał francuski w Polsce międzywojennej. Stan badań i postulaty badawcze," *UR Journal of Humanities and Social Sciences* 4, no. 1(10) (2019): 29–52, https://doi.org/10.15584/johass.2019.1.3. Cf. Anna Ambrochowicz-Gajownik, "Polsko-francuskie stosunki gospodarcze w okresie międzywojennym: nowe postulaty badawcze," *Przegląd Środkowo-Wschodni* 1 (2016): 182–211, https://doi.org/10.32612/uw.2543618X.2016.pp.182-211.

31 Peter J. Cain and Antony G. Hopkins, *British Imperialism, 1688–2015* (London and New York: Routledge, 2016), 59.

32 E.g. Zenon Szmidtke, *"Skarboferm" 1922–1939: związki polityki z gospodarką* (Opole: Państwowy Instytut Naukowy, 2005); Jerzy Łazor, "'Broń dyplomatyczna pierwszej rangi?' Powstanie polsko-francuskiego Banku Śląskiego SA po I wojnie światowej," *Roczniki Dziejów Społecznych i Gospodarczych* 81 (2020): 289–320, https://doi.org/10.12775/RDSG.2020.10; Jerzy Łazor, "Pierwsza francusko-polska koncesja kolejowa z 1924 r. Przyczynek do relacji finansowo-gospodarczych Polski i Francji po pierwszej wojnie światowej," *Kwartalnik Historyczny* 128, no. 3 (2021): 785–812, https://doi.org/10.12775/KH.2021.128.3.03.

33 David Mclean, "Finance and 'Informal Empire' Before the First World War," *The Economic History Review* 29, no. 2 (1976): 291–305; David Todd, *A Velvet Empire: French Informal Imperialism in the Nineteenth Century* (Princeton: Princeton University Press, 1978); Emily S. Rosenberg and Norman L. Rosenberg, "From Colonialism to Professionalism: The Public-Private Dynamic in United States Foreign Financial Advising, 1898–1929," *The Journal of American History* 74, no. 1 (1987): 59–82.

34 Teichova, *An Economic Background*, 380

35 Jeffry A. Frieden, "International Investment and Colonial Control: A New Interpretation," *International Organization* 48, no. 4 (1994): 559–93, 561, https://doi.org/10.1017/S0020818300028319. Cf. Rosenberg and Rosenberg, "From Colonialism."

36 Georges-Henri Soutou, "L'impérialisme du pauvre: la politique économique du gouvernement français en Europe Centrale et Orientale de 1918 à 1929. Essai d'interprétation," *Relations internationales* 3, no. 7 (1976): 219–39.

37 Mylène Mihout-Natar, "L'intervention des capitaux français dans la Pologne de la Seconde République (1918–1939): contribution à l'histoire de l'impérialisme économique français en Europe centrale" (PhD, Université Charles de Gaulle – Lille III, 2002).

38 Philippe Marguerat, "Les investissements français dans le Bassin danubien durant l'entre-deux-guerres: pour une nouvelle interprétation," *Revue historique* 39, no. 1 (2004): 121–62, https://doi.org/10.3917/rhis.041.0121.

39 Gusztáv Kecskés D., "The Anatomy of an Attempt to Create a Sphere of Influence: French Policy towards Central and Eastern Europe in the 1920s," in *Wars and*

Betweenness: Big Powers and Middle Europe, 1918–1945, ed. Aliaksandr Piahanau and Bojan Aleksov (Budapest: Central European University Press, 2020), 27–40.

40 Franciszek Ryszka, "Przywileje kapitału zagranicznego w Polsce burżuazyjno-obszarniczej," *Czasopismo Prawno-Historyczne* 6, no. 1 (1954): 302–48. Cf. Merja-Liisa Hinkkanen-Lievonen, "Exploited by Britain? The Problems of British Financial Presence in the Baltic States after the First World War," 335–36.

41 Zbigniew Landau and Jerzy Tomaszewski, *Anonimowi władcy: z dziejów kapitału obcego w Polsce: 1918–1939* (Warszawa: Wiedza Powszechna, 1968); Landau and Tomaszewski, *Kapitały*, 22.

42 Jan Ciałowicz, *Polsko-Francuski Sojusz Wojskowy: 1921–1939* (Warszawa: Państwowe Wydawnictwo Naukowe, 1971); Kukułka, *Francja*.

43 Ambrochowicz-Gajownik, "Polsko-francuskie stosunki," 211; cf. Aldcroft, *Europe's Third World*, 84.

44 John A. Hobson, *Imperialism: A Study* (New York: James Pott & Company, 1902), 100.

45 Piotr Stefan Wandycz, *The Twilight of French Eastern Alliances, 1926–1936: French-Czechoslovak-Polish Relations from Locarno to the Remilitarization of the Rhineland* (Princeton: Princeton University Press, 1988); Piotr Stefan Wandycz, *France and Her Eastern Allies 1919–1925: French-Czechoslovak-Polish Relations from the Paris Peace Conference to Locarno* (Minneapolis: The University of Minnesota Press, 1962); Teichova, *An Economic Background*.

46 Máté Rigó, *Capitalism in Chaos: How the Business Elites of Europe Prospered in the Era of the Great War* (Ithaca and London: Cornell University Press, 2022).

47 Anna Sosnowska, *Explaining Economic Backwardness: Post-1945 Polish Historians on Eastern Europe*, trans. Jasper Tilbury and Anna Sosnowska (Budapest: Central European University Press, 2019); cf. Daniel Chirot, *Social Change in a Peripheral Society: The Creation of a Balkan Colony* (New York: Academic Press, 1976); Aldcroft, *Europe's Third World*, 19–20.

48 Henryk Szlajfer, "Editor's Introduction," in *Economic Nationalism in East Central Europe and South America, 1918–1939*, ed. Henryk Szlajfer (Genève: Librairie Droz, 1990), 8; Kofman, *Economic Nationalism*, 30. Cf. Iván T. Berend, *The Crisis Zone of Europe: An Interpretation of East-Central European History in the First Half of the Twentieth Century*, trans. Adrienne Makkay-Chambers (Cambridge: Cambridge University Press, 1986), 22.

49 Łazor and Murgescu, "Economic Development," 318–26.

50 Jacek Luszniewicz, "Etatism of the Economy of the Second Polish Republic in the Period of Parliamentary Democracy: Conditions, Stages, Evaluation (Part 2: 1923–1926)," *Studia i Prace KES* 2018 4, no. 36 (2018): 65–84.

51 Kofman, *Economic Nationalism*, 78, 129–31, 137.

52 Jan Kofman, "How to Define Economic Nationalism? A Critical Review of Some Old and New Standpoints," in *Economic Nationalism in East Central Europe and South America, 1918–1939*, ed. Henryk Szlajfer (Genève: Librairie Droz, 1990), 98–99.

53 Jan Kofman, *Economic Nationalism and Development: Central and Eastern Europe between the Two World Wars* (London and New York: Routledge, 2018), 12–14, 192 (quote); Kofman, "How to Define," 50; Henryk Szlajfer, "Economic Nationalism of the Peripheries as a Research Problem," in *Economic Nationalism in East Central Europe and South America, 1918–1939*, ed. Henryk Szlajfer (Genève: Librairie Droz, 1990), 101–3.

54 Kofman, "How to Define," 49–50.

55 Murgescu, *Economic Revival*, 76.

56 Kofman, *Economic Nationalism*, 14, 34.

57 Peter B. Evans, *Embedded Autonomy: States and Industrial Transformation*, Princeton Paperbacks (Princeton, NJ: Princeton University Press, 1995), 8.

58 John Toye and Richard Toye, "The Origins and Interpretation of the Prebisch-Singer Thesis," *History of Political Economy* 35, no. 3 (2003): 437–67, https://doi.org/10.1215/00182702-35-3-437; Immanuel Wallerstein, *World-Systems Analysis. An Introduction* (Durham and London: Duke University Press, 2004), 24–29. Cf. Paul Bairoch, *Economics and World History: Myths and Paradoxes* (Chicago: University of Chicago Press, 1995), 140.
59 Peter Nolan, Jin Zhang, and Chunhang Liu, "The Global Business Revolution, the Cascade Effect, and the Challenge for Firms from Developing Countries," *Cambridge Journal of Economics* 32, no. 1 (2007): 29–47, https://doi.org10.1093/cje/bem016.
60 Alfred Chandler, *Scale and Scope: The Dynamics of Industrial Capitalism* (Cambridge, MA: Harvard University Press, 1990).
61 Evans, *Embedded Autonomy*, 7; Erik S. Reinert, *How Rich Countries Got Rich – And Why Poor Countries Stay Poor* (London: Constable, 2007).
62 Raymond Vernon, "International Investment and International Trade in the Product Cycle," *The Quarterly Journal of Economics* 80, no. 2 (1966): 190–207, https://doi.org/10.2307/1880689.
63 Bairoch, *Economics*, 140.
64 Carlota Perez, *Technological Revolutions and Financial Capital: The Dynamics of Bubbles and Golden Ages* (Cheltenham: Edward Elgar, 2002).
65 Freeman and Louçã, *As Time Goes by*, 257.
66 Christophe Laforest, "La Stratégie Française et La Pologne (1919–1939). Aspects Économiques et Implications Politiques" (PhD, Université Paris 1 Panthéon-Sorbonne, 2001).
67 Łazor and Murgescu, "Economic Develoment," 321; Cecylia Leszczyńska, "Level of Living of Polish Citizens in the Interwar Period, and Its Diversification," *Roczniki Dziejów Społecznych i Gospodarczych* 76 (2016): 93, https://doi.org/10.12775/RDSG.2016.04; Aldcroft, *Europe's Third World*.
68 Leszek Jerzy Jasiński, *Bliżej centrum czy na peryferiach? Polskie kontakty gospodarcze z zagranicą w XX wieku* (Warszawa: Centrum Europejskie Natolin, Wydawnictwo Trio, 2011), 101–5.
69 Eric Lethbridge, "National Income and Product," in *The Economic History of Eastern Europe 1919–1975, v. I. Economic Structure and Performance Between the Two Wars*, ed. Michael Charles Kaser and E. A. Radice (Oxford: Clarendon Press, 1985), 532–97, 569.
70 Aldcroft, *Europe's Third World*, 28, 49; Wojciech Roszkowski, *Land Reforms in East Central Europe after World War One* (Warsaw: Institute of Political Studies, Polish Academy of Sciences, 1995).
71 David, *Nationalisme*, 253.
72 Aldcroft, *Europe's Third World*, 48, 78.
73 Janusz Żarnowski, *Polska 1918–1939: praca, technika, społeczeństwo*, 2nd ed. (Warszawa: Książka i Wiedza, 1999).
74 Wallerstein, *World-Systems Analysis*, 56–57.
75 Ha-Joon Chang, *Kicking Away the Ladder: Development Strategy in Historical Perspective* (Anthem Press, 2002), 126.
76 Chang, *Kicking*, 59.
77 Alexander Gerschenkron, *Economic Backwardness in Historical Perspective: A Book of Essays* (Cambridge, MA: Harvard University, 1962), 41–42.
78 Chang, *Kicking*, 127.
79 Evans, *Embedded Autonomy*, 10.
80 Chang enumerates, apart from tariff protection: "export subsidies, tariff rebates on inputs used for exports, conferring of monopoly rights, cartel arrangements, directed credits, investment planning, manpower planning, R&D supports and the promotion of institutions that allow public-private cooperation" (Chang, *Kicking*, 65).

81 Cf. Joseph E. Stiglitz and Bruce C. Greenwald, *Creating a Learning Society: A New Paradigm for Development and Social Progress* (New York: Columbia University Press, 2014), https://doi.org/10.7312/stig15214.
82 Evans, *Embedded Autonomy*, 14.
83 Evans, *Embedded Autonomy*, 6, 31.
84 Ha-Joon Chang, *Bad Samaritans: The Myth of Free Trade and the Secret History of Capitalism* (New York: Bloomsbury Press, 2008), 92.
85 Chang, *Kicking*, 199.
86 Evans, *Embedded Autonomy*, 81.
87 Chang, *Bad Samaritans*, 92.
88 Chang, *Kicking*, 137.

2 Profits and costs of alliance

Mechanisms of Franco–Polish interwar economic relations

On 31 October 1935, the Polish deputy minister of finance Adam Koc asked for a meeting with the French Ambassador Léon Noël. In a long, "well-rehearsed" speech, the close collaborator of the recently deceased Józef Piłsudski admitted that Warsaw's financial situation was dire.[1] Both countries bore the brutal cost of staying on gold throughout the Great Depression, and the Bank of Poland's reserves were running dangerously low, threatening a currency collapse. The Poles needed "oxygen," which the French could provide by lending money. Noël answered that while France was, in principle, always happy to help its ally, doing so would require improving relations, undermined by recent conflicts. Without external help, and with the Bank of Poland bleeding out reserves, within six months the Poles introduced exchange control, thus leaving the gold standard. This period included Koc's brief stint as president of the Polish central bank. His conversation with Noël shows the double meaning of this chapter's title. Diplomats in both Poland and France tried to use the political anchor afforded by the alliance to gain advantages in the economic sphere. And both had to pay an economic price: either by providing loans and credits to their ally, or by granting privileges to its companies. Neither side was particularly happy about the arrangement. As a Polish newspaper editor raged a year earlier:

> We paid a steep price for the liberation of Poland, for the military convention, for scummy loans, for worn military matériel. France's ministers, her consul, and even private citizens intervened at the Ministry of Foreign Affairs, always successfully. The alliance of sovereign and vassal imposes charges, and the vassal has to cover all the costs of the so-called friendship.[2]

The French were likewise embittered, thinking that their monetary sacrifices to Poland would never truly be appreciated, and that Warsaw strove to deny them their rightful profits.[3]

In this chapter, I look at French investment in Poland from the point of view of inter-governmental relations: I attempt to understand both sides' goals and tools, and the influence of the political and economic hierarchy on mutual

DOI: 10.4324/9781003375586-2

relations. I argue that for both countries security considerations informed the alliance, and while both tried to use it for economic purposes, these attempts were ultimately more important for Poland. Initially, the economic relationship changed in step with the political one, but in the 1930s the influence also went in the other direction, as major Polish conflicts with French-owned companies undermined political relations. Since the French government did not engage money in Poland directly, other than by providing loans and credits, I look at them in more detail, and show that they had limited impact on Polish development, with the vast majority of money going towards military spending. Moreover, a comparison with loans and credits granted by France to other states in Central and Eastern Europe points to the weakness of the Franco–Polish relationship, and the financial limits to the efficiency of French policy in the region.

Financial history, starting with the failure of Latin American bonds in the 1820s, gives many examples of bankruptcies caused by high government debt, showing the difficulty of effectively using money from abroad.[4] In this chapter, I argue that debtor nations face another problem – indeed another vicious circle. As they import capital from states higher in the global hierarchy, they necessarily enter into asymmetrical relationships. In such cases, the stronger side is likely to be able to force its will on the borrowing country. It might dictate the way in which the funds in question are used, or obtain other privileges, impacting local development policy and the ability to challenge the hierarchy. These influences are stronger, if, as in the Polish case, the weaker party is unable to borrow from private investors, and gets money from foreign governments. This suggests an even greater importance of well thought-through policy towards foreign capital.

However, before we delve into these mechanisms, or the loans extended to Warsaw by Paris, let us start with a brief history of the Franco–Polish relationship, to serve as context for further analyses.

2.1 Marriage of (in)convenience

For most of the interwar period, the Franco–Polish alliance hardly functioned as intended.[5] While it continued to be the cornerstone of Poland's security policy, the 1925 Locarno treaties and Aristide Briand's policy of rapprochement with Germany in the second half of the decade weakened the agreement, further undermined by Józef Piłsudski's mistrust of the French. Little changed with Hitler's coming to power in 1933, but the relationship gained new life with the remilitarization of the Rhineland in 1936, a year after Piłsudski's death. In September 1939, Paris reluctantly joined London and declared war on Germany after its invasion of Poland.

The alliance grew out of the fall of empires after World War I. With the February 1917 revolution in Russia, Paris moved towards cooperation with the Poles, and, through Raymond Poincaré's decree from June of that year, provided for the creation of their army on French territory.[6] After the Armistice,

France backed Polish territorial demands. Since the results of the peace conference depended on the Great Powers, and Warsaw was unlikely to find friendly ears in London, Poland needed French support for all of its borders. The two countries also cooperated in the military sphere, and a French Military Mission contributed to the creation and training of the new Polish army, not to mention the significant deliveries of matériel on credit.[7] Strengthening Poland achieved three goals. First, it bolstered France's eastern "replacement ally," which became important especially once the French found themselves without the British and American guarantees they counted on. Second, as Warsaw looked to push its borders outwards, backing its claims to Danzig or Upper Silesia weakened Germany. Third, the French hoped to use this opportunity to expand their already sizeable economic holdings in the country, and replace German and Austrian capital.[8]

The two countries formalized their relationship with a political agreement on 19 February 1921, followed two days later by a secret military convention. The former saw the two states pledge cooperation on all questions of foreign relations. It also promised "united action and mutual help" in economic matters. The military convention was more explicit. It added obligations of "efficient and rapid help" in case of a German attack on either party or a Soviet attack on Poland. France promised to send matériel and technical personnel, and assure lines of communication, but it would not commit to delivering troops. Poland engaged itself to field at least 30 divisions of infantry, to unify the armaments used by its army following the French model, and to develop its war industry. France promised to help, and to provide 400 million French francs of credits towards this goal.[9] The agreement and the convention were to come into force after the signing of three economic treaties, with which Paris wanted to solidify its position in Poland. This economic blackmail – unheard of in French treaties in Central and Eastern Europe – encapsulated the unequal standing of the allies.[10] The Poles found the way French diplomats supported their economic interests and their companies' pursuit of short-term profits "harsh and disquieting."[11]

The alliance with Poland formed part of France's wider designs in Central and Eastern Europe – its "Eastern barrier."[12] In January 1924, France formalized its relationship with Czechoslovakia in a treaty of alliance and friendship. Both Poland and Czechoslovakia were also allies of Romania, and the last two countries formed the Little Entente together with the Kingdom of Serbs, Croats, and Slovenes (Yugoslavia since 1929). France supported the alliance, "a political expression of the expansive efforts of Czechoslovak business and banking circles," signing treaties of friendship with Romania and future Yugoslavia in 1926 and 1927.[13] Attempts to include Poland in the group ended in a stalemate due to bad relations between Warsaw and Prague.[14] These dated to 1919 and the conflict surrounding Cieszyn Silesia (Těšín in Czech, Teschen in German), a highly industrialized territory with significant coal reserves, which both countries claimed for themselves. Polish speakers made up the majority of its population, but Prague took the area by force, which Warsaw was pushed to accept during the critical phase of its war with Soviet Russia in 1920.[15] Despite Paris's repeated attempts to promote rapprochement between its two major eastern allies, Warsaw and Prague, both hoping to play the role of a Central European leader, looked at each other with distrust. The conflict ended in tragedy in 1938, with the Polish military taking Czech territories forcefully, as Hitler was dismantling Czechoslovakia.

The French signed the alliance with Poland with some hesitation, not convinced by its military rationale. The Poles in turn worried about the one-sided economic agreements. Nonetheless, once Raymond Poincaré became Prime Minister in early 1922, and as the Polish military pushed its government to make quick decisions, the three agreements were finally signed, and the alliance came into force. Thus began the best period of the alliance, with both parties treating it as a significant part of their security policies, and with multiple meetings between the highest echelons of their militaries. It culminated in a May 1923 visit of Ferdinand Foch to Poland.[16]

The Franco–Polish honeymoon ended with the electoral victory of the Cartel des Gauches in May 1924. A gradual reorientation of French policy under Édouard Herriot's government put a stop on the French military's attempts to register the alliance with the League of Nations, and the Quai d'Orsay started raising issues with the army about cooperation with Poland. Then, the Locarno treaties from 1925, guaranteeing French eastern borders, effectively left Paris's eastern allies behind. As George-Henri Soutou observed, "since the elections in 1924, the French government did not truly interest itself in the 'eastern barrier,'" and two years later Aristide Briand and other high officials thought that a revision of Poland's borders was conceivable.[17] Polish attitudes changed as well. Having stabilized their currency and territory, the authorities in Warsaw were less eager to listen to the French. Under the premiership of Władysław Grabski they made tough negotiators, even declining the final tranche of the 400 million francs credit.[18]

On 12 May 1926, Marshall Józef Piłsudski seized power in Warsaw after a bloody coup d'état. Initially, together with foreign minister August Zaleski he tried to assuage any French fears that Poland would leave the alliance.[19] Soon, however, the distance between Paris and Warsaw grew. Piłsudski changed the country's foreign policy, seeing the Soviet Union as the greatest threat to Polish independence.[20] Paris did not perceive Poland's eastern focus as helpful, especially since France's policy at the time lost its anti-Bolshevik edge. More importantly, while Piłsudski treated the alliance as "life insurance," he was not content with Poland playing the role of pupil to France's tutor, and strove towards greater independence.

The next decade thus saw a lessening of military contacts between the two countries. The French were unwilling to discuss their mobilization plans, and provide the Poles with armament loans, while Piłsudski disliked the influence of the Military Mission in Warsaw, and was unwilling to do the required planning and staff work. The general staffs consulted but once between 1924 and 1932.[21]

In 1932, despite the end of Briand's term in office, relations soured even more. In January, the Poles demanded the liquidation of the French Military Mission.[22] In late April, after a murder of the managing director of a French-owned linen factory in Żyrardów, the press in Poland launched a violent attack on the company and on French capital in general. On 2 November 1932, Józef Beck replaced August Zaleski as head of Foreign Affairs, signalling a further change in Polish policy. There was little love lost between the new minister and France. Newspapers in Paris reacted to his nomination in an "almost insulting" manner, and Beck was hardly interested in curtailing anti-French attacks in the Polish press.[23]

In January 1933 Hitler came to power. As Piłsudski's attempts to coordinate actions with the French against Germany (the "preventive war") brought no results, he decided to reorient Polish policy, looking for a *modus vivendi* with Hitler. In January 1934 Poland signed a non-aggression pact with Germany, marking a low point in the already strained relationship with France.[24] The Poles doubted the French would support Warsaw in case of war with Berlin, yet they did nothing to strengthen the alliance – either foster cooperation between the two armies, plan for a potential war, or regularly share intelligence. There was also little potential for understanding on the other side. Paris would not act without cooperation with the United Kingdom – the guarantor of its borders under Locarno.

Piłsudski died in May 1935. His rule "ended with Franco–Polish relations in an atmosphere of built-up mutual doubts, bitterness, and disappointment."[25] After his death, a power struggle unfolded in Poland. From it, several key figures emerged with markedly more pro-French attitudes as a counterbalance to Beck. They included President Ignacy Mościcki, the soon-to-be new Marshall Edward Rydz-Śmigły, and the Deputy Prime Minister Eugeniusz Kwiatkowski. The Poles realized that their army needed urgent modernization, and only France could help. They found an interested listener in Léon Noël, the new ambassador who came to Warsaw from Prague.[26] Then in March 1936 German forces marched into Rhineland, while Berlin renounced the Locarno agreements. This brought Poland and France closer, with Paris willing to talk about further cooperation. After intense negotiations, on 6 September 1936 the two sides signed a treaty in Rambouillet, in which Poland was promised 2 billion francs in loans and credits. Due to the devaluation of the franc the following month, this amount was increased to 2.6 billion. Rambouillet revitalized the alliance, despite problems with French deliveries of Polish purchases.[27] Nonetheless, as Paris and London continued with appeasement, the alliance did little to stop Hitler. The takeover of Czechoslovakian soil by the Poles after Munich greatly undermined the Polish position, but after German demands in 1939, now the United Kingdom led the allies to closer cooperation with Warsaw in the final months before the beginning of the war.

2.2 Goals

Throughout the interwar period, French authorities pursued goals informed by a mixture of security and economic considerations.[28] In the first years after the war, Paris wanted to use the geopolitical situation to strengthen its economic presence in Central and Eastern Europe, and take the place of German and Austrian investors. Important French companies were seen as beacons of influence, and government officials would provide help, "necessary to stop German infiltration."[29] Taking over key parts of the Polish economy, and thus making the country dependent on the French, was a way of guaranteeing that Warsaw remained a useful ally. These arguments (such as "In economic terms, to take over a country's coal is to become its master"[30]) reappeared throughout the interwar period. Sometimes they came from the ministry, sometimes from private investors hoping to win its support. Both milieux at first overestimated Polish economic potential, which affected their actions. The authorities also wanted French companies to profit in Poland, but this goal was subservient to more strategic considerations.

With limited resources, and with control in mind, authorities in Paris carefully defined their foreign investment policy. The Ministry of Finance – operating from the Louvre – had already been conservative before the war. Now, due to wartime restrictions on capital exports, and the general post-war push towards "decontrol and retrenchment," its policies decidedly shaped and limited French investment abroad.[31] To preserve capital, the Quai d'Orsay and the Louvre opposed portfolio investments, which would bring nothing beyond limited profits to select investors. The authorities preferred either majority stakes in companies, or at least guarantees of dominant French representation in their management, "which give the most serious assurance of a clearly French orientation." Other uses of capital, such as issuing bonds on the French market, were also discouraged. As a result, between 1918 and 1925, the total value of loans from Central and Eastern Europe floated in Paris amounted to only 250 million francs, with only one (worth 155 million) going to a French ally, Romania.[32] Much more important were the strictly political credits afforded by the French government to the region, worth 5.1 billion francs by 1923 – however these were often earmarked for military purchases. Here, Yugoslavia got the most: over a third of all credits, followed by Romania. Poland – France's only ally in the region at the time, placed third with just over a billion francs (we will come back to this at the end of the chapter).[33]

Even once the franc stabilized, Paris broadly continued to follow this careful policy. In 1928 Raymond Poincaré, with Aristide Briand's full support, formulated the rules for French financial engagement on other markets, aimed at gaining influence over their economies.[34] The Minister of Finance argued that the best approach was to either found new companies, or take full control over established enterprises. Sometimes, the use of French private savings to fund a foreign state loan could also translate into influence (such as the Polish railway bonds from 1931), but private issues were discouraged.[35]

The rules regulating investment, sensible as they were from Paris's financial perspective, were at odds with the idea of keeping (or increasing) French influence in Poland. Indeed, particularly in 1924 French companies lost bids in Poland (and Serbia) due to insufficient government help from Paris, much to the chagrin of Prime Minister Raymond Poincaré, over-ruled by Finance Minister Frédéric François-Marsal.[36] There is a wider parallel between the French position in Central Eastern Europe – won after the war, and then gradually lost, as Paris was unable to bear the associated costs – its empire, where ideas of colonial reform and modernization ultimately fell through in the same period, and the French economy, where "Time after time in the 1920s the parsimonious finance ministry refused subsidies or capital outlays because the treasury could not afford them."[37]

French Ambassador Jules Laroche in particular thought that these rules hindered French policy. He argued that the Poles, likely to play a big role in European history, would have to import capital for development. If Paris did not provide the needed money, someone else would, thus reducing France's influence won in the early 1920s.[38] Laroche saw the need for the French to act boldly in Poland, lead international investors, and show good will.[39]

More broadly, the French were afraid of losing their position in Poland to other countries. Directly after the war, they feared the seemingly better-organized British in Upper Silesia, and the Americans in Galicia.[40] Soon, Germany became the principal locus of French anxiety, reflecting a deeper German complex.[41] Paris considered its eastern neighbour to be more dynamic, entrepreneurial, and difficult to defeat in direct competition. These fears mirrored a more general sense of French weakness and isolation, dating to pre-war days.[42] As a result, authorities in Paris put much effort in making sure that French companies stayed French. Any contact with the former enemy was treated as suspicious. Owners of French companies allegedly working with the Germans would send letters to the Quai d'Orsay, explaining their actions, objecting to accusations, and proclaiming their patriotic feelings. Some declared a "sacred hatred" towards the enemy, who "robbed their houses, destroyed their factories, offended and deported their wives, killed their sons."[43]

Beyond strategic goals, the French tried to protect the property rights and rents of their investors. This can be seen most clearly in responses to autonomous Polish economic actions, especially if they went against French interests and policy recommendations.[44] The Polish historian Maria Pasztor showed that the French had little faith in Poland's management.[45] In Warsaw they saw incompetence and bad will, and complained about the "constant, almost childlike resistance" of central and local Polish authorities, needlessly complex procedures, and unprofessionalism.[46] These negative perceptions found analogues in comments made by private investors, worried about the "hesitant" Polish government, with French industry "in constant danger."[47]

In diplomatic documents this sphere was linked to alleged Polish nationalism, xenophobia, *étatisme* (or statism) and fiscalism. The first two terms, ostensibly noneconomic, were used by the French to describe any Polish actions which strengthened domestic companies at the expense of those with foreign capital. Statism was used as a form of criticism even in the oil sector, where the French authorities exercised extraordinary control. Fiscalism was raised in the context of remuneration of capital (or the so-called "normal profits"), to which the French considered themselves entitled due to their contributions in Polish post-war reconstruction and economic development.

The emphasis shifted with time. Initially the French complained about mismanagement and fiscalism, but by the end of the 1920s they focused on Polish nationalism, which, according to chargé d'affaires in Warsaw Jean Tripier "threatened the future of all foreign-owned firms in the country."[48] The Quai d'Orsay seemed to agree and in 1929 it claimed that "in the current political and economic state of Poland, we can do nothing but advice French finance to stay away from such a fool's bargain."[49] By late 1933 even Laroche became worried about the scale of attacks on foreign capital.[50]

Reacting to these fears, the authorities in Paris set out to shield French companies from expropriation, and guarantee their ability to make profits and transfer them back home. In the 1920s, this translated into attempts to obtain the most favoured nation status for French firms, or, preferably, win immunity from local laws on foreign exchange, import and export tariffs, special taxes, or hiring foreigners. By the next decade the goal shifted to protecting French holdings and the rights won earlier.

Did the French consider the economic development of Poland as a part of their goals? Christophe Laforest argues that they did, in the sense that a successful economy in Poland would translate into stable Polish politics, and thus guarantee the country remained a useful French ally.[51] Despite reoccurring declarations of Franco–Polish friendship, even such instrumental arguments for development are rare in archival documents, and it is easier to find calls for greater control. This remains true even in cases where an improved Polish economy would unequivocally render the country more powerful as an ally, such as the development of its armaments industry. To paraphrase the proverb: rather than teach the Poles how to fish, Paris would sell them fish on credit. In this, the authorities agreed with the owners of private French companies, who were certainly not interested in helping create future competitors in Central Europe.

Discussions of development appear in another interpretative context: calls for helping Poland as "the frontier of Western civilization."[52] Even the most sympathetic French officials viewed the country as backwards. Jules Laroche thought the Poles owed everything modern in their country to foreigners. He eulogized the "remarkable technology, way of work, activity" of French industrialists in Dąbrowa. Once the Germans left Silesia, he saw "a certain negligence, already a bit oriental" in Katowice, and he doubted whether "our Poles," if left to their own devices, would be able to keep those factories running.[53] This reflected a wider tendency to essentialize the Poles, and present them in orientalizing ways.[54] As I discuss elsewhere, a French officer stationed in Poland provided a representative example in his writing:

> They are like big children, very talkative, very proud, and very sensitive; they think they know everything; they are sometimes insincere, and not always honest. They cannot do anything practical because their brains are still poorly furnished and they lack persistence.[55]

From this point of view, the French presence in Poland appeared almost as a civilizing mission, not unlike what the authorities in Paris thought they were doing in the colonies.

If any Polish development (or "civilizing") was the effect of foreign investment, and Paris had placed so much capital on Polish lands before World War I, then the French had contributed a lot. In consequence, both the authorities and private owners believed that investors now had the right to "normal profits" from their holdings in Poland. The discourse on civilizing thus served as an argument for protecting rents, although some French commentators, such as Jules Laroche, realized the tension between the argument and the new political situation: "Our industrialists cannot give the impression that they are exploiting Poland like a colony."[56]

Moving on to Poland, the goals of its authorities can also be broadly divided into security and economic aims, with some projects straddling the division. On a general level, the relationship with France was a way to strengthen Poland's geopolitical position. Going beyond grand strategy, Warsaw's principal goal was to use Paris's funds and (especially in the early 1920s) expertise to field an army capable of defending Poland's borders. In practical terms, this meant getting credits and loans to either purchase equipment, or create a military industry with the help of French companies, and using French officers for training.[57] The choice between buying weapons and making them in Poland was a matter of timing and money: creating industry took time, whereas simply purchasing planes meant that Warsaw could use them sooner.[58] In later years, Poland also hoped that the French could help finance certain key investments, which had both economic and security implications. The harbour in Gdynia, the Coal Trunk Railway, and the electrification of the Central Industrial Basin stand out in this category.

The Poles also had strictly economic goals, and when talking about them it is useful to distinguish between policies towards new foreign capital and towards existing investments. Starting with new capital, Polish policy was broadly consistent throughout the interwar period. The authorities and pundits treated the influx of foreign funds as crucial.[59] Initially it would help rebuild the economy after the war, create the new state's structures, and plug the budgetary and trade deficit. Later, the goals shifted to economic modernization. Moreover, for liberal commentators, foreign investors would counterbalance the growing Polish state sector. The Poles thus both sought foreign loans, and tried to attract private FDI.[60]

Regarding loans, initially Warsaw scrambled to get any outside financing. Later, governments pursued a "big" foreign loan to strengthen the financial system (which happened in 1927). Moreover, officials hoped that getting and successfully servicing such a loan would convince foreign investors that Poland was a safe location for capital, and thus lead to more FDI and financing. Officials and commentators thought that "foreign capital should become a factor helping the modernization of the Polish economy; its influx, no matter the intended use, would also increase the supply of foreign exchange."[61] At first Polish authorities welcomed both FDI, which would create new industry, and cash loans to be used for government-led industrial investment. As economic nationalism gained ground in the last years of the 1930s, some commentators argued for loans rather than FDI, as they gave the authorities more influence over investment, and made the state less beholden to foreign owners.

The state's economic position in Poland continued to grow throughout the interwar period, despite repeated declarations of liberal policy. To explain this discrepancy, Polish historians coined the term "unwanted statism," arguing that the rise of state ownership was not the result of a plan, but either a combination of various stopgap measures, aimed at solving specific problems, or, as Zbigniew Landau put it, the only possible solution given the limited availability of private capital in the country.[62] By 1922, authorities took the first steps towards state-led industrialization, with forays into military production. Later, Prime Minister Władysław Grabski made state entrepreneurship a normal part of the economy, consolidated state-owned banking into a major part of the sector in 1925, and pushed for cartelization of the crucial coal sector. His government also oversaw the beginning of two of the three major infrastructural investments mentioned above.[63] After 1926, subsequent governments broadly followed these precepts. The onset of the Great Depression greatly increased the scale of intervention, with state-owned companies taking over failing enterprises. Moreover, the authorities themselves founded fully state-owned or mixed companies, from banks to prospecting firms. The sector's growth was stunning, from some 30 companies, worth about 50 million złoty in 1927, to almost 160 companies worth ten times as much a decade later.[64] Despite extensive criticism, the state turned out to be a decent owner, with companies belonging to it reporting reasonable results.[65]

The increasingly vocal proponents of state intervention included Eugeniusz Kwiatkowski and Sanacja officials grouped in the so-called First Economic Brigade (Pierwsza Brygada Gospodarcza). Chief among the latter group was Stefan Starzyński, who, as government commissioner and later president of Warsaw, led the attack on the Warsaw power plant in the 1930s.[66] With the death of Piłsudski in 1935, this approach became more mainstream, and under Kwiatkowski as Deputy Prime Minister, government actions evolved into a broad policy of state-led development, focused on the Central Industrial Basin (Centralny Okręg Przemysłowy). Located in the southern part of the country, between the rivers Vistula and San, it was a large, underdeveloped, almost exclusively agricultural area, home to some 6 million people. It was close to the country's resources (coal and iron to the west, oil to the east), yet farther from the border with Germany than the exposed Upper Silesia. Military considerations fuelled the investment programme, and new factories would bolster the country's armaments production.[67]

If in the 1920s FDI was seen as an antidote for state ownership, now proponents of statism argued the opposite. A well-constructed intervention programme would allow a smaller impact of foreigners on the Polish economy, in line with the ideology of economic nationalism. However, as pursuing such a project required money, which at least to some degree had to be acquired from abroad, as well as technology, which had to be imported, this still left much space for foreign investors. Moreover, in the mid-1930s no sources of capital other than Paris were available, giving the French a strong negotiating position – enough to secure some projects for their companies through the Rambouillet agreement (more on this in the last section of this chapter).[68] This offers a good vista on how French and Polish goals would interact, and on paradoxes faced by countries wanting to combine development with capital imports.

Polish goals towards existing investment were not as obvious, especially in the first years of the interwar period. Companies with foreign capital were, at least de jure, treated in the same way as purely domestic ones, and could operate freely provided they followed the law. However, after World War I the nationality of capital mattered, and the Poles were wary of firms owned by ethnic Germans – both foreigners and Polish citizens. This led to complicated relations, with much lobbying, especially by companies from Upper Silesia.[69] In certain key sectors, such as coal production, the Poles were willing to support domestic and French companies to limit German influence (see Chapter 5).

The situation changed with the Great Depression and the emergence of economic nationalism. Now the Polish authorities decided to consolidate their control of some strategic sectors. In some cases this meant the creation of obligatory cartels (oil, coal), in others, the nationalization of domestic and foreign-owned companies (aviation). More generally, the authorities now expected investors to not only abide by the letter of the law, but also remain "loyal" to Poland, which resulted in further conflicts and takeovers. I will return to these matters in later chapters.

2.3 Tools and mechanisms

Moving on to tools, let us start by noting that the French government did not, as a rule, engage in the economy directly. No companies in Poland were co-owned by Paris, and private firms had to undertake all investment. With the strict financial rules I mentioned, they could not count on financing or government guarantees.[70] The French minister in Warsaw Hector André de Panafieu argued that, as a result, the French stood little chance against firms from "richer or less timid countries."[71] Moreover, while the French in Poland had to contend with the growing state sector, the success of Paris's policy often hinged on private companies agreeing to follow the government's lead. Corralling them usually took the form of informal meetings at one of the interested ministries, the use of lobby groups, or personal connections. Without financial incentives, the system worked slowly, with political and patriotic arguments often falling on deaf ears, as authorities were unable "to mobilize others around the message of national interest."[72] After a few spectacular failures, such as the attempt to create a Franco–Polish holding company in Upper Silesia (which I discuss in Chapter 6), private investors became even more wary. Nonetheless, in certain key areas connected to security, Paris and its representatives became very active, convincing the Poles to grant concessions to French companies, and limit the influence of capital coming from other countries. Moreover, as I will show in Chapter 4, the French government and military were not neutral, and sometimes picked winners from among French companies.

The French pursued the safeguarding of property rights and rents primarily through a series of economic agreements signed in the early 1920s, which "protected French interests in Poland without reciprocity."[73] As we will discuss in the next chapter, the so-called rights and interests treaty regulated pre-war investments; the oil treaty granted special rights to oil companies; the commercial treaty specified the status of all French firms. The French avoided basing even the mildest rights on reciprocity, as this would limit their domestic policies, and preferred secret agreements to avoid investors from other countries profiting through the most favoured nation clause.[74]

The French were able to force the three unequal agreements using conditionality, which remained their primary negotiating technique throughout the interwar period. Paris's representatives would relentlessly link ongoing negotiations with other outstanding, often unconnected issues. In this way, a single topic, such as the fate the state-owned oil refinery in Drohobycz, lowering Polish tariffs on wines, or solving the conflict in Żyrardów, would continue to reappear as a condition for many new loans or agreements. Both sides regularly compiled lists of such outstanding issues used in talks, and private investors were aware of this dynamic.[75] In August 1920, a week before the battle of Warsaw, a French businessman and politician observed with satisfaction: "We can hope that thanks to the current circumstances, our government can obtain guarantees of protection for French interests."[76] It was in this way that the three economic agreements were forced onto the Poles as a condition for the alliance, added at the last minute by Aristide Briand. In the French Senate, the oil agreement was self-righteously described as proof or pledge (*gage*) "of Polish friendship."[77]

There is nothing untypical about conditionality in diplomacy, but the one-sidedness of the Franco–Polish case stands out. While the French did pursue specific goals in Poland which hinged on Warsaw's agreement (such as the protection of their companies' oil interests), the dynamic of the two countries' relationship was skewed towards Poland asking for things (mostly money), and the French setting the rules. Thus, in many cases, Paris was able to set the agenda for discussions, even when it was Warsaw which initiated the talks, leaving the Poles to defend their position: trying to reduce the price they had to pay for French support. The result was annoyance coming from both capitals. Officials in Warsaw were annoyed that the French forced the Poles to pay through the nose for the so-called "friendship," while their counterparts in Paris found the Poles unreasonable and difficult to negotiate with.

Three situations illustrate how exceptions to this dynamic were significant enough to be noticed by diplomats. First, when the Poles also attempted to use conditionality in negotiations with the French, Paris's representatives rebuked them, arguing that there was no need to link separate issues. Later, after the collapse of Crédit Général des Pétroles in 1930, as the French negotiated with its creditors in Austria, they asked the Polish state-owned Bank of the National Economy (Bank Gospodarstwa Krajowego, BGK) to provide a financial guarantee. It was a rare example of the French soliciting money, rather than the other way around. They received it without much trouble, surprising Laroche, who declared that if the Poles had always been this agreeable in financial matters, they would have found more welcome ears in Paris.[78] Finally, in 1938 the French threatened Polish officials with cutting access to foreign capital unless they relented in their fight against the Warsaw power plant (Compagnie d'Électricité de Varsovie). The head of MSZ's Legal Department (and future US academic) Władysław Kulski came to the conclusion that unless the French were planning to provide Poland with additional credit, the threat was meaningless, and should Paris persevere, the Poles were free to retaliate by reneging on the 1922 rights and interests treaty.[79]

The last example serves to illustrate that the efficacy of French interventions depended on the state of the Franco–Polish relationship, and the scale of Polish needs at the time. When Warsaw was fighting for its survival in 1920, or precariously rebuilding in 1921, the Poles were willing to pay almost anything. As Mylène Mihout-Natar put it in the context of infrastructural investment: "liberty has no price."[80] In comparison, since Czechoslovakia was in a better position than Poland, it could count on better treatment, even if Prague was also forced to grant privileges to the French.[81] And even for Warsaw, the sword of conditionality lost its edge when the Poles felt more confident, either due to the geopolitical situation, or because of the consolidation of their government and the position of the Prime Minister or Minister of Foreign Affairs. Hence Władysław Grabski or Józef Beck made tougher negotiators, less likely to agree to French demands (and as such – hardly liked in Paris). Arguably, more agreeable Polish politicians, such as Eugeniusz Kwiatkowski, found it easier to convince their French partners.[82]

To finish the discussion of conditionality, let us note the multifaceted contribution of French loans to Paris's policy. They helped the authorities directly, by strategically strengthening their eastern ally in useful areas (hence the considerable control the French exerted over the use of the 400-million-franc credit). Moreover, thanks to conditionality, loans and credits allowed other advantages, and forced the French position in various conflicts. Finally, they helped get new contracts to French firms – as in the case of Schneider et Compagnie in an armaments factory in Starachowice.

The meagre value of loans extended to French Central and Eastern European countries was thus a significant limit to the spread of French influence in the region. Looking at the matter more broadly, Paris's policy was pursued via diplomacy and "occasional loans," to use Charles Lipson's wording. In comparison to the informal empire build by Great Britain in 19th century Latin America, there was not enough trade policy, or the opening of the French market to products from the region, which could have helped Paris strengthen its position. Lipson observed that with Paris holding relatively little sway in Warsaw or Prague, "For the most part, foreign investments in Eastern Europe were protected by the conservatism of the local governments."[83]

The Poles, as the junior partners who mostly asked for assistance, necessarily took a different approach than the French. In some cases, Warsaw's economic diplomacy was direct, as when its representatives offered economic concessions in Upper Silesia to get further French support in the province and create networks between Polish and French investors (I discuss this more broadly in Chapter 6). Moreover, throughout the interwar period they attempted multiple times to get the French government to grant Poland loans, credits, financial guarantees, and allow the issue of Polish bonds on the market in Paris, sometimes using their contacts with French private investors to lobby their allies.[84]

Other strategies adopted by Warsaw were the consequence of the preponderant French position, and the advantages Paris's representatives had won for their companies directly after the war. The Polish reaction was gradual and indirect, aimed at limiting earlier French victories. The Poles would delay responding to French requests, slow the ratification process of some agreements, ignore particularly jarring stipulations in others (see Chapters 5 and 6). As Warsaw gained confidence, its methods became less timid. By the end of the 1920s, Polish authorities annulled a major concession won by a Franco–Polish group, and in the next decade vigorously pursued actions against certain French companies.

When officials in Warsaw tried to attract investment, they ran into recurring problems. The interwar period was a poor time to hinge development on money from abroad, especially in Central and Eastern Europe.[85] World War I and the collapse of the classical Gold Standard led to economic disintegration, and undermined European financial markets. Countries in the region faced higher spreads than around the turn of the 19th century, and borrowed less money than their authorities had hoped.[86] Private investors were likewise wary of greenfield investment in the region, and preferred short-term placements. The Great Depression exacerbated the problem, with a sudden stop to much of the capital flows, and attempts from investors to pull out. Poland was seen as a particularly risky market due to conflicts with all its neighbours, long-unsettled borders, hyperinflation, and late currency stabilization.[87]

Officials in Warsaw could do little about the state of global finance. If they wanted to get foreign capital and float private loans in Paris, they needed to manage investor perceptions.[88] This was done mostly through macroeconomic policy. At first, currency stabilization was the primary goal. Officials thought that adopting the recommendations of the 1922 Genoa Conference would serve as a "Good Housekeeping Seal of Approval," and translate into greater trust in the Polish economy.[89] Nonetheless, the frequent use of exchange control remained a problem until 1927.[90] In later years, the Poles followed a broadly liberal, fiscally conservative economic policy. Examples include the careful use of the 1927 stabilization loan to bolster the currency, or the orthodox approach to the Great Depression, including membership in the Gold Bloc. The Poles also tried to assure investors that their holdings were safe. For instance, after Piłsudski's coup in 1926, the government in Warsaw was particularly eager to close all outstanding negotiations, hoping to showcase the new authorities' high regard for foreign investors. This included settling a serious conflict with the Franco–Polish consortium building the harbour in Gdynia.[91] I discuss other tools used by Warsaw in its relations with private companies in Chapter 3.

2.4 Polish state loans

With limited access to foreign markets, Warsaw hoped it could rely on Paris to provide funds. As I mentioned, private banks were loath to engage themselves in Poland, and the French Ministry of Finance was averse to Polish attempts to place bonds in Paris, citing the poor state of the market. Poland did not place any bonds abroad before 1924, and on the French market before 1927 (2 million dollars), with the only major loan granted in this manner in 1931 (400 million francs). As in the rest of the region, real interest rates were high.[92]

These results are unsurprising. Before the war, France had been the second-largest provider of foreign capital in the world after Great Britain, with some 9.7 billion dollars tied in long-term investment in 1914, mostly in Europe. After 1918, its importance diminished. By 1938, France's total foreign long-term investment amounted to less than 4 billion dollars, a quarter of it in Europe.[93] The US and Great Britain took up the mantle of providing funds to Central and Eastern Europe, and between 1919 and 1932, were responsible for over two thirds of Polish, Czechoslovakian, and Hungarian bond issues, while France provided only a tenth of their total value (its position was stronger in the Balkans).[94] Most of French lending occurred once the country finally stabilized the franc in 1928, yet before the Great Depression started affecting the market in Paris. In other words, when Poland and other countries of the region needed funds the most, it was nearly impossible to issue bonds in France.[95]

As a result, if Poland wanted to get loans from its Western partner, especially in the early days after the war, it needed to get direct financing from the French government. This made loans purely political, and under the full

Table 2.1 Value of French state loans for military and state purposes

Type of loan	*Date*	*Value (million current French francs)*
Credits for financing Polish army abroad	1917–1923	442
Loans and credits for purchase of French military equipment	1919–1920	425
Loan for purchase of French military equipment	1919	5
Loans and credits for running of Polish National Committee in Paris and repatriating Siberian prisoners	1918–1920	2
Cost of occupying plebiscite zone in Upper Silesia	1920–1922, set in 1930	179
Credits promised in the Franco–Polish alliance	1924–1926 1931–1935	400
Rambouillet loans and credits	1936–1939	2 060
August 1939 commodity credit	1939	430
September 1939 cash credit	1939	600

Sources: CAÉF, B 31.929, P-V de clôture des travaux des commissions française et polonaise chargées d'établir le montant des sommes dépensées par la France pour le recrutement, l'équipement et le transport en Pologne de l'armé Haller, 26 November 1923, n.p.; CAÉF, B 31.922, Accord pour le réglement de la dette de guerre de la Pologne envers la France au titre des soldes impayés des frais d'occupation de la zone de plebiscite de Haute-Silésie, 20 January 1930, n.p.; Landau, *Polskie zagraniczne pożyczki*, 100–117; Stawecki, "Pożyczka," 64; Mihout, "L'intervention," 804.

control of Paris. With few other sources of money available to Poland (except relief funds from the US), this gave the French even more power. By 1933, out of a total state foreign indebtedness of 4.8 billion złoty, France was responsible for 20 per cent – almost a billion, much more than any country other than the United States.[96]

The majority of financing extended in this manner to Warsaw in the interwar period was earmarked for military spending, at a nominal interest rate of 5–6 per cent. As Table 2.1. shows, in the early years, two positions were responsible for most of the so-called Polish "war debt": money spent on the purchase of French stocks (1919–1920), and the financing of Polish armies in France and in Russia (dating to 1917, final amount set in 1923).[97] These purchases were crucial for the continued existence of Poland as a state, and for the defence of its borders, but proved expensive, especially for the low quality of stocks the French provided, at often elevated prices. As Polish Treasury Minister Leon Biliński wrote about a Polish general, he

> was not seen fondly in the French army's headquarters, since he had the good (for me at least) habit of searching for goods that were cheap, and haggling for those goods that were expensive. That's something the French don't like in general, and their army – in particular.[98]

This financing almost exclusively took the form of commercial credit, and had little value for Polish development.[99] France was responsible for c. 60 per cent of all funds used for military purposes in Poland, and c. 22 per cent of all funds (second after the US) between 1918 and 1921.[100] Yet, as I mentioned, despite its role in French security plans, by 1923 Poland received less money than both Yugoslavia and Romania, with the difference being even starker in per capita terms.[101] As these debts were a significant burden on the Polish budget, Warsaw did not service them. After long negotiations, in January 1930 the two countries agreed to restructure the debt, setting its value at 1.9 billion francs Poincaré, or just under 75 million dollars, to be paid by 1992.[102]

The next round of military credits – 400 million francs – was promised in the alliance treaty. As I mentioned, it took until 1924 for the promise to materialize.[103] Much to the Poles' chagrin, they were required to provide additional security for the credit, which moreover had to be spent on purchases in France vetted by the French Military Mission. Table 2.2. details its use. A significant portion of this credit was spent on artillery purchases, and only about an eighth on the military industry. This was not only less than planned, but some of it was wasted by French companies, for instance by Schneider in Starachowice. When it came to equipment, the Poles again complained about the quality and selection, and about French control over spending.[104] Warsaw temporarily renounced the 4th tranche, asking for the money again during the Great Depression.[105] The first 300 million was serviced until 1931/1932, and cut short due to the Great Depression. An agreement from 1937 arranged further service until 1956, but World War II ended it.[106]

After a failed bid in 1929–1930, the Poles managed to get major military funding from France in September 1936.[107] The treaty of Rambouillet afforded 2.6 billion francs at 5 per cent interest (c. 133 million dollars when it was granted, or some 45 million by 1939 due to the franc's devaluations), split almost equally between cash loans and credits.[108] This arrangement had a complex structure, shown in Table 2.3, and it combined strictly military expenditure with spending on infrastructure. The largest position, commodity credit, was supposed to be used for military spending in France (although this included small orders of machine tools used in industry). It quickly ran into problems, and only a small part was realized before the war (perhaps 150–190 million

Table 2.2 The use of the 400 million francs credits (1924–1926, 1931–1935)

Category	*Plan from 1924*	*Effective realization*
Weaponry	123	133
Army	117	180
Military industry	120	49
Transport	40	15
Payment for earlier purchases	0	23

Sources: Mihout-Natar, "L'intervention," 796.

Table 2.3 The scope of Rambouillet loans and credits

Category	*Plan from 1936*	*Effective realization (per cent)*
Commodity credit	1,000	15
Credit for military construction works of French companies in Poland	250	100
Bond issue of the Franco–Polish Railway Company	540	100
Bond issue of the Franco–Polish Railway Company (cash credit)	405	50
Cash loan for the Polish government	405	100
Total	2,600	62

Sources: Mihout, "L'intervention," 803.

francs).[109] The second-largest position were loans, backed by bonds of the Franco–Polish Railway Company. Some of them financed the Coal Trunk Railway, the rest was free to use by the Polish government. The Poles managed to use most of these loans, and the completion of the railway was a major boon. Warsaw also got another direct cash loan. With difficulties in buying equipment abroad, the money not destined for construction was mostly used to bolster Bank Polski's reserves and thus finance domestic lending. Paris made sure that a sizeable portion of government orders in Poland would be placed with French-owned companies. The last part of the loan would be used to finance the construction of military industrial facilities by French firms. Two ammunition factories within the Central Industrial Basin were chosen: in Kraśnik and Dęba. However, with the contracts signed in March 1938, and plans for the works to take over two years, they were not completed before the war. Likewise, the Poles did not use the new credits granted in August 1939.[110]

These last projects – particularly railway construction – straddled military expenditure and loans and credits granted for industrial purposes. Financing without a military purpose was almost non-existent, and amounted to only 12.5 million francs, lent (in German marks) to cover the Polish participation in certain Upper Silesian mixed companies. As I explain in more detail in Chapter 6, for the French this was also a security tool, and a way to spread the influence of their companies, rather than any appreciable input into Polish development.[111]

As Table 2.4 shows, the only other French financing of civilian nature were loans and credits for monetary goals, used by the Poles to stabilize or prop up their currency. Officials in Paris were worried about Polish inflation in the early 1920s, and considered sending a money doctor to help, but without financial backing, they abandoned the plan.[112] For the same reasons, all Polish attempts to place bonds in Paris were torpedoed. The lack of French financial help

Table 2.4 French loans for development and monetary purposes

Type of loan	*Date*	*Value*	*Interest rate*
Silesian loans	1921–1922	12.53 million francs	5 per cent
French part of the Polish stabilization loan	1927	2 million USD	7 per cent
Rolling credit granted by Banque de France to Bank Polski, backed by a gold deposit in France	1931–1939	100 million złoty, in 1932 increased to 175 million złoty	6.5 per cent, decreased to 3 per cent in 1937
Credit granted by Banque de France to Bank Polski backed by bills of exchange	1935	50 million złoty	4 per cent

Sources: AdC, CPC PL, 370, Avances à la Pologne autre que la dette de guerre proprement dite, Avances de sommes en Marks à la Pologne, 28 February 1931, 17; Leszczyńska, *Polska polityka*, 308; Landau, *Polskie zagraniczne pożyczki*, 201–202.

undermined Paris's position both in Warsaw and on global markets. In reaction, France tried to engage in "bankers' diplomacy": a series of European stabilization loans. In Poland this took the form of the 72 million dollar loan from 1927.[113] The United States provided two thirds of the money, while France gave only 2 million dollars after an arduous process of assembling a group of private banks willing to float the bonds in Paris.[114] French authorities bemoaned the state of their market, as they saw the loan as both as ways to keep their influence in Poland, and perhaps get Warsaw to service the old war bonds. Later, during the Great Depression, Poland pursued orthodox monetary policy: costly, but looked upon favourably by the Bank of France.[115] To help Poland stay on the Gold Standard, the formally private Banque de France provided rolling credit to the likewise private Polish central bank.[116]

This overview of financing extended to Poland by France serves to illustrate that the vast majority of loans and credits were earmarked for military purposes, with very little left for development. From the developmental point of view this was a negative outcome. With high servicing costs, the money was unproductive, and only undermined Warsaw's ability to pursue economic intervention, especially since it served as a tool of political influence for Paris. On the other hand, the large expenses on defence – further increased by the end of the 1930s in a "desperate but remarkable" gamble – were linked to Warsaw's precarious geopolitical position.[117]

2.5 Conclusions

During heated negotiations in 1924, the Polish Prime Minister Władysław Grabski complained that "With the French it is always the same…they never have the money."[118] This quote encapsulates the Polish experience of attempting to use French funds for anything other than military spending – and even then, the amounts extended to Warsaw were significantly smaller than what the Poles wanted. Arguably then, the price paid by Paris for the alliance was quite small. While good for the country's finances, the situation nonetheless undermined French security policy in Central and Eastern Europe (as the practice was similar in other countries of the region). It also hurt Paris's ability to influence the Poles, since promises of money combined with conditionality remained the principal political and diplomatic tool used by France.

The economic aspect of the relationship between the French and Polish governments was determined by politics. The flow of credits and loans depended on external circumstances: French elections, the Polish coup d'état, the Locarno treaties, or the remilitarization of the Rhineland. Combined with the influence the Paris government held over the domestic loan market, this meant that the process of obtaining funds by Warsaw was mostly political.

From the Polish point of view, French funding was insufficient both to improve Warsaw's military significantly, and to allow the government to invest in industry – unsurprisingly, as Paris was uninterested in promoting the growth of future rivals. Moreover, the price Warsaw had to pay by privileging and protecting private French companies was high – perhaps too high for what it got. Ultimately, if the Poles were looking to finance their industry using French funds, they could hardly count on state loans.

Notes

1 Archives Diplomatiques, La Courneuve [henceforth: AdC], Correspondance politique et commercial, 1918–1940, Pologne [henceforth: CPC PL], 409, Noël to MAÉ, 31 October 1935, 186–90.
2 AdC, CPC PL, 401, Laroche to Barthou, 15 August 1934, 157v.
3 AdC, CPC PL, 237, Briand to Laroche, 6 July 1927, 57v.
4 Cf. Murat Birdal, *The Political Economy of Ottoman Public Debt: Insolvency and European Financial Control in the Late Nineteenth Century* (London: I.B. Tauris, 2010).
5 Franco–Polish political relations are very well researched, The best account in English is still: Piotr Stefan Wandycz, *France and Her Eastern Allies 1919–1925: French–Czechoslovak–Polish Relations from the Paris Peace Conference to Locarno* (Minneapolis: The University of Minnesota Press, 1962); Piotr Stefan Wandycz, *The Twilight of French Eastern Alliances, 1926–1936: French–Czechoslovak–Polish Relations from Locarno to the Remilitarization of the Rhineland* (Princeton: Princeton University Press, 1988). Kalervo Hovi also gave a good general account of the beginning of the relationship: Kalervo Hovi, *Cordon Sanitaire or Barrière de l'est?: The Emergence of the New French Eastern European Alliance Policy, 1917–1919*, trans. Sirkka Battarbee and Keith Battarbee (Turku: Turun yliopisto, 1975); Kalervo Hovi, *Alliance de Revers: Stabilization of France's Alliance Policies in East Central Europe 1919–1921*, trans. Kaija London and Gary London (Turku: Turun yliopisto, 1984). Polish accounts came in two generations. The first two comprehensive works were mostly based on Polish sources: Józef Kukułka, *Francja a Polska Po Traktacie Wersalskim: 1919–1922* (Warszawa: Książka i Wiedza, 1970); Jan Ciałowicz, *Polsko-francuski sojusz wojskowy: 1921–1939* (Warszawa: Państwowe Wydawnictwo Naukowe, 1971). Later, Henryk Bułhak published two well-researched volumes on political history, based on both Polish and French sources: Henryk Bułhak, *Polska – Francja: z dziejów sojuszu 1922–1939. Cz. 1, (1922–1932)*

(Warszawa: Wydawnictwa Fundacji "Historia pro Futuro," 1993); Henryk Bułhak, *Polska – Francja: z dziejów sojuszu 1933–1936* (Warszawa: Wydawnictwo Neriton, 2000). The best French works were written by Georges-Henri Soutou, particularly: "L'Alliance franco-polonaise (1925–1933): ou Comment s'en débarrasser," *Revue d'Histoire Diplomatique* 95, no. 2, 3, 4 (1981): 295–348.

6 Wandycz, *France*, 11; Cf. Gusztáv Kecskés D., "East-Central European Nationalities and French Foreign Policy during the First World War," in *Nationalisms in Action: The Great War and Its Aftermath in East-Central Europe*, ed. László Szarka and Attila Pók, trans. Péter Barta (Komárom: J. Selye University – Faculty of Education, 2023), 41–61.

7 Tomasz Schramm, *Francuskie misje wojskowe w państwach Europy Środkowej: 1919–1939* (Poznań: Uniwersytet Adama Mickiewicza, 1987), 23–95.

8 Wandycz, *France*, 131–37.

9 Zbigniew Landau, *Polskie zagraniczne pożyczki państwowe 1918–1926* (Warszawa: Książka i Wiedza, 1961), 115–16; Mylène Mihout-Natar, "L'intervention des capitaux français dans la Pologne de la Seconde République (1918–1939): contribution à l'histoire de l'impérialisme économique français en Europe centrale" (PhD, Université Charles de Gaulle – Lille III, 2002), 796.

10 Jan Ciałowicz, *Polsko-francuski sojusz*, 49, 53.

11 Wandycz, *France*, 220.

12 Georges-Henri Soutou, "L'Alliance," 298; Hovi, *Cordon*, 75.

13 Alice Teichova, *An Economic Background to Munich: International Business and Czechoslovakia 1918–1938* (London: Cambridge University Press, 1974), 54–55.

14 Wandycz, *France*, 207, 241.

15 Jochen Böhler, *Civil War in Central Europe, 1918–1921. Reconstruction of Poland* (Oxford: Oxford University Press, 2018), 115–21.

16 Bułhak, *Polska – Francja*, 1993, 17–22; Georges-Henri Soutou, "L'impérialisme du pauvre: la politique économique du gouvernement français en Europe Centrale et Orientale de 1918 à 1929. Essai d'interprétation," *Relations internationales* 3, no. 7 (1976): 219–39, 296–97.

17 Soutou, "L'Alliance," 303, 305–11; Wandycz, *France*, 313–14, 329, 362–63.

18 Christophe Laforest, "Kulisy zrzeczenia się przez Polskę czwartej raty pożyczki francuskiej w 1925 r.," trans. Maria Pasztor, *Dzieje Najnowsze* 31, no. 3 (1999): 91–99; Ciałowicz, *Polsko-francuski sojusz*, 120.

19 Jules Laroche, *La Pologne de Pilsudski: Souvenirs d'une ambassade 1926–1935* (Paris: Flammarion, 1953), 41–42.

20 Wandycz, *France*, 368.

21 Ciałowicz, *Polsko-francuski sojusz*, 144; Henryk Bułhak, "Polskie starania o francuską pożyczkę na cele obrony narodowej. Okres uzgadniania koncepcji i sposobów jej realizacji w latach 1929–1930," in *W kręgu idei, polityki i wojska. Studia ofiarowane profesorowi Januszowi Farysiowi w siedemdziesiątą rocznicę urodzin*, ed. Tomasz Sikorski, Henryk Walczak, and Adam Wątor (Szczecin: Wydawnictwo Naukowe Uniwersytetu Szczecińskiego, 2009), 361–72.

22 Schramm, *Francuskie misje*, 125.

23 AdC, CPC PL, 401, Memo from meeting with Chłapowski, 21 August 1934, 244.

24 Bułhak, *Polska – Francja*, 2000, 10–11, 28–29, 51–53; Jameson W. Crockett, "The Polish Blitz, More than a Mere Footnote to History: Poland and Preventive War with Germany, 1933," *Diplomacy & Statecraft* 20, no. 4 (2009): 561–79, https://doi.org/10.1080/09592290903455667. Cf. Anna Ambrochowicz-Gajownik, "Koncert życzeń – żądania francuskie w negocjacjach gospodarczych z Polską w latach 1933–1935," *Studia z Historii Społeczno-Gospodarczej XIX i XX Wieku* 23 (2020): 75–93, https://doi.org/10.18778/2080-8313.23.04.

25 Ciałowicz, *Polsko-francuski sojusz*, 210.

26 Léon Noël, *L'Agression allemande contre la Pologne: Une ambassade à Varsovie, 1935–1939* (Paris: Flammarion, 1946).
27 Piotr Stawecki, "Pożyczka francuska z 1936 roku," *Kwartalnik Historyczny* 1 (1967): 49–68.
28 Christophe Laforest, "La stratégie française et la Pologne (1919–1939). Aspects économiques et implications politiques," *Histoire, économie et société* 22, no. 3 (2003): 395–411, 397, https://doi.org/10.3406/hes.2003.2328.
29 AdC, CPC PL, 234, Millerand to François-Marsal, 3 March 1920, 86; AdC, CPC PL, 238, de Monplanet to Pichon, 16 December 1918, 9–11.
30 AdC, CPC PL, 212, La Haute Silésie. Étude économique, 26 June 1920, 29.
31 Soutou, "L'impérialisme," 221; Richard F. Kuisel, *Capitalism and the State in Modern France: Renovation and Economic Management in the Twentieth Century* (Cambridge: Cambridge University Press, 1981), 59, 62, 65.
32 Soutou, "L'impérialisme," 222; Derek H. Aldcroft, *Europe's Third World: The European Periphery in the Interwar Years* (Aldershot and Burlington: Ashgate Publishing, 2006), 44; AdC, CPC PL, 234, MAÉ to Lévy, 5 July 1919, 13–15; AdC, CPC PL, 234, de Panafieu to Briand, 20 April 1921, 127–29; AdC, CPC PL, 235, Poincaré to François-Marsal, 27 May 1924, 68–68v; AdC, CPC PL, 234, de Lasteyrie to Poincaré, 22 December 1922, 175–75v.
33 Mihout, "L'intervention," 795.
34 AdC, CPC PL, 232, Briand to Laroche, 15 Octover 1928, 163–64.
35 AdC, CPC PL, 232, Briand to Chéron, 13 November 1928, 169–69v.
36 AdC, CPC PL, 231, Politique de la France en Pologne et en Serbie, 15 May 1924, 36.
37 Kuisel, *Capitalism*, 65; Martin Thomas, "French Empire Elites and the Politics of Economic Obligation in the Interwar Years," *The Historical Journal* 52, no. 4 (2009): 989–1016, https://doi.org/10.1017/S0018246X09990379.
38 AdC, CPC PL, 235, Laroche to Briand, 27 October 1928, 115–16, and 17 November 1928, 123; AdC, CPC PL, 251, Laroche to MAÉ, 23 October 1926, 250v; AdC, CPC Pl 426, Laroche to Briand, 12 April 1930, 19–24.
39 AdC, CPC PL, 426, Laroche to Briand, 12 April 1930, 19–24.
40 AdC, CPC PL, 251, Noulens to Pichon, 10 March 1919, 16–17; AdC, CPC PL, 247, Vicaire to Noulens, 13 March 1919, 19; AdC, CPC PL, 217, Le Rond to MAÉ, 2 March 1922, 2–5.
41 E.g. AdC, CPC PL, 216, Actions allemandes et anglaises en Pologne, 24 December 1921, 165–66.
42 David Stevenson, "France at the Paris Peace Conference. Addressing the Dilemmas of Security," in *French Foreign and Defence Policy, 1918–40: The Decline and Fall of a Great Power*, ed. Robert Boyce (London and New York: Routledge, 1998), 15.
43 AdC, CPC PL, 256, Vincent to Briand, 25 April 1921, 113.
44 AdC, CPC PL, 238, Noulens to Millerand, 5 July 1920, 59; AdC, CPC PL, 238, PLP to MAÉ, 20 July 1920, 63; AdC, CPC PL, 253, La situation dans le bassin de Dombrowa, en Pologne, 26 March 1921, 102–2v.
45 Maria Pasztor, *Polska w oczach francuskich kół rządowych w latach 1924–1939* (Warszawa: Wydawnictwo Akademickie Dialog, 1999).
46 AdC, CPC PL, 253, de Barante to Pichon, 23 August 1919, 60–64; AdC, CPC PL, 230, de Panafieu to Poincaré, 1 August 1923, 75.
47 AdC, CPC PL, 238, de Monplanet to Pichon, 16 December 1918, 9–11.
48 AdC, CDC PL, 252, Tripier to Briand, 30 November 1928, 197v and 3 December 1928, 198–99v.
49 AdC, CDC PL, 252, MAÉ to FEW, 25 May 1929, 229v.
50 AdC, CPC PL, 429, Laroche to Paul-Boncour, 21 December 1933, 165–68.
51 Laroche, "La stratégie" (article), 397.
52 AdC, CPC PL, 408, Laroche to Briand, 6 August 1930, 36.

53 AdC, CPC PL, 251, Laroche to MAÉ, 23 October 1926, 245–50v.
54 Cf. Larry Wolff, *Inventing Eastern Europe: The Map of Civilization on the Mind of the Enlightenment* (Stanford: Stanford University Press, 1994).
55 Maria Pasztor, "Główne elementy obrazu Polaka w oczach francuskich elit politycznych w okresie międzywojennym," *Dzieje Najnowsze* 31, no. 3 (1999): 113–26, 118; Jerzy Łazor, "'A Colony of Alien Capital.' French Investments, Polish Identity, and a Story of Murder in 1930s Warsaw," *Slavic Review* 81, no. 1 (2022): 122–41, https://doi.org/10.1017/slr.2022.79.
56 AdC, CPC PL, 251, Laroche to MAÉ, 23 October 1926, 250; AdC, CPC PL, 252, Laroche to Briand, 1 December 1927, 78v.
57 A good summary: Schramm, *Francuskie misje*.
58 For detailed discussions concerning such decision: Wojciech Mazur, *Pod wiatr. Francja i lotnictwo wojskowe II Rzeczypospolitej (1921–1938)* (Kraków: Ksiegarnia Akademicka Publishing, 2015), https://doi.org/10.12797/9788376386577.
59 Zbigniew Landau, "The Inflow of Foreign Capital into Poland after the Coup d'etat of May 1926," *Acta Poloniae Historica* 46 (1982): 159–77.
60 Zbigniew Landau, *Polskie zagraniczne pożyczki państwowe 1918–1926* (Warszawa: Książka i Wiedza, 1961); Landau, *Plan*; Jan Kofman, "Koła wielkoprzemysłowe a kwestia kapitałów obcych w okresie 1920–1939," *Kwartalnik Historyczny* 82, no. 2 (1975): 303–20.
61 Quoted from Leszczyńska, *Polska polityka*, 229. Cf. Władysław Marian Zawadzki, "Polityka finansowa w okresie 1931–1935," ed. Zbigniew Landau and Jerzy Tomaszewski, *Kwartalnik Historyczny* 6, no. 1 (1965): 134, 139.
62 Zbigniew Landau and Wojciech Roszkowski, *Polityka gospodarcza II RP i PRL* (Warszawa: Wydawnictwo Naukowe PWN, 1995), 47–56; Józef Nowicki, *Teoria ekonomii II Rzeczypospolitej* (Warszawa: Książka i Wiedza, 1988), 176–84; Stanisław Czaja and Bogusław Fiedor, *Oblicza polskiego etatyzmu gospodarczego: spór o miejsce państwa w gospodarce w okresie międzywojennym, powojennym i po 1990 roku: liberalizm versus etatyzm* (Wrocław: Wydawnictwo Uniwersytetu Ekonomicznego we Wrocławiu, 2021), 59–60.
63 Jacek Luszniewicz, "Etatism of the Economy of the Second Polish Republic in the Period of Parliamentary Democracy: Conditions, Stages, Evaluation (Part 1: 1918–1923)," *Studia i Prace KES* 9 3, no. 35 (2018): 35–60; Jacek Luszniewicz, "Etatism of the Economy of the Second Polish Republic in the Period of Parliamentary Democracy: Conditions, Stages, Evaluation (Part 2: 1923–1926)," *Studia i Prace KES* 9 4, no. 36 (2018): 65–84.
64 Tadeusz Bernadzikiewicz, *Udział państwa w spółkach handlowych* (Warszawa: Towarzystwo Wydawnicze Młodych Prawników i Ekonomistów, 1938), 86–89. Cf. Stanisław Kruszewski, *Majątek państwa polskiego według stanu na dzień 1 stycznia 1927 r.* (Warszawa: Ministerstwo Skarbu, 1931). Jerzy Gołębiowski, ed., *Kapitał państwowy w spółkach prawa handlowego u schyłku Drugiej Rzeczypospolitej. Szczegółowe sprawozdanie z działalności przedsiębiorstw o kapitale mieszanym za rok 1937 wzgl. 1937/1938* (Kraków: Wydawnictwo Naukowe Akademii Pedagogicznej, 2004).
65 This point is contentious. See: Janusz Kaliński, "State Entrepreneurship in Interwar Poland," *Studia Historiae Oeconomicae* 41, no. 1 (2023): 43–78, https://doi.org/10.14746/sho.2023.41.1.003; Jerzy Gołębiowski, *Sektor państwowy w gospodarce Polski międzywojennej* (Warszawa—Kraków: Państwowe Wydawnictwo Naukowe, 1985), 238–87; Czaja and Fiedor, *Oblicza*, 72–74.
66 Piotr Janus, *W nurcie polskiego etatyzmu. Stefan Starzyński i Pierwsza Brygada Gospodarcza 1926–1932* (Kraków: Wydawnictwo Avalon, 2009); Grzegorz Piątek, *Sanator. Kariera Stefana Starzyńskiego* (Warszawa: W.A.B., 2016); Tadeusz Grabowski, *Rola państwa w gospodarce Polski (1918–1928)* (Warszawa: Państwowe Wydawnictwo Ekonomiczne, 1967), 238–87.

67 Adam Leszczyński, *Leap into Modernity: Political Economy of Growth on the Periphery, 1943–1980* (Frankfurt am Main: Peter Lang Edition, 2017).
68 Zenon Szmidtke, *"Skarboferm" 1922–1939: związki polityki z gospodarką* (Opole: Państwowy Instytut Naukowy, 2005), 244.
69 Cf. Zbigniew Landau and Bronisława Skrzeszewska, eds., *Wojciech Korfanty przed Sądem Marszałkowskim: Dokumenty* (Katowice: Wydawnictwo "Śląsk," 1964).
70 Cf. AdC, CPC PL, 261, Clementel to Herriot, 29 October 1924, 38.
71 AdC, CPC PL, 261, de Panafieu to Herriot, 15 September 1924, 7–7v.
72 Mihout-Natar, "L'intervention," 733.
73 Archiwum Akt Nowych, Warsaw, [henceforth: ANN], Ministerstwo Spraw Zagranicznych [henceforth: MSZ], 3858, Notatka w sprawie elektrowni, 3 June 1938, 357; AdC, CPC PL, 238, Dispositions urgents pour la sauvegarde des biens et des intérêts français en Pologne, 16 December 1918, 5–8; AdC, CPC PL, 238, de Monplanet to Pichon, 16 December 1918, 9–11.
74 AdC, CPC PL, 253, MAÉ to FCK, 19 April 1923, 128; AdC, CPC PL, 230, MSZ to FLW, 13 September 1923, 100–101; AdC, CPC PL, 252, Laroche to MAÉ, 6 March 1929, 215–16.
75 E.g. AdC, CPC PL, 280A, Règlement des réclamations françaises en Pologne, 16 January 1924, 79–83; AdC, CPC PL, 400, Briand to Flandin, 29 November 1931, 17–17v; AAN, MSZ, 3839, Instrukcja dla Posła Chłapowskiego, [1924], 5–11.
76 AdC, CPC PL, 238, Noulens to [MAÉ], 7 August 1920, 77–78.
77 *Rapport fait au nom de la Commission des affaires étrangères et de politique générale des colonies et protectorats, chargée d'examiner le projet de lois adopté par la Chamber des Députés, portant approbation de la Convention conclue à Paris le 6 février 1922, entre la France et la Pologne, et relative au régime des industries du naphte, par M. Louis Dausset, Sénateur*, Sénat 1923, no 627, 10 July 1923, 19.
78 AdC, CPC PL, 404, Laroche to MAÉ, 1 October 1931, 62 and 24 May 1932, 74.
79 AAN, MSZ, 3858, W. Kulski, Notatka w sprawie elektrowni, 3 June 1938, 355–58.
80 Mihout-Natar, "L'intervention," 758.
81 Jan Kofman, *Economic Nationalism and Development: Central and Eastern Europe between the Two World Wars* (London and New York: Routledge, 2018), 56.
82 AdC, CPC PL, 397, Laroche to Briand, 24 December 1930, 58–60.
83 Charles Lipson, *Standing Guard: Protecting Foreign Capital in the Nineteenth and Twentieth Centuries* (Berkeley: University of California Press, 1985), 71–72.
84 Centralne Archiwum Wojskowe, Rembertów, I Oddział Sztabu Głównego, I 303.3.559, Memorandum on a conversation with André Citroën, 10 February 1931, 303–304.
85 See Rudolf Nötel, "International Credit and Finance," in *The Economic History of Eastern Europe 1919–1975, v. II. Interwar Policy, The War, and Reconstruction*, ed. Michael Charles Kaser and E.A. Radice (Oxford: Clarendon Press, 1986), 170–295.
86 Jari Eloranta, Stefan Nikolić, and Flóra Macher, "Between Disintegration and Convergence, 1918–1939: Flows of Capital, Goods, and Labor," in *The Economic History of Central, East, and South-Eastern Europe: 1800 to the Present*, ed. Matthias Morys (London and New York: Routledge, 2021), 216–42, 221.
87 Landau, *Polskie zagraniczne pożyczki*, 15.
88 Leszczyńska, *Polska polityka*, 103–10, 228.
89 Michael D. Bordo and Hugh Rockoff, "The Gold Standard as a 'Good Housekeeping Seal of Approval,'" *The Journal of Economic History* 56, no. 2 (1996): 389–428.
90 In the 1920s, the Poles used exchange control between February 1919 and August 1924, and from May 1925 to November 1927. It was the most restrictive intermittently before 1921, in the first half of 1923, after December 1925. Cf. Leszczyńska, *Polska polityka*.
91 Zbigniew Landau, "Stosunek rządów pomajowych do napływu kapitałów zagranicznych do Polski," *Śląski Kwartalnik Historyczny Sobótka*, no. 3–4 (1962): 408–25.

92 Aldcroft, *Europe's Third World*, 54.
93 Charles H. Feinstein and Katherine Watson, "Private International Capital Flows in Europe in the Inter-War Period," in *Banking, Currency, and Finance in Europe Between the Wars*, ed. Charles H. Feinstein (Oxford University Press, 1995), 94–130, 97. https://doi.org/10.1093/0198288034.003.0004.
94 Calculations based on Eloranta, Nikolić, and Macher, "Between Disintegration," 220.
95 The Poles did manage to get some minor financing from railway companies and private banks: Leszczyńska, *Polska polityka*, 308; Landau, *Polskie zagraniczne pożyczki*, 201–2; Mihout, "L'intervention," 792.
96 Leopold Wellisz, *Foreign Capital in Poland* (London: George Allen & Unwin, 1938), Appendix A.
97 AdC, CPC PL, 239, Grabski to Komitet Narodowy Polski, 17 December 1917, 1–2; Landau, *Polskie zagraniczne pożyczki*, 50.
98 Leon Biliński, *Wspomnienia i Dokumenty. Tom II, 1915–1922* (Warszawa: Księgarnia F. Hoesicka, 1925), 262.
99 Schramm, *Francuskie* misje, 81–82.
100 Mihout-Natar, "L'intervention," 793.
101 Mihout-Natar, "L'intervention," 206.
102 Centre des archives économiques et financières, Savigny-le-Temple [henceforth: CAÉF], B 31.922, Réglement de la dette de guerre de la Pologne envers la France, 26 November 1930, n.p. For negotiations and calculations: CAÉF, B 31.931; Christophe Laforest, "La stratégie française et la Pologne (1919–1939). Aspects économiques et implications politiques" (PhD, Université Paris 1 Panthéon-Sorbonne, 2001), 47.
103 AdC, CPC PL, 212, Convention entre la France et la Pologne relative à trois avances de 100 million de francs chacune consenties par le Tresor français au Gouvernement polonais, 28 August 1924, 313–18.
104 Laforest, "Kulisy"; Ciałowicz, *Polsko-francuski sojusz*, 125.
105 Józef Łaptos and Mariusz W. Majewski, "Francuska pomoc w wyposażeniu armii polskiej (1919–1939)," *Annales Universitatis Paedagogicae Cracoviensis. Studia Historica* 14 (2013): 102–16, 113; Ciałowicz, *Polsko-francuski sojusz*, 162–64.
106 Landau, *Polskie zagraniczne pożyczki.*
107 Laforest, "La Stratégie," 68–70; Henryk Bułhak, "Polskie starania".
108 Stawecki, "Pożyczka."
109 See Stawecki, "Pożyczka", 64; Mihout, "L'intervention," 803, Laforest, "La Stratégie," 83, 97; Jakub Skiba, "Polska polityka finansowa wobec zbrojeń w latach 1935–1939," in *Pieniądz, historia, polityka. Studia ofiarowane prof. dr. hab. Wojciechowi Morawskiemu w 70. rocznicę urodzin*, ed. Łukasz Dwilewicz and Jerzy Łazor (Warszawa: Oficyna Wydawnicza SGH, forthcoming in 2024).
110 Tadeusz Grabowski, *Inwestycje zbrojeniowe w gospodarce Polski międzywojennej* (Warszawa: Wydawnictwo Ministerstwa Obrony Narodowej, 1963), 173–77; Szmidtke, *Skarbferm*," 244; Mihout, "L'intervention," 276, 802 bis.
111 Cf. Jerzy Łazor, "'Broń dyplomatyczna pierwszej rangi?' Powstanie polsko-francuskiego Banku Śląskiego SA po I wojnie światowej," *Roczniki Dziejów Społecznych i Gospodarczych* 81 (2020): 289–320, http://doi.org/10.12775/RDSG.2020.10; Zbigniew Landau and Jerzy Tomaszewski, "Misja Prof. A. Benisa," *Teki Archiwalne* 6 (1959): 29–225.
112 AdC, CPC PL, 229, Briand to de Panafieu, 11 October 1921, 225–27.
113 Landau, *Plan.*
114 Documents in: AdC, CPC PL, 237; Richard Hemmig Meyer, *Bankers' Diplomacy; Monetary Stabilization in the Twenties* (New York: Columbia University Press, 1970), 58–100; Zbigniew Landau, *Plan Stabilizacyjny 1927–1930. Geneza, Założenia, Wyniki* (Warszawa: Książka i Wiedza, 1963).

115 Banque de France, Direction Générale des Études, Dossiers Pays: Pologne, 1370199803, 1, Introduction de l'étalon-or en Pologne, 1933, n.p.; Nikolaus Wolf, "Should I Stay or Should I Go? Understanding Poland's Adherence to Gold, 1928–1936," *Historical Social Research* 32, no. 4 (2007): 351–68.
116 Banque de France, Direction du Reseau, 1064199002, 150, file "Renouvellement d'un crédit de złotys or, 1933–1939;" Leszczyńska, *Polska polityka*, 308.
117 Aldcroft, *Europe's Third World*, 65–66, 113 (quote).
118 AdC, CPC PL, 260, de Vaux to Poincaré, 9 May 1924, 194.

3 French companies in interwar Poland

Distribution, results, and economic environment

In 1920 Joseph Noulens, president of the Banque Franco-Polonaise in Paris, unsuccessfully petitioned the Quai d'Orsay to grant his company the right to use the French Military Mission's courier service, and thus allow it to avoid the Polish postal service. The French Minister in Warsaw Hector de Panafieu was worried that the bank would use the privilege to bypass Polish currency export controls, and thus gain an edge over other French companies. Characteristically, he did not mind the illegality of such actions. Noulens, a former minister and ambassador, knew the workings of the French government. He approached officials from other government services, promised not to break the law, and got the General Staff to authorize his request. Soon couriers started complaining about the weight of "correspondence" sent by the bank in a padlocked suitcase, and the military ordered the firm to use envelopes instead.[1]

The Poles found out that the bank had been avoiding their foreign exchange laws in early 1924 and arrested its director Louis George. Understanding the severity of the situation, Prime Minister Raymond Poincaré asked de Panafieu not to intervene, and to cooperate with the Poles without handing over any documents. The bank reacted by sacking its managers in Poland. In a conversation with Jules Laroche at the Quai d'Orsay, Noulens admitted that his firm had broken the law, but attacked the ministry for allowing the arrest of a French citizen, and suggested retaliation, as it was "necessary not to give the Poles an impression of weakness."[2] Ultimately, Noulens was right. Sending a French director to prison was unlikely. The Poles realized that French diplomats did not knowingly deceive them, and were themselves the bank's victims. By 1925, the bank's new management had excellent relations with diplomats both in Warsaw and Paris, and by 1926 returned to trying to get the French authorities to protect it from Polish fiscal controls.[3]

Banque Franco-Polonaise was an outlier in many ways. The only French bank operating in Poland directly, it played a dominant role in supporting French companies in the country, and enjoyed significant political backing, especially in the early 1920s. Nonetheless, its approach to Polish laws, and the reliance on French diplomatic support, was not extraordinary. The scale of its illegal activities seems small in comparison to what the Poles alleged happened in Zakłady Żyrardowskie or the Compagnie d'Électricité de Varsovie. What

DOI: 10.4324/9781003375586-3

makes the bank's story notable was Noulens' subterfuge, and the use of the French military for suspect economic activity. The rejection of this approach by the Quai d'Orsay and the outrage and anxiety visible in diplomatic correspondence on this subject underline a crucial distinction. While private investors cooperated with the French authorities, and used them as a shield against Polish regulations, they were not merely the arm of government policy. They had different goals and plans, sometimes at odds with those of Paris, wide-ranging contacts with both the Poles and investors from other countries, and complex arrangements of ownership and lobbying. This makes them *sui generis* economic actors in Poland, influenced by both governments, but following a separate path.

The goal of this chapter is to analyze the scope and financial results of these private investments, and the economic environment in which they functioned. As I argue, while the size of French holdings in the Polish economy was significant, much of these were formed before the war, with a lot of new ventures limited to brownfield investment. The latter were a sign of the geopolitical situation after the Great War, rather than any significant push towards Polish development. Moreover, their technological background was often archaic, with very few ventures into leading interwar products. The two factors together explain much of the companies' results: higher dividend payments in the late 1920s (as owners pushed their ventures to their limits, looking for compensation for the lost years of the war and post-war rebuilding) and lower than average results during the Great Depression, which greatly affected resource extraction and industries based on old technologies. While it is difficult to show a firm link between privileges extended to French companies and their results, the protection extended by the government in Paris greatly facilitated the firms' functioning in Poland.

The story underlines the necessity and geopolitical limits of both industrial policy and rules governing the functioning of foreign capital. As I show, the only area where Warsaw pushed for reasonable regulations – the employment of foreigners in companies operating in Poland – was hotly contested by the French. As the weaker side, the Poles were forced to limit their policy well into the late 1930s. It is also notable that a similar situation occurred in French-owned Škoda in Czechoslovakia, despite stricter regulations in Prague, and a stronger position of the country in relation to Paris.[4] It is yet another example how the hierarchical relationship which necessarily appears between capital exporters and importers distorts the investment process, and interferes with the weaker side's policy.

3.1 Scope and structure of French investment in Poland[5]

The value of foreign investments is notoriously difficult to estimate. Some of the difficulty stems from problems with determining a company's nationality. It can, of course, be defined simply through "the place of incorporation or by the location of central administration/headquarters ('real seat')."[6] This approach works well for free-standing companies, with a clear structure of ownership, but it becomes inadequate for large multinationals, with their multiple cross-border connections.[7] The French and Polish governments themselves struggled to find a better approach in 1922. In one agreement they defined French companies as those owned in majority by the French, while in another they left it to themselves to confirm each firm's nationality.[8]

Neither France, nor Poland organized foreign investment censuses. What remains are incomplete interwar Polish statistics based on self-reporting, whose creators struggled to counter biases and difficulties arising from the complex structures of capital. As an example, subsidiaries of French-owned Polish firms would not report themselves as foreign.[9] Moreover, all the major interwar investments formed part of larger conglomerates, with many interconnected companies providing capital for a common endeavour. Such capital groups invested in multiple firms, forming large holdings. Schneider with its investments throughout Central and Eastern Europe was the most extensive, and estimating the value of its various holdings is no easy task.

Turning to French sources does not alleviate these problems. Even officials tasked with dealing with investment were not always sure about the extent of their national holdings in Poland.[10] Moreover, the size of French engagement played a rhetorical role, and was thus misused and misrepresented in diplomatic and government correspondence. Any estimates are further complicated by types of investment which fully escaped statistics, such as controlling firms through short-term credit.

Table 3.1 presents estimates of French investment on future Polish land in 1914. The nominal share value of the c. 30 companies in question reached some 280–300 million francs (54–58 million dollars).[11] Except for the sizeable oil sector in Austrian Galicia, the French mostly invested in the Kingdom of Poland (representing a sixth of their holdings in Russia).[12] Their interests covered coal mining and the metallurgical industry in the Dąbrowa Basin, as well as the textile industry, predominantly located in Łódź and Częstochowa. The French often cooperated with Belgian capital.

What changed after the war? Unfortunately, there is no reliable information on foreign investment in Poland before 1927 and after 1937.[13] Between these two

Table 3.1 French capital invested in future Polish lands, current prices, 1914

Sector	*Value (million francs)*	*Value (million USD)*	*Partition*
Oil extraction and refining	75	14.5	Austrian
Textile industry	70	13.5	Predominantly Russian
Mining and metallurgy	110–130	21.2–25.1	Predominantly Russian
Other	25	4.8	Russian

Sources: Calculated based on Mihout-Natar, "L'intervention," 380, 900–5; Girault, *Emprunts*, 516; Christophe Laforest, "La stratégie française et la Pologne (1919–1939). Aspects économiques et implications politiques" (PhD, Université Paris 1 Panthéon-Sorbonne, 2001), 13, 16, 35.

dates, almost half of all capital in joint-stock companies was reported as foreign-owned, with the share growing during the Great Depression, and falling again after 1935.[14] Estimates point to c. 234 million British pounds as the total value of foreign capital in the country in 1930, of which almost a third was in the form of short-term placements. The per capita value of c. 7 pounds was low, but generally in line with the rest of Central and Eastern Europe. However, the highest share of short-term credit in the region (together with Hungary) put Polish businesses and the country's balance of payments in a precarious position.[15]

More granular data on foreign investment is elusive. Table 3.2 summarizes Mieczysław Smerek's estimates for 1930. It covers three forms of investment: equity and reserve capital in domestic joint-stock and limited liability companies, the same values for foreign companies operating in Poland, and cash credits afforded to these two categories of firms. The first two are uncontroversial. I included cash credits as a form of investment, since they were predominantly used within holdings and multinationals.[16] France, with almost 1 billion złoty (or 109 million dollars) placed in Poland, emerges as the most important foreign owner, ahead of Germany and the US, and accounts for almost a quarter of all foreign investment in the country. Unlike owners from other states, the French achieved their position primarily through equity investment, with the lowest share of cash credits in their portfolio among all the major investors. As credits are the most volatile form of capital engagement, their smaller role in French investment suggests that Paris was a stable source of funds–arguably due to the strong position of pre-war industrial holdings.

Leopold Wellisz prepared the second major estimate of foreign investment in Poland for the year 1933.[17] Like Smerek, he relied on self-reported data, but his results are more problematic, as he could not name the source of most credits. However, if we assume that their structure was analogous to that in 1930, the overall share of investors from various countries remains the same as

Table 3.2 Value of foreign capital in Polish domestic and foreign companies, 1930

Country	*Number of companies*	*Share and reserve capital (million złoty)*	*Cash credits (million złoty)*	*Total (million złoty)*	*Total (million USD)*	*Share in total foreign capital investment (%)*
Austria	96	95	153	248	28	6
Belgium	58	263	119	381	43	9
France	100	680	289	969	109	23
Germany	123	498	318	816	92	19
Switzerland	50	80	197	277	31	6
UK	63	105	257	362	41	9
USA	28	415	239	654	73	15
Other	152	190	365	555	62	13
Total	505	2,326	1,937	4,262	478	100

Sources: Calculated from Smerek, "Bilans" 1933, 16, 30, 33.

in Smerek's estimates, with French holdings rising to 1.1 billion złoty or 123 million dollars.[18]

Both interwar commentators and later historians argued that Smerek's and Wellisz's data was wrong. They claimed that German owners had infiltrated the Polish economy to a greater extent than statistics showed, hiding behind capital coming from other countries, such as the United Kingdom, the United States, or France. There is little proof of this process in French archives. The government in Paris was even more paranoid than the Poles when it came to competition from Germany (see Chapter 5).[19] Some later studies disproved rumours of German control: Daniel Stone found no proof of such influence in Giesche, a major American-owned zinc and coal producer headquartered in Katowice, despite many claims to this effect.[20] Nonetheless, one notable exception makes Polish claims plausible: Compagnie d'Électricité de Varsovie, which stayed at the centre of a major Franco–Polish conflict, hid its German origins throughout the interwar period. More research on this issue is needed in company archives and in Germany.

Table 3.3 shows Smerek's data on the structure of French investment. The majority of funds were in resource extraction, split between the oil sector (33 per cent) and mining (28 per cent). The former dated to the early 20th century,

Table 3.3 The role of French capital in different Polish sectors, 1930

Sector	*French capital*[a]			*Sector total*[b]		
	Number of companies	*Value (million złoty)*	*Value (million USD)*	*Total value (million złoty)*	*Share of French capital (%)*	*Share of foreign capital (%)*
Oil extraction	14	222	25	300	74	85
Mining	12	190	21	610	31	65
Metallurgy	5	106	12	689	15	86
Chemical industry	14	25	3	347	7	61
Textile industry	17	52	6	667	8	27
Paper industry	3	25	3	102	25	38
Private banks	5	42	5	309	14	31
Other	30	17	2	2,045	1	27
Total	100	680	76	5,067	13	46

Notes:

[a] Includes share and reserve capital of domestic joint-stock and limited liability companies, as well as foreign companies operating directly in Poland. The distribution of the last component is estimated based on incomplete data.

[b] Sector total includes domestic and foreign joint-stock companies, and foreign capital in domestic limited liability companies.

Sources: Calculated from Smerek, "Bilans" 1933, 17, 19, 33; RPPiH 1932; *Rocznik Statystyczny Rzeczpospolitej Polskiej* [henceforth: RSRP] 1930.

when the Galician Oil Basin briefly became the third-largest producer in the world, and to directly after World War I. Mining included the extraction of coal and zinc, and was mostly the result of 19th century investments I mentioned above, their reconstruction after the war, and politically motivated takeovers in Upper Silesia. Including interwar investment, French companies were responsible for almost a quarter of all coal mined in the country. In zinc, they accounted for about two-fifths of production, and competed with the Silesian company Giesche, owned by the American magnate Averell Harriman and the Anaconda Copper Mining Company.[21] About a quarter of private French capital in Poland in 1930 represented various branches of industry–mostly in metallurgy and textiles (16 and 8 per cent respectively). The textile sector is notable for greenfield investments in 1929 and 1930. There was also little French investment in the banking sector.

As I mentioned in Chapter 1, there is nothing inherently detrimental to development in resource extraction – and many of today's rich states had relied on such exports in the past.[22] Long term, however, such countries need to invest in industry to improve their place in the global division of labour. Consequently, France's holdings in energy resources were of little use for Polish development in the interwar period, especially since these were generally brownfield investments, often based on old technology. Applying Carlota Perez's approach to French investment in industry also gives unimpressive results.[23] Almost all major French holdings belonged to the third (metallurgy, most of chemical companies) or even the second Kondratiev (majority of textiles), and saw little refitting to new technologies in the interwar period. There were certainly exceptions. Škoda's Warsaw plant, specializing in aviation, became a leading producer in the country, investments in the Gdynia Shipyards were also potentially important, as were the multiple approaches to car production. In terms of total capital, however, they were but a small part of French holdings. I will discuss them in more detail in the next chapter.

While the structure of French investment in the interwar period remained broadly the same as before the war (albeit with a bigger role of the oil sector), its economic niche changed. In Mira Wilkins's framework, investors either orient towards the market (focus on demand in the host country) or towards supply (focus on exports).[24] Before the war, French holdings in the Polish lands were predominantly market-oriented, based on producing coal, steel, or textiles within (mostly) the Russian Empire, and selling them on that market. Interwar Poland's economy could not support such ambitions, forcing investors to reconsider the purpose of their companies. Gradually, their orientation changed towards supply, with, for instance, French coal producers leading the internationalization of Polish coal sales.[25] As resources and low-tech products were a poor match for the interwar period's general stagnation, this explains much of French capital's unimpressive results, which we'll discuss in the next section. On the other hand, the most important post-war investment, which catapulted the French to domination in the oil sector, was initially supply-oriented, a way for Paris to win access to oil. However, with high extraction costs, and expensive freight, the sector soon moved towards competition on the domestic Polish market, with exports treated as a necessary, loss-inducing evil.

As the main sectors with strong French presence formed dense clusters on the Polish map, French investment was geographically concentrated in just a few voivodeships (see Map 3.1).[26] Over half of all French companies had headquarters in Warsaw or in the Lwów voivodeship, and over a third in the regions of Łódź, Kielce (which included the Dąbrowa Basin and Częstochowa), and Upper Silesia. In terms of share capital, the voivodeships of Lwów and Kielce accounted for three-quarters of its value. There was no French investment along Poland's eastern borders, in the poorest parts of the country.

To look beyond official statistics, I moved to company-level data, which I accessed through interwar Polish industry yearbooks. Six volumes of such publications appeared before World War II (in 1929, 1930, 1932, 1934, 1936, and 1938), compiling self-reported data on share capital, dividends, production, basic financial results, and others.[27] Based on files collated by Mylène Mihout-Natar, archival sources, and information within the yearbooks, I created a list of 100 companies with French capital (in 94 of which French capital was likely the sole or dominant owner).[28] I excluded simple trading firms, and companies operating in more complex holdings with a non-dominant French position.[29] Based on this list, I found 416 yearbook entries (c. 50 each for 1929 and 1930, and c. 80 for the other years). Later entries often included information on past performance and company history, allowing more precise comparisons.

I first tested the yearbook data by recreating Smerek's 1930 statistics. With fewer companies, I arrived at a very similar level of French share ownership, and a similar structure of investment. This was expected, as larger companies, representing the majority of French capital in Poland, were more likely to be included in the yearbook. I lacked adequate cash credit and reserve capital data. Nonetheless, since my estimates of share capital were robust, I extended them to cover 1927 and 1936, as seen in Table 3.4. For 1936, they show slightly more investment than in aggregated Polish statistics.[30]

The data shows that the French dominated among the largest companies, accounting for a third of what the Poles considered very large firms (with a capital over 20 million złoty), and about a fifth of the so-called large firms (8 to 20 million).[31] Moreover, it confirms an expansion of French holdings directly before the Great Depression, which is consistent with narrative sources. As the crisis hit, major pre-war French investments stayed in business, albeit at the cost of decapitalization, while private banking collapsed (with three major bankruptcies), and the textile sector underwent horizontal integration.

To chart a more precise timeline of French investment, I used my dataset, but excluded the oil sector, where significant restructuring of companies blurs the information (I discuss the timeline of French investment there in more detail in Chapter 5). Table 3.5 presents the relevant data on the entry of French capital into companies on my list, and the capital held by those among them that survived until 1936. The results are consistent with both narrative and

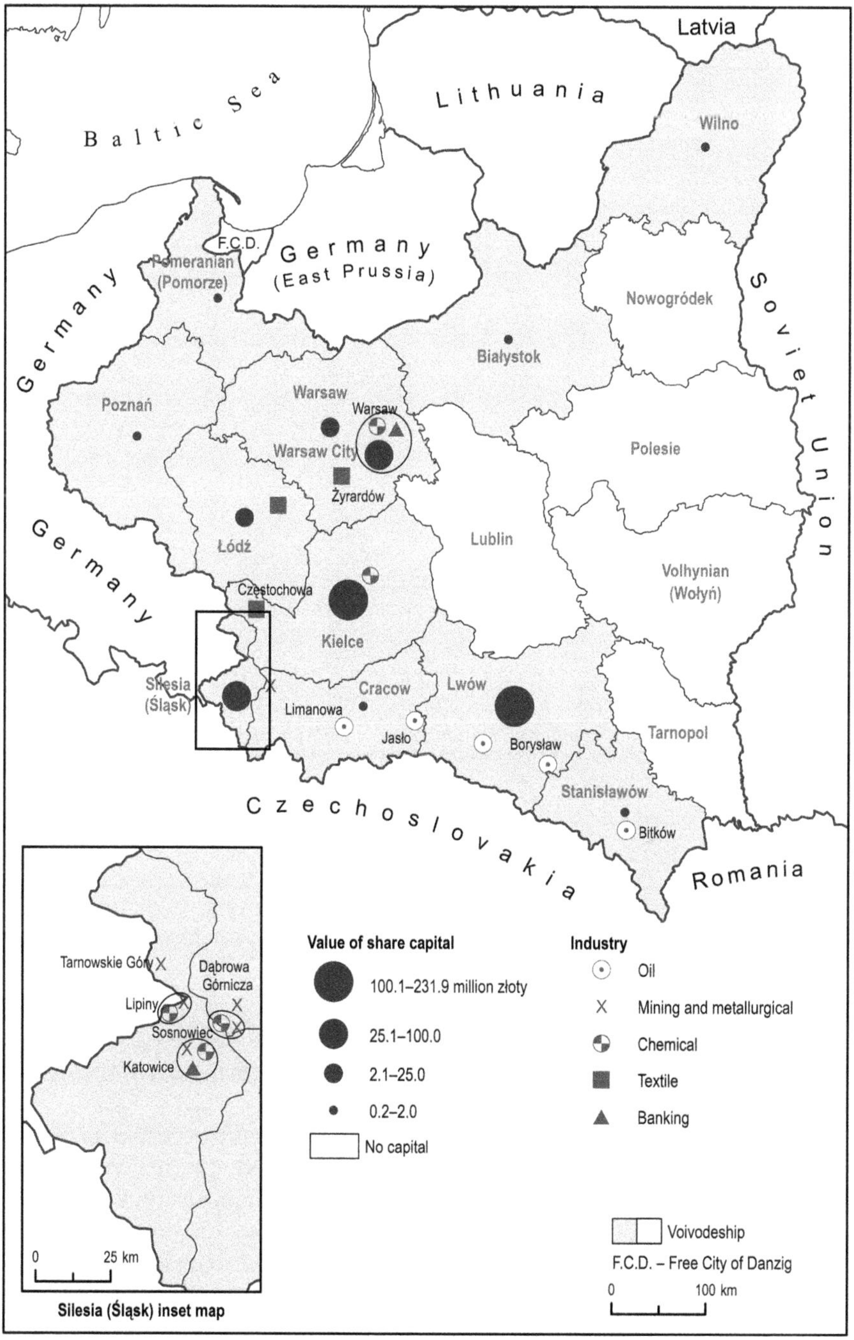

Map 3.1 Geographical concentration and principal locations of French industry in interwar Poland.

Table 3.4 The structure of French investment in Poland based on company reporting, 1930 and 1936

Sector	*1927*		*1930*		*1936*	
	Number of companies	*Share capital (million złoty)*	*Number of companies*	*Share capital (million złoty)*	*Number of companies*	*Share capital (million złoty)*
Oil extraction	11	149	30	172	31	173
Mining	10	98	11	111	9	109
Metallurgy	4	58	4	88	4	68
Chemical industry	2	1	8	13	11	18
Textile industry	9	37	11	50	6	63
Private banks	5	11	4	25	2	6
Other	5	18	16	36	16	16
Total	46	371	84	496	79	452

Sources: Calculations based on RISA 1929; RPPiH 1932, and 1938.

Table 3.5 Chronology of French investment in Poland (excluding the oil sector)

Time of investment	*Number of companies*	*Share capital in 1936 (million zł)*
Before 1918	20	218.0
1918–1925	17	32.9
1926–1930	15	39.6
1930–1935	6	0.4

Sources: Calculations based on RPPiH 1928, 1929, 1930, 1932, 1934, 1936; Mihout-Natar, "L'intervention," 895–922.

statistical sources.[32] Thus the dominant role of pre-war investment, and the much weaker capital position of firms from the 1920s (some of which went bankrupt by the early 1930s). In the next decade, new firms, even if visible in some sectors (such as construction), were even smaller.

This data suggests that French investment in Poland occurred primarily before the Great War. The story is more complicated. During World War I, Berlin and Vienna put French firms under forced administration, extending it to Russian Poland after its occupation in 1915. Companies in the last territory, which constituted most of French investment, were faced with forced requisitions and organized plunder of their resources and equipment. The resulting decapitalization produced, in the words of an interwar owner, "a state of agony," with both heavy and light industry almost non-operational after the Armistice.[33] As an employee of a French textile factory in Łódź testified after the war: the Germans "took everything…apart from goods stored in a well-hidden secret storeroom."[34] The Germans in the Dąbrowa Basin also requisitioned and looted houses of French employees, who later claimed damages of tens of thousands of francs.[35] Afterwards, businesses in Poland had to cope with war, inflation and hyperinflation, currency integration, and monetary reforms. Companies operating within the former empires needed to find their place in the new borders. Some, like the powerful coal and metallurgy group Huta Bankowa, had lost their investment in Russia after the October revolution; for others, such as Air Liquide or the insurance company L'Urbaine, the remaining businesses in Poland were but small remnants of much larger enterprises. The return of these firms to operations required significant additional investment which mostly occurred between 1919 and 1922, sometimes through the issue of new stock. For instance, the Société Anonyme Mines de Czeladź doubled its stock capital from the pre-war 9.75 million francs to 19.5 million in 1920.[36] Thus, while in interwar Poland pre-war French companies dominated over others, their capital owed much to rebuilding directly after the war.

In the interwar period, the French invested in three distinct phases. First, directly after the Armistice, takeovers in the oil sector accompanied purchases in textile production, joint Franco–Polish endeavours in Upper Silesia, and forays into construction.[37] The second phase, in the late 1920s, saw further investment in the textile sector, with some small new companies, and expansion into electricity production and the chemical sector (with many small cosmetics companies in Warsaw). Finally, the 1930s resulted in the creation of new companies in the civil engineering sector, as Warsaw moved towards state-directed investment in infrastructure. The introduction of exchange control in 1936 put a damper on new ventures, as the French were afraid (as in other markets) to be stuck in a risky country with no easy way to liquidate their assets.[38]

Poland was not the only country in Central and Eastern Europe with significant French investment. Paris obtained a similar level of economic control in Czechoslovakia and Yugoslavia, as illustrated in Table 3.6. French capital also had a considerable stake in Romania, with all four countries belonging to Paris's political sphere of influence. When we consider these together with Poland, Warsaw and Prague appear closer to each other than to Bucharest or Belgrade. In the two Central European states, foreign capital had a minority stake in all joint-stock company capital (some 29 per cent in Czechoslovakia in 1937, and 43 per cent in Poland in 1936), and specifically in the banking sector (15 per cent and 29 per cent respectively). These numbers were in stark contrast to the situation in Romania and Yugoslavia. In both counties, three-quarters of all capital in banking came from abroad, and the numbers for industrial joint-stock companies amounted to 60–80 per cent, although there seemed to be a downward trend in the 1930s.[39]

The similarity between Warsaw and Prague disappears when we look specifically at French investment, shown in Table 3.7. In pre-Roosevelt dollars, Poland received around five times as much money as its southern neighbour, while its population was only around twice as large as Czechoslovakia's. The latter saw a much greater engagement in banking and the engineering industry

Table 3.6 Source of foreign investment in equity capital in Central and Eastern Europe, 1937

Country of investor	*Czechoslovakia*[a]	*Poland*[b]	*Yugoslavia*[c]
Austria	13.1	3.5	—
Belgium	7.1	12.5	5.3
Czechoslovakia	—	1.6	8.5
France	21.4	27.1	27.5
Germany	7.2	13.8	6.2[d]
Switzerland	4.5	7.2	7.3
UK	30.8	5.5	17.3
USA	3.5	19.2	12.0
Other	12.4	9.6	15.9

Notes:
[a] Industry and trade.
[b] Industry and banking.
[c] Private industry.
[d] Including Austrian investment.

Sources: Alice Teichova, "*Industry,*" in *The Economic History of Eastern Europe 1919–1975, vol. I. Economic Structure and Performance*, ed. Michael Charles Kaser and E.A. Radice (Oxford: Clarendon Press, 1986), 222–322, 293.

Table 3.7 Direct French capital investment in Czechoslovak enterprises, 31 December 1937

Sector	*French investments (in million Kč)*	*French investments (in million USD)*	*Percentage of total French investment (%)*	*French share in total foreign investment in branch (%)*
Banking	100	3.5	15	45
Mining and metallurgy	174	6.1	26	15
Mineral and vegetable oil industry	43	1.5	6	11
Chemical industry	78	2.8	12	25
Textile industry	35	1.3	5	16
Engineering industry	164	5.8	24	74
Sugar industry	59	2.1	9	34
Other	20	0.7	3	7
Total	674	23.8	100	21

Sources: Teichova, *An Economic Background*, 48.

(which included Škoda), with no comparable investment in Poland (the shipyards in Gdynia, partially controlled by those in the Free City of Danzig, were a poor replacement).[40] There was also relatively little invested in resource extraction. This made the structure of French investments in Czechoslovakia more beneficial for industrial development. Moreover, while Teichova identified Czechoslovakia as the locus of operations of international cartels, which influenced other countries of the region, we do not see a similar development in Poland.[41] On the other hand, as in Poland, the most important holdings in Czechoslovakia were the result of post-war takeovers, rather than greenfield investments. The structure of French holdings thus reflected the economic development of both countries, rather than aimed to change it.

3.2 Financial results of French companies

The business cycle in interwar Poland saw huge swings, which affected the performance of companies. The period can be roughly divided into six stages. Until 1921, the country was in a state of war, and economic activity was mainly concerned with reconstruction and supplying the military, with significant levels of state control. Once the wars ended, further reconstruction was accompanied by inflation, which in 1923 changed into hyperinflation. Stabilization came in 1924, quickly translating into a post-stabilization slump and a second monetary crisis, which ended only in 1927. The next three years saw the best economic performance of the interwar period, with fast growth throughout the Polish economy. The Great Depression brought a huge fall in production, and lasted into 1935. Only afterwards did economic growth restart albeit with a larger role of state intervention.

To see how French companies performed in this context, I returned to the dataset created from Polish industry yearbooks. The 416 entries contained 280 balance sheets and 136 data points on dividends. While getting access to so many balance sheets is significant, the data they contain remain unreliable. Interwar Polish accounting requirements were lax, resulting in low quality, unrevealing balance sheets, made without uniform practices, under limited supervision.[42] As an example, the Towarzystwo Przędzalni Czesankowych S. A. in Łódź (which remained under French control), reported its capital as worth 2.1 million złoty. However, a critical analysis of its balance sheet in 1932 reduced the value to only 0.1 million, putting the company one step away from bankruptcy. Such false reporting was endemic.[43] Without data to correct the sheets I accessed, I focused on relatively uncontroversial information: profits, dividends, working capital, and the balance sheet total.

Table 3.8 combines information on profits from the yearbooks with statistics for the entire Polish economy. Based on this data, the French seemed to have done better than average in the years before the Great Depression, yet worse during the crisis. They did not start to recover until 1936, later than other firms in Poland. It is likely that some companies systematically underreported profits, and transferred capital abroad through unequal agreements

Table 3.8 Profits and losses of companies with French capital, 1927–1936

Year	*1927*	*1928*	*1930*	*1932*	*1934*	*1936*
Companies with French capital						
Value of profits reported (million złoty)	36.0	31.7	12.5	6.4	2.9	8.7
Value of losses reported (million złoty)	0.4	1.9	20.0	22.3	17.1	15.4
Ratio of profits to equity in companies reporting profits	9%	6%	3%	2%	1%	3%
Ratio of losses to equity in companies reporting losses	1%	12%	5%	3%	5%	3%
Ratio of companies reporting losses	14%	21%	62%	75%	54%	59%
Ratio of the value of losses to profits in French companies	1%	6%	160%	347%	597%	177%
Total for the Polish economy						
Ratio of domestic companies reporting losses	23%	24%	52%	69%	53%	37%
Ratio of the value of losses to profits in domestic and foreign companies	25%	21%	141%	369%	191%	74%

Sources: Calculations based on RISA 1929 and 1930; RPPiH 1932, 1934, 1936, and 1938; RSRP 1930; MRS 1939.

with firms in France. Sometimes this is easy to spot. French companies operating directly in Poland, for which I have both French and Polish balance sheets, reported losses in Poland ten times. Among them, seven announced concurrent profits in France, even if their entire business rested on Polish production. This practice must have been more prevalent before 1928, when such firms did not even prepare balance sheets for their Polish businesses.[44] Nonetheless, beyond these expected results, we can say little. Information about profits serves as an indication of trends, rather than rigid data.

For context, it is interesting to look at foreign credits. Unfortunately, I do not have robust data, as official Polish publications did not cover all of the period, and values from different estimates are not comparable.[45] Nonetheless, according to Smerek's estimates, French companies paid some 29 million złoty in interest in 1929 based on the total value of cash credits reaching 241 million. These payments accounted for around 30 per cent of all such payments to foreign capital owners, representing the largest share among all countries.[46] It is unlikely that France kept the same share in other years, but it is notable that the value of such interest payments was comparable to total profits reported by French companies in their best years.

A look at dividends allows comparisons with companies with owners from other countries. For France, official data (Smerek again) only provides detailed values for 1929 and 1930: 8 and 5 million złoty respectively, representing only some 1.9 and 1.2 per cent of all French capital engaged in Poland. In 1930 this made the French perform worse than any other national group of investors (with Belgium earning 2.7 per cent, Germany 3.2 per cent, and the US an impressive 4.5 per cent).[47]

Turning to my company dataset, I calculated dividend payments for the same years, getting similar amounts to Smerek's. I then extended them to cover

Table 3.9 Dividends paid out to French investors, 1927–1936

Year	*1927*	*1928*	*1929*	*1930*	*1931*	*1932*	*1933*	*1934*	*1935*	*1936*
Dividends (million złoty)	15.3	16.4	8.1	5.1	4.5	0.7	2.4	3.1	5.1	2.8
As % of total share capital	4.7%	4.2%	2.1%	1.2%	1.1%	0.2%	0.6%	0.8%	1.3%	0.7%
Total outflow of funds from Poland due to capital ownership in companies (million złoty)	57	68	53	54	41	28	15	16	14	20
French dividends as share of this outflow	27%	24%	15%	9%	11%	2%	17%	19%	35%	14%

Notes:

Estimates based on 136 datapoints on the level of dividends, multiplied by the value of French-owned share capital in each company. Capital in years not covered by data interpolated from neighbouring years. The value of all foreign dividends taken from official publications on the balance of payments.

Sources: Calculations based on data from RISA 1929 and 1930; RPPiH 1932, 1934, 1936, and 1938; Landau and Tomaszewski, *Kapitały*, 15.

a decade, as shown in Table 3.9. The results strengthen my conclusions derived from the analysis of profits. French-owned companies compared poorly to the rest of the Polish economy during the Great Depression, and to companies controlled by capital from other countries. Their results were also significantly lower than what the British reported at the time. Alice Teichova argued that long-term foreign investment provided high stability in the 1930s, especially when compared with trade.[48] This suggests either that the French cooked their books more than any other group of investors, or that their holdings were particularly vulnerable to the Depression, especially as their results directly before the crisis were actually better than those of other capital groups.

Smerek explained France's poor results during the Depression with the lack of dividends in the oil sector, possibly due to capital transfers through other means and window dressing.[49] This is a plausible explanation, although the sector was experiencing structural difficulties due to high production and transportation costs. Moreover, other major fields of French investment, such as coal mining and the textile industry, were among the worst-performing sectors of the Polish economy at the time. It was thus the structure of French investment, focused as it was on resource extraction and old technology, which directly contributed to its exceptionally bad results.

I based the analysis so far on data covering all companies found in the yearbooks. They allow a general discussion of French investments, but the evolving list of firms for which I had data makes it difficult to show trends. To conclude this discussion, I thus turn to a list of 26 companies, for which I have balance sheets for the entire period.[50] They represent around 80 per cent of share capital of the firms on my list, and include 9 companies in the oil sector, 8 in other types of mining, 4 in metallurgy, 3 in the textile industry, and 2 in electricity production. They were all either wholly owned by the French, or remained under dominant French control.

Even apart from dwindling profits, the data presented in Table 3.10 shows a grim state of the companies after 1930. Let us start with investment. Most firms in the interwar period did not subtract amortization from fixed assets, but instead added the amount to amortization capital, included in the table in

Table 3.10 Balance sheets of 26 companies with French capital, 1927/1928–1936 (in million złoty)

Year	*Balance sheet total*	*Assets*			*Liabilities*			
		Fixed assets	*Debtors*	*Losses*	*Share capital*	*Reserve capital*	*Creditors*	*Profits*
1927/1928	1,017	540	148	0	347	216	308	24
1930	1,103	698	161	12	355	299	342	8
1932	1,115	734	137	16	355	325	330	3
1934	1,104	733	151	14	359	353	281	2
1936	1,103	763	120	15	356	393	262	6

Sources: Calculated from RISA 1929 and 1930; RPPiH 1932, 1934, 1936, 1938.

reserve capital. Only in the case of fully amortized assets did companies remove their value from both sides of the balance sheets, but they avoided doing so during the Great Depression. Moreover, they did not change the valuation of fixed assets in step with changing prices. As a result, any change in fixed assets reported in the balance sheets is equal to investment. After 1930, fixed assets in French companies grew by only 1.1 per cent a year, well below the 6 per cent considered to be the standard rate of amortization at the time, and slower than in the entire Polish economy.[51] In other words, the companies were shrinking, despite reporting stable balance sheet totals. Moreover, their combined working capital shifted from positive in 1928 to negative throughout the rest of the period. It reached its nadir (negative 5 per cent of the balance sheet total) in 1932, with 15 out of 26 firms in the red.[52] This result was nonetheless better than the Polish average.[53]

3.3 Economic environment in Poland

French private companies in Poland functioned in an environment shaped by Polish laws and policies, bureaucratic decisions, international treaties, arbitrage, and diplomatic intervention. As a result, it was to some degree negotiated by Warsaw and Paris, and evolved with the changing dynamic of the Franco–Polish relationship. The environment was hostile directly after the war, before Paris was able to send its diplomats to intervene, then became friendlier, as the French were able to force their allies to grant certain privileges to their companies, and soured once again as the Great Depression hit, and Warsaw moved to consolidate its influence over the economy.

Moreover, after World War I, with its mass requisitions and takeovers envisaged in the Treaty of Versailles, "owner nationality mattered."[54] Investors from countries considered unfriendly were frowned upon. Sometimes, as in the Romanian oil sector, the result was an "obsession with the ownership structure of industrial assets."[55] Reborn Poland had to deal with both truly foreign companies, and those which had been domestic within the three empires, but whose owners suddenly became foreign citizens or members of national minorities. In both Warsaw and Paris, such German-owned firms were seen as a problem. The Poles were quick to talk about unfriendly capital, using the adjective "alien" instead of "foreign" (*obcy* rather than *zagraniczny*).[56] The hope of replacing such ownership either with domestic or friendly foreign capital continued to influence policy.

As we discussed in the previous chapter, one of the most important economic Polish goals in the interwar period was attracting FDI. The Poles used few tools, restricted by their relatively orthodox economic policy. As with private loans, they were mostly limited to striving for macroeconomic stability, sticking to gold for as long as possible, and assuring everyone of the safety of their potential investments.[57] In other words, they were signalling about the reliability of property rights and future rents. However, no government agency routinely dealt with foreign capital, and there was no long-term information policy or marketing targeting investors. As French authorities attempted to win privileges for their companies, the resulting agreements sometimes included boons specifically given to future investors (such as an exemption from certain extraordinary taxes for oil companies). These were, however, chance consequences of French goals, rather than a part of any planned Polish policy. The same was true for Upper Silesian mixed companies, which were granted special privileges for political reasons.

Nonetheless, the Polish authorities did try to approach foreign private investors in two ways, both based on guaranteed rents. First, Warsaw created markets for some producers by long-term government purchases linked to investment in crucial industries – a dominant Polish intervention tool.[58] In automobile production, aviation, or the military industry, the process was similar, with the state signing contracts with foreign firms for the delivery of goods, requiring a growing proportion of production to take place in Poland. The French participated in these endeavours with mixed success, as I explore in Chapter 4. Second, in the first half of the 1920s, the Poles were willing to sell foreign investors the country's "family heirlooms," such as the tobacco or match monopolies, or timber concessions. The practice was controversial, but accepted as a necessary evil for fiscal reasons. While the French attempted to win some of these rights, they could not match the offers from other countries.

Beyond these policies, French firms in Poland had to follow Polish regulations, which did not discriminate against foreign-owned companies. Nonetheless, some aspects of the firms' functioning were contentious, including the specifics of their legal form. They were joint-stock or limited liability companies, but before the war, some had been registered in France (to avoid the onerous process of registration in St Petersburg), while others were Russian, German, or Austrian, regulated by the different commercial codes of the three empires.[59] Even before Polish independence, minister of Foreign Affairs Stephen Pichon suggested that firms registered abroad should reincorporate in France, and thus gain a measure of safety from future Polish authorities. Some owners were interested, but the legal process was cumbersome and expensive, and the Poles opposed it.[60] Despite a 1922 Franco–Polish agreement giving pre-war owners the right to move their firms to France, only 15 companies functioned under French law. They were mostly in the textile and heavy industries in Russian Poland, with Banque Franco–Polonaise the only new business among them. As I mentioned, this arrangement was particularly beneficial to French owners, allowing them, via transfer prices and other tools, to easily avoid taxes in Poland, and move capital out of the country.

The 1922 agreement in question, known as the goods, rights, and shares convention, was one of the three economic treaties tied to the coming into force of the Franco–Polish alliance. It focused on the security of French property rights, guaranteeing the return of pre-war French companies and privileges to their owners.[61] Crucially, it confirmed all concessions granted to the French before the war, and envisaged their prolongation by at least six years. Conflicts would be referred to international arbitration, as in the long battle between the Warsaw municipality and Compagnie d'Électricité de Varsovie.

The second agreement concerned the oil sector, essentially guaranteeing French rents. French companies, having invested millions of francs, sought to consolidate and protect their holdings. After forceful negotiations, the Quai d'Orsay obtained for them the freedom of exports, imports, and exemption from Polish exchange control. The Poles defended the right to levy special taxes on firms from the sector, although new investments were protected from them. The French in the coal sector unsuccessfully pushed for similar privileges, but they did not enjoy the same level of Quai d'Orsay support.[62]

Finally, the 1922 commercial treaty smuggled its important provisions in an accompanying secret exchange of letters. Some dealt with rents, some with less tangible rights. It guaranteed French firms in the textile sector access to coal, and the right to freely import semi-finished products. Moreover, all French companies would profit from three forms of special treatment. First, they would be able to employ as many foreigners as they wanted. Second, those that owned mining concessions received more extensive rights regarding assets on the territories under concession than Polish citizens and companies. Third, all French firms would be near-exempt from Polish limitations on the purchase of real estate by foreigners if supported by the French minister in Warsaw.[63] The significant scope of these privileges, repeated in the same form in the 1924 commercial agreement, explained why Paris hid them in secret letters: otherwise all firms from countries enjoying the most favoured nation clause would benefit from them as well.[64]

In practice, the Poles tried to erode the scope and applicability of these privileges, and thus limit the rents of French owners and their freedom of action. One of the tools they used was diplomacy: Warsaw relied on delaying tactics to postpone implementation of some benefits. Such was the fate of the oil agreement, which did not come into power until 1924. There were also privileges that the Poles ignored despite repeated French interventions (as in the case of the Bank of Silesia). At least some conflicts concerning these privileges were the result of miscommunication between Warsaw and the local Polish administration. Clerks working in central offices, especially in the ministries of Foreign Affairs, and Industry and Trade, seemed to understand the dynamics of the Franco–Polish relationship, and were less likely to make decisions negatively impacting French companies. The same was not true for the local administration, often manned by clerks from the Austrian partition, whom the French considered Francophobic.[65]

Between the actions of local authorities and the waning importance of the economic agreements, asking Paris for intervention remained the most powerful tool in the arsenal of French companies. It was often supported by lobby organizations, such as the Groupement des Industriels français en Pologne, the powerful Comité des Houillères, or the Association National des Porteurs Français de Valeurs Mobilières. Petitioned in this manner, French authorities took little convincing. They mostly acted through the ambassador in Warsaw, who often got instructions taken verbatim from letters received by the ministry.

The Polish government received hundreds of such complaints, mostly concerning larger firms, connected to all aspects of their activities. This included taxation, tenders, employing foreigners, relations with local authorities, arrests of managers, Polish cartels, or the firms' concessions. Apart from highly publicized conflicts, such as the Żyrardów Affair, these interventions were also surprisingly effective. For instance, in some of the more startling cases, Paris forced Warsaw to annul two tenders for the purchase and production of military trucks (Chapter 4), or to limit the publication of press articles attacking French companies. However, most French companies seemingly did not resort to such interventions, which remained the domain of bigger, more prominent firms.

Some types of conflicts continued to appear in diplomatic documents. As expected, the principal one concerned taxes – de facto the value of rents available to capital owners. Here, the French complained about unreasonable Polish fiscalism, especially extraordinary levies and taxes on assets. It seems that some of these protests stemmed from overzealous Polish clerks, and certain companies, such as Zincs de Silésie, were able to get their tax valuations overturned.[66]

The second topic concerned French freedoms from Polish laws concerning the employment of foreigners, or more generally the idea of "Polonization," which went beyond the legal status discussed earlier, and can be seen as an example of pro-developmental industrial policy. At the beginning of the interwar period, French companies employed many foreigners in key positions. Some – especially Germans and Russians – were gradually let go, with Poles hired in their place, sometimes seemingly to placate the authorities.[67] Polish officials often felt that the process was too slow, especially in Upper Silesia, where the French were more likely to work and maintain social relations with Polish citizens of German ethnicity. For example, five years after the Polish takeover of eastern Upper Silesia, the major zinc and coal producer Zincs de Silésie did not have a single ethnic Pole among its management, which was dominated by Germans, despite Franco-Belgian ownership. At the time, neither the director of the Bank of Silesia Max David, nor the French consul Georges Terver had ever visited a Polish home, focusing their social life on the German minority. In the latter case, it took an intervention of the Quai d'Orsay for the diplomat to change his ways.[68]

Polish attitudes towards foreigners continued to evolve. In the 1920s, they could work in Poland based on a residence permit and visa, which remained at the discretion of voivodes and consuls. New regulations from 1931 barred foreigners from working in non-managerial positions in much of the economy without a permit from the voivode. The decision theoretically depended on the state of the local labour market (a common practice today), but de facto remained at the discretion of local authorities.[69] This was a sensible policy, aiming to use foreign investment to limit unemployment, increase the number of posts available to highly qualified workers in Poland, and likely foster positive spillovers. Despite guarantees for French companies, after 1926 the Poles continued to pressure them. Procedures got tougher, especially for long-term employees, and despite diplomatic interventions, some workers lost the right to stay in Poland. By the mid-1930s, some local authorities required foreign employees to speak Polish, or help train Polish replacements.[70] These were rare cases, but they told the French what to expect.

The third problem represented rising government regulation, which took its most drastic forms in the oil and coal sectors – both with a significant French presence. Unsurprisingly, therefore, some French companies in the sectors helped finance the big industry lobby organization Lewiatan, which protested against state intervention, while also giving money to local Sanacja officials. Others were not convinced the results were worth the money.[71] In these two sectors, due to their strategic importance and precarious economic position, Polish authorities forced the creation of obligatory cartels, which limited domestic competition. Thus, despite significant foreign presence, these sectors became some of the most regulated, with a clear limit on French rents.

On the back of rising conflicts with certain French and German firms, in 1934 the Sanacja regime declared a new approach to foreign-owned companies, based on the notion of "loyal cooperation." The authorities explained in the semi-official press that since investors thought Poland was a risky market, Warsaw would accept higher return on investment (or "normal profits") for foreigners. Nonetheless, their companies needed to follow local laws, and allow the authorities to surveil their actions for abuses. If the firms did not cooperate, or if their actions were deemed detrimental to the Polish interest, the authorities would act swiftly.

The Polish approach, hardly designed to win friends, was tied to the wider problem of Warsaw framing problems with foreign capital in moral rather than economic terms. Capital thus became "loyal" or "disloyal," and was either welcome, or punished. As Jan Kofman observed, such a policy was unlikely to produce results.[72] Governments can influence investors not by bringing up ethics, but by creating a system of incentives and regulations to steer them towards desired outcomes, as I discussed in Chapter 1. Focusing on morals allowed the Poles to express rage when faced with foreign abuses, and to bolster the regime's authority, but did little to reform labour inspection, adopt a long-term foreign-investment policy, or rethink private-public cooperation. The authorities' approach resulted in a rising anger of Polish public opinion against the French. While a useful tool in domestic politics, it proved problematic once the Poles decided to negotiate with the French. Now public opinion limited the scope of government policy, making agreements with Paris a costly political endeavour. On the other hand, the spectre of nationalization, long court battles, and arrests of foreign managers eroded the confidence of outside investors in the safety of the Polish market, further weakened by the introduction of exchange control in April 1936. Such attitudes towards existing investment made it more difficult for the Poles to achieve the more general goal of attracting foreign capital.

This erosion of confidence was connected to the final issue in Franco–Polish relations: the expansion of the state sector, which evolved in tandem with Polish economic nationalism. As I mentioned in Chapter 1, despite the Polish authorities' turn towards self-sufficiency, they still considered outside investment indispensable for development. Nonetheless, after 1926, high-level officials, particularly in military circles, increasingly saw certain types of production as strategically important, and sought to shield them from foreign capital. For example, the Poles consolidated state control in the aviation sector, leading to a takeover of the Škoda-owned (and thus Schneider-controlled) factory in Warsaw.

In 1940, during World War II, the Polish government-in-exile created a committee tasked with studying the background of the defeat in 1939. While biased, some depositions explored the problems of the interwar state sector. Leon Małecki, the CEO of an optics firm Polskie Zakłady Optyczne, focused on how the practice of revolving doors between the state apparatus and state-owned companies fostered the growth of the latter. Bureaucrats who supported creating state companies rather than hiring private enterprises got well-remunerated posts. This created a systemic bias against private enterprise.[73] For instance, Polskie Zakłady Optyczne was highly successful in its work with the French, but Małecki complained that he had "never received any recognition from authorities for introducing reliable foreign capital into the country." On the other hand, he "often heard accusations that the factory was French, that the French were squeezing Poland dry, etc."[74] The seemingly low level of organization culture among Sanacja's higher military commanders was another factor. As Tadeusz Cyprian pointed out, there was a noted lack of adequate industrial planning, "unwelcome under Marshall Piłsudski, who considered it mere paperwork with little hope for later use, as war brought too many surprises."[75] Likewise, military circles lacked expertise in industry, trade, or the economy, and had a limited appreciation for the nuances of international negotiations.[76]

It is therefore not surprising that without a clear, long-term policy of attracting foreign capital, the Poles failed to convince more investors to open shop in the country. On the other hand, while there are no clear connections between French privileges in Poland, and the poor results of the companies we covered, it appears that "French imperialism" did not translate into exceptional results. With increased Polish regulation, by the late 1930s, not much remained of French plans to control Poland's economy.

3.4 Conclusions

Perhaps my biggest surprise when researching this chapter came from compiling a list of companies with French capital, and comparing it with an inventory of interventions in Paris and Warsaw. The latter was shorter, while the former contained companies about which I had never read in the archives, or which were only mentioned in passing. Interventions were thus primarily the domain of large well-connected companies, which either enjoyed special privileges, or were important enough to present a special interest to the government in Paris.

The second surprise came from seeing that French companies consistently underperformed in the 1930s. Based on claims from the Polish literature on French imperialism or exploitation, I expected better results. The data from which I inferred these results were admittedly imperfect. However, even if French companies were cooking their books, investors from other countries were likely doing the same, and I do not believe that my sources reflect any systemic bias.

There also seemed to be no clear connection between the privileges of French companies, or the sometimes-hostile Polish policy towards them, and their financial results. The French performed badly, because the sectoral and technological structure of their investment – dating to the previous techno-economic paradigms – was particularly susceptible to problems caused by the Great Depression. In a global deflationary economy, investing in late-life cycle products and competing on price had little chance of success. Somewhat ironically, the very same argument can be made regarding the French impact on Polish development. The sectoral structure of investment did not lend itself to any meaningful industrial transformation. Besides, most holdings were brownfield investments. There is thus little to sustain Christoph Laforest's thesis of French "Schumpeterian," entrepreneurial imperialism – at least not in the interwar period.[77]

The third surprise came with the chronology of French FDI, and the realization that, except for the oil sector, most had come before the war. Moreover, in absolute terms, their dollar value did not greatly change between 1914 and 1930, which attests to the devastating consequences of World War I and the costs of reconstruction. In general, French FDI appears as a faltering remnant of 19th century investing – still able to perform well in good times, but struggling during crises. This goes against the established notion of significant French expansion in interwar Poland.

For stories of French investment important for Polish development, or cases where Paris successfully pressured the Poles into significant policy changes, we need to turn to forms of French activity which did not represent FDI, or to transactions that were small enough so that they did not meaningfully register in the data I discussed in this chapter.

Notes

1 Archives diplomatiques, La Courneuve [henceforth: AdC], Correspondance politique et commercial, 1918–1940, Pologne [henceforth: CPC PL], 234, de Panafieu to Briand, 15 December 1921, 149–49v; AdC, CPC PL, 235, Affaire de la Banque Franco-Polonaise, 27 February 1924, 32–32v; Centre des archives économiques et financières, Savigny-le-Temple, B 31.928, Deschamps to Cloquemin, 10 September 1920, n.p.

2 AdC, CPC PL, 235, Visite de monsieur Noulens, 26 January 1924, 29–31.

3 "Nowa afera bankowa. Aresztowanie dyrektora Banku Franko-Polskiego," *Kurjer Poranny* 20 February 1924, 5; AdC, CPC PL, 235, de Panafieu to Poincaré, 20 February 1924, 17–19v; AdC, CPC PL, 235, Dupont to Maginot, 26 February 1924, 51–51v; AdC, CPC PL, 235, Poincaré to Maginot, 18 March 1924, 59–59v; AdC, CPC PL, 235, Briand to de Panafieu, 13 March 1926, 96–96v.

4 Alice Teichova, *An Economic Background to Munich: International Business and Czechoslovakia 1918–1938* (London: Cambridge University Press, 1974).

5 An early version of this section appeared as Jerzy Łazor, "Wpływ kapitału francuskiego na modernizację Polski międzywojennej," in *Przemiany modernizacyjne w Drugiej Rzeczypospolitej*, ed. Paweł Grata (Rzeszów: Wydawnictwo Uniwersytetu Rzeszowskiego, 2020), 195–209.

6 Alfred Reckendrees, Boris Gehlen, and Christian Marx, "International Business, Multinational Enterprises and Nationality of the Company: A Constructive Review of Literature," *Business History* 64, no. 9 (2022): 1567–99, 1569, https://doi.org/10.1080/00076791.2022.2118718.
7 Geoffrey Jones, "The End of Nationality? Global Firms and «Borderless Worlds»," *Zeitschrift Für Unternehmensgeschichte* 51, no. 2 (2006): 149–65, https://doi.org/10.1515/zug-2006-0203.
8 DzU RP 1923, nr 106, poz. 832; DzU RP 1922, nr 71, poz. 149.
9 Archiwum Państwowe w Łodzi [henceforth: APŁ], Zakłady Przemysłu Włókienniczego "Polana" Spółka Akcyjna w Łodzi, 16, Kwestionariusz, 3 January 1939, 5.
10 AdC, CPC PL, 253, MAÉ to Bérenger, 30 November 1919, 78–78v; AdC, CPC PL, 252, Lancial to Briand, 11 October 1929, 242v. See vastly different estimates: AdC, Fonds Nominatifs, Léon Noël, 2, Noël do MAÉ, 17 July 1936, n.p.; AdC, CPC PL, 397, Laroche do MAÉ, 22 February 1932, 167–72.
11 Mylène Mihout-Natar, "L'intervention des capitaux français dans la Pologne de la Seconde République (1918–1939): contribution à l'histoire de l'impérialisme économique français en Europe centrale" (PhD, Université Charles de Gaulle – Lille III, 2002), 380; Irena Pietrzak-Pawłowska, "Les investissements français en Pologne," in *La position internationale de la France: aspects économiques et financiers, XIXe–XXe siècles*, ed. Maurice Lévy-Leboyer (Paris: Éditions de l'École des hautes études en sciences sociales, 1977), 319–24; Feliks Hilchen, "Rola kapitału zagranicznego w Polsce," *Ekonomista*, no. 1 (1920), 76; AdC, CPC PL, 253, Établissements industriels Française en Pologne, [October–November 1919], 75–77.
12 René Girault, *Emprunts russes et investissements francais en Russie, 1887–1914; recherches sur l'investissement international* (Paris: A. Colin, 1973), 580.
13 Zbigniew Landau and Jerzy Tomaszewski, *Kapitały obce w Polsce 1918–1939: materiały i dokumenty* (Warszawa: Książka i Wiedza, 1964), 15.
14 Cf. Mieczysław Smerek, "Bilans płatniczy Polski za rok 1930," *Statystyka Polski* Seria B, no. 17 (1933); Józef Kożuchowski, *Kapitał zagraniczny w przemyśle polskim* (Warszawa: Tygodnik "Przemysł i Handel," 1928); *Mały Rocznik Statystyczny* [henceforth: MRS] *1939*, 108.
15 Teichova, *An Economic Background*, 5; Aldcroft, *Europe's Third World*, 54.
16 Cf. Teichova, *An Economic Background*, 37.
17 Leopold Wellisz, *Foreign Capital in Poland* (London: George Allen & Unwin, 1938).
18 Polish economic historians assumed instead that the structure of these credits was similar to that of share capital (Landau and Tomaszewski, *Kapitały*, 22). However, as Table 3.2 shows, the use of credits as an investment vehicle was different for investors from different countries. The use of proportions from 1930 is more appropriate, even if it doesn't take into account the likely different reactions to the Great Depression of owners from different countries.
19 AdC, CPC PL, 251, Poincaré to de Panafieu, 3 July 1922, 155–56; AdC, CPC PL, 252, Laroche to Briand, 1 December 1927, 77v.
20 Daniel Stone, "The Giesche Company: Anaconda Copper's Subsidiary in Interwar Poland," *Slavic Review* 56, no. 4 (1997): 679–97, https://doi.org/10.2307/2502117.
21 Stone, "The Giesche Company." Cf. Archiwum Akt Nowych, Warsaw [henceforth: AAN], Ministerstwo Spraw Zagranicznych [henceforth: MSZ], 3845, Memo on the Zincs de Silésie, [1927], 201–215; AdC, CPC PL, 218, Note sur la Société des Mines et Usines à Zinc de Silésie, 11 May 1929, 291–92.
22 Paul Bairoch, *Economics and World History: Myths and Paradoxes* (Chicago: University of Chicago Press, 1995), 140.
23 Carlota Perez, *Technological Revolutions and Financial Capital: The Dynamics of Bubbles and Golden Ages* (Cheltenham: Edward Elgar, 2002); Chris Freeman and Francisco Louçã, *As Time Goes by: From the Industrial Revolutions to the Information Revolution* (Oxford: Oxford University Press, 2001).

24 Mira Wilkins, *The Maturing of Multinational Enterprise: American Business Abroad from 1914 to 1970* (Cambridge, MA: Harvard University Press, 1974), x.
25 Jerzy Łazor, "French Capital, Gdynia, and the Position of Polish Coal on International Markets in the Interwar Period," in *Fueling the World Economy: Seaports, Coal, and Oil Markets during the Early Globalization*, ed. Daniel Castillo Hidalgo and Cézar Honorato (Chaim: Palgrave Macmillan, 2023): 99–121, https://doi.org/10.1007/978-3-031-32565-6_6.
26 Based on estimates in: Smerek, "Bilans" 1933, 20; cf. MRS 1939, s. 114.
27 The first two volumes appeared as *Rocznik Informacyjny o Spółkach Akcyjnych w Polsce* [henceforth: RISA], and only contained information about joint-stock companies, the rest, under the title of *Rocznik Polskiego Przemysłu i Handlu* [henceforth: RPPiH] also included limited companies, and even partnerships in later editions.
28 Mihout-Natar, "L'intervention."
29 For instance, Wytwórnia Sygnałów i Urządzeń Kolejowych S.A. remained under the control of the Czech firm Vítkovické horní a hutní těžířstvo, itself – via the Allied Assurance Co. Ltd in London – owned in about a third by the French. (Teichova, *An Economic Background*, 84–85).
30 Józef Kożuchowski, *Przebudowa gospodarcza Polski* (Warszawa: Towarzystwo Pracy Społeczno-Gospodarczej, 1938), 111.
31 Cf. Bohdan Cywiński, *Przemysł polski i nasze położenie gospodarcze. Uwagi na tle bilansów przemysłowych spółek akcyjnych z lat 1928–1933* (Warszawa: Skład Główny w Domu Książki Polskiej, 1934), 28.
32 M. Smerek, "Bilans" 1933, 16; Claude Beaud, "Une multinationale française au lendemain de la Première Guerre mondiale: Schneider et l'Union Européenne Industrielle et Financière," *Histoire, économie et société* 2, no. 4 (1983): 625–45, https://doi.org/10.3406/hes.1983.1345.
33 AdC, CPC PL, 253, Marchal to Ministère de la Guerre, 4 June 1919, 52–53; AdC, CPC PL, 253, État des mines de charbon et des haute-fourneaux en Pologne russe, 9 December 1918, 35.
34 APŁ, Francuska Spółka Akcyjna Generalna Kompania Przemysłu Przędzalniczego Towarzystwo Anonimowe Zakładów Allart Rousseau i Spółka w Łodzi [henceforth: Allart Rousseau], 128, Testimony of Jakób Stein, [1919], 169.
35 E.g. Archiwum Państwowe w Katowicach [henceforth: APK], Towarzystwo Bezimienne Kopalń Węgla "Czeladź" w Czeladzi – Piaskach [henceforth: Czeladź], 441, Reklamacje strat wojennych pana Denisa Pigre, [1920], 13–15.
36 *Société Anonyme des Mines de Czeladz. Assemblée Générale Ordinaire du 31 Mai 1920*, (Paris: Imprimerie Devalois, 1920), 41.
37 AdC, CPC PL, 238, Memo of undersecretary of state, Ch. Sargent, 25 January 1919, 3; AdC, CPC PL, 234, Pralon to Pichon, 13 October 1919, 55–55v; AdC, CPC PL, 238, MAÉ to Pralon, [January 1920], 42.
38 See discussions: APŁ, Allart Rousseau, 276, Aperçu sur la situation actuelle en Roumanie, [December 1938], 8–11.
39 Teichova, *An Economic Background*, 16; Victor Axenciuc, *Evoluția economică a României: cercetări statistico-istorice, 1859–1947. Vol. 1. Industria* (București: Editura Academiei Române, 1992), 453; John R. Lampe and Marvin R. Jackson, *Balkan Economic History, 1550–1950: From Imperial Borderlands to Developing Nations* (Bloomington: Indiana University Press, 1982), 428–29, 509–10. See also Jerzy Łazor and Bogdan Murgescu, "Economic Development," in *The Routledge History Handbook of Central and Eastern Europe in the Twentieth Century: Challenges of Modernity*, ed. Stanislav Holubec, Władysław Borodziej, and Joachim von Puttkamer (London and New York: Routledge, 2020), 313–84, 371–78.
40 The International Shipbuilding and Engineering Co Ltd in Danzig, created in 1922, was dominated by British and French interests (30 per cent of shares each), with a

smaller role played by the Danzigers and the Poles (20 per cent each). I talk about some of the company's political connections in Chapter 6.

41 Teichova, *An Economic Background*, xx, 43.

42 Cf. Aleksandra Banaszkiewicz, *Bilans w polskiej perspektywie historycznej – wiek XIX i XX* (Toruń: Wydawnictwo Naukowe Uniwersytetu Mikołaja Kopernika, 2019), 109–72.

43 APŁ, Allart Rousseau, 266, Analiza i krytyka bilansu Towarzystwa Przędzalni Czesankowych Spółki Akcyjnej, w Łodzi, 29 March 1932, n.p.; Tadeusz Bernadzikiewicz, *Nowe prawo o bilansach: geneza – system – ocena* (Warszawa: Towarzystwo Wydawnicze Młodych Prawników i Ekonomistów, 1934); Cywiński, *Przemysł*, 52–53.

44 APK, Czeladź, 551, Walne Zgromadzenie z 28 grudnia 1938, Sprawozdanie Członka Komisji Rewizyjnej, 28 Decembre 1938, 148.

45 Cf. Roman Seidler "Bilans płatniczy Polski za rok 1928," *Kwartalnik Statystyczny* 7, no. 4 (1930): 1469–541.

46 Mieczysław Smerek, "Bilans płatniczy Polski za rok 1929," *Kwartalnik Statystyczny* 8, no. 1 (1931): 279. Cf. Landau, Tomaszewski, *Kapitały*.

47 Smerek, "Bilans," 1931, 271; Smerek, "Bilans," 1933, 28.

48 Teichova, *An Economic Background*, 10–11.

49 Smerek, "Bilans," 1931, 271.

50 As seven companies were missing one balance sheet, I obtained these by averaging the results from two neighbouring dates. Since the data from the first two yearbooks was patchy, I combined the two, using the latter result if I had both. There were two more companies for which I had consistent data throughout the period, but which I removed as outliers. One was a bank, and the other a textile company in the process of restructuring, which reported huge swings from year to year (for instance, it went from reporting no fixed assets to 16 million złoty).

51 Cywiński, *Przemysł*, 34–51.

52 Working capital was calculated by subtracting fixed assets from equity capital, which was in turn the sum of share and reserve capital.

53 Cywiński, *Przemysł*, 61.

54 Alfred Reckendrees, Boris Gehlen, and Christian Marx, "International Business, Multinational Enterprises and Nationality of the Company: A Constructive Review of Literature," *Business History* 64, no. 9 (2022): 1568, https://doi.org/10.1080/00076791.2022.2118718.

55 Murgescu, "Economic Revival," 76; Aldcroft, *Europe's Third World*, 89.

56 Zbigniew Landau and Jerzy Tomaszewski, *Kapitały obce w Polsce 1918–1939: materiały i dokumenty* (Warszawa: Książka i Wiedza, 1964).

57 Jan Kofman, "Koła wielkoprzemysłowe a kwestia kapitałów obcych w okresie 1920–1939," *Kwartalnik Historyczny* 82, no. 2 (1975): 303–20.

58 Tadeusz Grabowski, *Rola państwa w gospodarce Polski (1918–1928)* (Warszawa: Państwowe Wydawnictwo Ekonomiczne, 1967), 182–84.

59 Leonard Górnicki, "Kodeks Handlowy," in *Prawo handlowe i gospodarcze II Rzeczypospolitej*, ed. Robert Jastrzębski (Warszawa: Wolters Kluwer Polska, 2019), 53–120; Irena Pietrzak-Pawłowska, "Zagłębie Dąbrowskie i Okręg Loary: penetracja kapitałów francuskich po 1870 r.," *Kwartalnik Historyczny* 72, no. 4 (1965): 797.

60 AdC, CPC PL, 280C, Tubes & Forges de Sosnowice to Klotz, 25 November 1919, 21–23v; AdC, CPC PL, 238, Note on Polish forced loans, [June 1920], 55.

61 DzU RP 1922, nr 71, poz. 149.

62 DzU RP 1923, nr 106, poz. 832.

63 AD, CPC PL, 249, Contre-lettre to the Commercial Convention, 6 February 1922, 7–11.

64 AdC, CPC PL, 252, Laroche to Briand, 18 May 1927, 26–26v.
65 AdC, CPC PL, 253, Marsy to FCK, 29 March 1923, 117–18.
66 AAN, MSZ, 3845, Legal opinion on the asset tax for Górnośląskie Towarzystwo Kopalń i Hut Cynkowych, [1925], 51–79; cf. AAN, MSZ, 3848, Three mining companies from the Cracow Basin to Czechowicz, 5 January 1927, 11–12.
67 AdC, CPC PL, 252, Memo on French companies in Sosnowice, [September 1919], 66; AdC, CPC PL, 251, Laroche to MAÉ, 23 October 1926, 240v; AdC, CPC PL, 252, Laroche to FCK, 20 November 1927, 79–80.
68 Mieczysław Grzyb, *Narodowościowo-polityczne aspekty przemian stosunków własnościowych i kadrowych w górnośląskim przemyśle w latach 1922–1939* (Katowice: Uniwersytet Śląski, 1978); Jerzy Tomaszewski, "Economic Differentiation and the National Question in Poland in the Twentieth Century," in *Economic Change and the National Question in Twentieth-Century Europe*, ed. Alice Teichova, Herbert Matis, and Jaroslav Pátek (Cambridge, U.K. and New York: Cambridge University Press, 2000), 338–56; Zenon Szmidtke, *"Skarboferm" 1922–1939: związki polityki z gospodarką* (Opole: Państwowy Instytut Naukowy, 2005), 183–86.
69 DzU RP 1931, nr 18, poz 98; cf.: Anna Kicinger, "Polityka migracyjna Polski 1918–2003" (PhD, Warsaw University, 2011), 125–26.
70 Edyta Majcher-Ociesa, *Interwencjonizm państwowy w przemyśle Drugiej Rzeczypospolitej w latach 1930–1939* (Kielce: Kieleckie Towarzystwo Naukowe, 2019), 259; AdC, CPC PL, 250, Laroche do FCA, 9 October, 1928, 140–42; AdC, CPC PL, 422, Laroche to Laval, 12 December 1934 r, 20–21; AAN, Ministerstwo Skarbu, 4259, Banque Franco-Polonaise to MS, 28 April 1939, n.p.
71 APK, Czeladź, 488, Markiewicz to Wierzbicki, 28 January 1929, 183 and APK, Czeladź, 488, Société Française et Italienne des Houillères de Dąbrowa to Markiewicz, 1 March 1929, 306–8.
72 Kofman, "*Koła*," 303–4; Jan Kofman, *Economic Nationalism and Development: Central and Eastern Europe between the Two World Wars* (London and New York: Routledge, 2018), 32; "Punkt ciężkości," *Gazeta Polska*, 20 December 1932; [Czesław Bobrowski], "Żyrardów," *Gospodarka Narodowa* 1934, nr 4, 55.
73 Polish Institute and Sikorski Museum, London [henceforth: PISM], B.I. 116/50, Zeznania Inż. L. Małeckiego, 14 February 1940, 705.
74 PISM, B.I. 116/50, Zeznania Inż. L. Małeckiego, 14 February 1940, 710.
75 PISM, B.I. 117/7, Dr Tadeusz Cyprian, Służba uzbrojenia, przemysł, 74.
76 PISM, B.I. 116/48, Protokół przesłuchania dr Tadeusza Łychowskiego, 1 October 1941, 678–87.
77 Laforest, "La stratégie."

4 French capital in interwar Polish state-led modernization

Infrastructure and high technology

A marketing brochure from 1929 shows a stylized red-gold flame flaring out of the darkness and dividing the frame into three parts. In each, a small drawing depicts economic activity: in a dimly lit mine colliers toil, a steam locomotive pulls into a station, and a graceful ship sails, steam billowing from its smokestacks.[1] While the brochure promotes the Franco–Polish company Skarboferm, it closely follows the mix of French investments in Poland, which linked coalfields and the new harbour in Gdynia with a major train route, the last two both built by the French. All three ventures united Western investors with the Polish government, which played the role of co-owner or principal investor. All represented old technology from the previous paradigm.

Ten years later, the Cracow-based "Ilustrowany Kurjer Codzienny" published the monumental *Twenty Years of Communication in Poland Reborn*.[2] Over 500 pages long, and with patronage from three members of the cabinet, it was an impressive propaganda piece, extolling Polish achievements on the seas and in the air. However, any car fan picking up the book would be disappointed. Discussions on motorization were hidden in a section about roads under apologetic titles, while car producers got the last few pages of the book. This relegation was not a mistake. Even by the end of the interwar period, the automobile was still a rare guest on Polish roads, with only 40,000 cars and trucks registered in the country, putting it at the tail end of European motorization. At the same time, the car played an oversized role in public consciousness, both as a symbol of modernity, and "an indispensable part of all stories about the rich and mighty."[3]

In this chapter, I discuss the Polish state acting as an investor, seeking to develop certain parts of the country's economy using foreign capital. I focus on the two groups of modernization endeavours described above: crucial transportation infrastructure and interwar hi-tech sectors – cars and aviation.[4] I argue that the former group, based on old technology, was a qualified success. The French provided some of the money and expertise, and were able to significantly speed up crucial projects. However, this came at the cost of more expensive financing and the exclusion of Polish contractors. It was only in the 1930s that the Poles were able to negotiate more favourable contracts.[5] On the other hand, there are no comparable long-term successes in cars and aviation. This failure is surprising,

DOI: 10.4324/9781003375586-4

considering France's remarkable competences in the sector – both technological and managerial – and the obvious security applications.[6] Polish attempts to cooperate with their allies were consistently undercut by French problems with financing, or failures to meet deadlines or quality standards. At the same time, the political sway the French held over Warsaw allowed their diplomats to block any cooperation with other countries. This pushed Polish historian Jerzy Gołębiowski to write about the "destructive influence of foreign capital" on the military sector.[7]

As I argue, the difference in outcomes can be explained by a combination of politics and private investment decisions. Such developmental endeavours, closely connected to both counties' security policies, could only be successful when both governments and private investors were interested in their success. Since this happened to be true in infrastructure, it proceeded more smoothly than many other French projects. In automobile production and aviation, French companies delayed Polish production by a decade, as they were uninterested in creating competitors in a leading hi-tech products.

Peter Evans writes about cars (but his words can easily be extended to aeroplanes), that the success of the sector hinges on access to cutting-edge technology, owned globally by only a few producers.[8] As a result, to successfully foster domestic production, the authorities need to focus on "building alliances with transnational capital," which "must be induced first to enter, then to increase local content, then to export, ideally all in alliance with local firms."[9] In the interwar period, these technologies were not as difficult to create as they are today, even if before World War I they were scarce in Central and Eastern Europe.[10] At the time, with lax intellectual property laws, and technologies which were not out of reach of determined engineers, states pursuing economic nationalism could break away from the influence of foreign capital and develop their own industries. Some would do it based on reverse-engineering, as was the case of Toyota, while others developed domestic technologies, as Poland ultimately ended up doing in aviation. The primary cost was time.

4.1 The harbour in Gdynia[11]

After Poland reappeared on the political map of Europe in 1918, its authorities faced the double task of integrating its lands coming from the Russian, Austrian, and German empires, and reorienting its economy away from the old imperial markets.[12] The trade war started by Germany in 1925 undermined the exports of coal, Poland's most important product, making the task crucial.[13] Such a reorientation required adequate transports: a harbour to ship goods overseas, and railways to connect it to Polish producers. Existing routes catered to old trade directions and borders. Moreover, the Free City of Danzig was a poor candidate for the principal Polish export port. Created at the insistence of the British, it leaned towards Germany, and could not be relied upon, as events during the Polish-Soviet war showed, when Danzig blocked transports to Poland.[14]

Polish authorities had little choice with their maritime investment due to the country's meagre coast. Ultimately, they settled on the tiny village of Gdynia to the north-west of Danzig as the site for a new commercial harbour.[15] Likewise, once the western border of Poland was settled in Upper Silesia, the Poles started looking into the necessary changes to their rail network to add missing connections. By 1923 they proposed the first plan for what would become the coal trunk line, linking coal producing regions and the sea.[16] Taken together, these projects would increase Poland's economic security, reduce transportation costs, and foster exports. While the French consul in Danzig, Édouard Gérardin, declared that there was "no wiser thing in Polish thought," building infrastructure is expensive.[17] The young state could hardly hope to raise enough money to finance construction, and the authorities were hoping to grant concessions to outside investors.

Map 4.1 Principal lines covered by the 1924 railway concession.

By 1924, two Franco–Polish consortia won both projects. In Gdynia, Société de Construction des Batignolles led a group made up of Société Anonyme Hersent Entreprises de Travaux Publics et Maritimes and Schneider, together with Polski Bank Przemysłowy and Polish engineers who initiated the project. When it came to the railway, Schneider was this time joined by one of the most important French civil engineering companies, Société Générale d'Entreprises, and the Poznań-based firm "Tri" Towarzystwo Robót Inżynierskich with Polish engineers.[18]

Let us start by looking at Gdynia. French diplomats and the military (including War Minister André Maginot) were enthusiastic about the Polish project, as was the Study Commission of the Superior Council of National Defence.[19] In 1924, the latter body saw it as an important project for French security policy, as it would allow supplying Poland, already a French ally, in case of war. Moreover, Gdynia could serve as a base for the future Polish navy and commercial fleet, would strengthen the country economically, and allow French companies to profit in the process.[20]

The consortium, which ultimately received the project with such overwhelming support, initially had limited French presence. It started when Polish engineers approached the Danish company Højgaard & Schultz, and the Belgian-Dutch firm Ackermans & van Haaren, which they had known from their work in tsarist Russia. These companies in turn invited the French firm S. A. Hersent, with which they had worked in Caen, Havre, Rouen, Rosario, or St Petersburg.[21] While Hersent did specialize in building harbours, the others probably invited the company for political and financial reasons: getting diplomatic protection in Poland, and access to the French financial market.[22] Both assumptions proved wrong. When Hersent asked the French government for help, its proposal was met with little enthusiasm due to the company's small role in the endeavour.[23] Nonetheless, support was reluctantly granted.

The head of the French Naval Mission in Poland, Commandor Eugène Charles Jolivet, did not agree. Due to the security importance of the harbour in Gdynia, he thought that no firms from other countries should take part in construction.[24] Jolivet convinced the French Navy Minister of the danger coming from both this consortium and from competing British firms. He also approached the Polish military, warning them about the consequences of giving the contract to foreign companies.[25] With the Minister's support, he put further pressure on the Poles through the Quai d'Orsay, and started looking for other French companies to invest in Gdynia. He was supported by the French Commercial Attaché, Armand-Guillaume de Gontaut-Biron. By early February 1924, the authorities managed to convince both Schneider and Batignolles to join Hersent. Their cooperation was nothing extraordinary – they had just received a concession together for works in the harbour in Piraeus. The scale of official French engagement was, on the other hand, rare. Highly placed officials at the ministries (such as Jules Laroche) approached the companies, which also got access to fast diplomatic telegrams and other benefits.

As the consortium was forming, another group emerged with a very different political strategy. It was represented in France by the engineer Adrien Godin. He visited the Quai d'Orsay in January 1924, and announced that his group, based on the Régie Générale des Chemins de Fer et des Travaux Publics, the Polish agrarian party of Wincenty Witos, and an unnamed British firm, was about to win the concession. Godin added that he did not want any support from the authorities, as it would only hurt his cause.[26] Godin's visit was peculiar, and his convictions misplaced. In 1924, with the strong position of the French military, domestic Polish political power was apparently not enough to overrule Paris. The original consortium was soon awarded the concession, and started negotiations to finalize the deal.

The French military and government thus ostensibly acted to exclude companies from other countries from taking part in the project. However, members of the consortium did not feel bound by these rules, and continued to talk to both Ackermans & van Haaren and Højgaard & Schultz. When the construction contract was signed, the consortium hired the Danes and Belgians as contractors, who subsequently carried out most of the work. Batignolles and Hersent focused on management and studies, while Schneider contended itself mostly with receiving a commission (similarly as in Piraeus). This was a shocking turn of events. France's endeavours did little beyond making the project more expensive for the Poles, as they had to pay for the intermediation of French companies – and wait for them to get the needed money.[27]

Financing remained a problem. This was a significant weakness of the French civil engineering sector in the interwar period. Powerful before the war, thanks to a thriving domestic market and large contracts abroad, it now faced difficulties in procuring loans for major foreign projects. As a result, the sector relied on political protection, and scored its largest contracts in Central and Eastern Europe thanks to French influence. Gdynia and the railway accounted for the majority of works in the region.[28]

In the case of Gdynia, the Banque de Paris et des Pays Bas and Banque de Pays du Nord were willing to provide the funding, but investors wanted the French government to guarantee their loans in addition to the Poles pledging income from state-owned forests and from the harbour itself. The government rejected all similar demands in the interwar period. Not so in Gdynia. With a personal intervention of Maginot, the authorities adopted a "bastard combination" of blocking a part of the 400 million francs military loan to use as a guarantee. The Poles reluctantly agreed. Ultimately, the French financial sector did underwrite the concession, but ended up resorting to very expensive financing from the US (from J.P. Morgan).[29]

The contract did not leave the Polish government much space for developmental policy.[30] It did not force the consortium to buy Polish materials – moreover, it required the government to compensate the concession-holders the difference in price should they ever be prohibited from importing. While it did require the employment of Poles (apart from rare cases in the initial period of construction), the institution overseeing construction could in no way intervene in economic conflicts between the consortium and its workers.

While the French and the Poles ran into some further problems (resulting, among others, in a temporary halt to works in 1925), construction in Gdynia proceeded smoothly, overseen by Polish engineers.[31] The consortium signed two more agreements for additional works in 1930 and 1936, this time including the Danes and the Belgians as full members.[32] Moreover, French firms from the consortium were soon able to get contracts for other maritime projects, often with Polish partners. In Gdynia, this included contracts for a military harbour (1925 and 1927), a navy repair basin (1931) and a fishing harbour (1928). In other developments, the Gdynia consortium signed further contracts for a fishing port in Wielka Wieś (1935), and a military harbour on the Hel Peninsula (1931). Getting these contracts required diplomatic help, undercutting the offers of Polish companies, or buying them off.[33]

The beginning of the trade war with Germany in 1925, and the resulting Polish surge towards maritime exports, underlined the need for the new Polish port. As works proceeded, the importance of Gdynia continued to grow, and by 1932 it overtook Danzig as the principal Polish export port for coal.[34] The city of Gdynia, also built from scratch, quickly grew. Its success and modernist architecture are well-remembered in Poland, and have recently brought both new books on the city's history, and comparisons to Tel Aviv – another coastal national project from the interwar period. It is thus amusing to see that when the Franco–Polish consortium won the project, the British minister in Warsaw W. Max Muller expressed joy that Britain "had nothing to do in encouraging the Polish government to spend their money on such a costly and, for the present at all events, unjustifiable undertaking."[35]

4.2 The coal trunk railway[36]

The story of the Coal Trunk Railway is both longer and more convoluted. In 1924, the French authorities were not as enthusiastic about the project as they were about Gdynia. Nonetheless, with support of de Panafieu, and after long and arduous negotiations led in Warsaw by Ernest Weyl from Schneider, by late 1924 the bid also proved successful. The Franco–Polish consortium received a concession to build and operate five railways, connecting Polish industrial basins to Warsaw and the northern part of the country, while avoiding German territory in Upper Silesia (Map 4.1). The group now faced the same problems with financing as in Gdynia. Since officials in Paris considered the project less interesting, they denied French companies financial guarantees. As a result, the group failed to sign a construction contract in 1924, and soon the Poles built some parts of the railway themselves, spurred on by the trade war with Germany.

Later developments attest to Polish stubbornness, and to a changing approach to foreign capital in Warsaw. Throughout 1925, 1926, and the first half of 1927, the French tried unsuccessfully to procure funding for the project. Their failure angered the Poles, as the results of the trade war hinged on Warsaw's ability to ship coal overseas. After the May 1926 coup, the new Polish government initially tried to show itself trustworthy to foreign capital.[37] However, by the end of the year, with seemingly growing interest of foreign capital, the Poles focused on obtaining a big loan abroad (which succeeded in 1927). Now, Warsaw moved to free itself from the concession given to the French. In June 1927, the government decided not to proceed with the promised process of giving a financial guarantee to the consortium. Following a series of legal attacks on the French, in February 1928 Polish authorities declared they would build a railway connecting the coal basins to Gdynia themselves, along a slightly different route. Despite multiple French interventions, the Poles would not budge, and soon construction started. This was the first time Polish authorities reneged on an earlier agreement with French companies. However, as the Poles lacked the necessary funds to finish the entire railway, by the time the Great Depression erupted, they were looking for an investor once again.

The railway was good business, so after a failed attempt of Batignolles in 1927, in 1930 Schneider returned to the talks (together with Banque de Pays du Nord), seeking to obtain a new concession. As the financial market in Paris was still doing well at the time, the group hoped to pay for the project by issuing bonds there, amounting to around 1 billion francs,[38] but needed a bank to underwrite the issue.[39] This time the French government was much more in favour of the project. Ambassador Jules Laroche argued that it allowed supporting the development of Poland "both as an ally, and as the frontier of Western civilization."[40] Once again it found backing from André Maginot and the army.[41] The French Commercial Attaché in Warsaw Bertrand Jochaud du Plessix argued that if Gdynia were like "lungs, which allow Poland to breathe freely," the railway would serve as "airways, which must grow in parallel to avoid suffocation."[42]

The Poles, enthusiastic about the project, were willing to guarantee profits throughout the period of the concession, but his was not enough, even despite the personal attempts of the French Minister of Finance Paul Reynard. French bankers sought a formal declaration of intent from the government, but, as in all similar cases in the interwar period, the government refused. After long talks, French companies and banks came to an agreement, and by April 1931 got the concession (see Map 4.2). The new Compagnie Franco-Polonaise des Chemins de Fer or Francusko-Polskie Towarzystwo Kolejowe (FPTK), owned in 8/15th by French investors and in 7/15th by Polish State Railways (PKP), would build and operate the railway for the next 45 years.[43]

Despite the French majority in FPTK, the Poles retained significant supervision over construction, and were guaranteed a third of profits arising from the railway, increasing to 90 per cent should they greatly exceed projected results. Crucially, from the point of development, Polish enterprises were guaranteed the delivery of all resources for construction, despite the French insisting on some purchases from their country. The Poles instead promised to buy

Map 4.2 The coal trunk line covered by the 1931 concession.

other products from France for 150 million francs over the next three years, provided the construction proceeded on schedule.[44] It was a sensible solution, since Warsaw hoped to buy more military equipment anyway. Moreover, in line with the Polish goal of protecting the labour market, the FPTK needed explicit authorization to hire foreigners, and initial construction gave work to some 7,500 people. Warsaw would also receive 90 million francs from the loan to use for other goals – something the Poles had trouble achieving on the market in Paris otherwise. In case of conflict, however, the two sides would resort to external arbitrage in The Hague, where Poland has historically lost – most famously in the case of the Warsaw power plant.

The concession was badly timed. The French managed to issue the first tranche of 400 million francs (at 6.5 per cent, sold for 94 francs per 100), but with banking and monetary crises erupting throughout Europe in 1931, further issues were impossible.[45] As a result, Schneider's consortium completed only the first phase of the construction, and the Polish State Railways operated the coal trunk line's single-track line starting in 1933. Schneider became a hostage of its investment, unable to draw funds back from Poland, or to finish construction.[46] Despite multiple attempts to secure financing, including a dramatic call for help by Deputy Treasury Minister Adam Koc in October 1935 (with which we started Chapter 2), the French government would not offer financial guarantees for the investment.[47] The Poles tried to use the introduction of exchange control in April 1936 to obtain capital for the railway through a clearing arrangement. There was little incentive for Paris to accept this solution, and the Poles were annoyed.[48]

Ultimately, the success of the "Gdynia Railway," as it was called in British correspondence, depended on politics rather than economics.[49] With the rapprochement between France and Poland, the treaty of Rambouillet in 1936 resulted in the French government providing the necessary funds–910 million francs–by itself, without resorting to banks. With money, the Franco–Polish company finished the project before the war, taking over the control of the line and the associated tidy profits. The construction was thus a success, and improved relations between the two countries.[50]

In these sections, I discussed the two most prominent infrastructural projects in which French companies were present. There were many more, ranging from attempts to build the Warsaw underground (with cooperation of French and Belgian capital),[51] to electrification projects, where the French competed against Averell Harrimann, to more modest hydroelectric plant construction.[52] Most of these were a failure, which itself is not remarkable in the case of international tenders. Arguably, however, the differentiating factor in the most important successful bids was the role of the French state, which shaped the consortia, provided guarantees, and finally even financed the railway. Crucial infrastructural investment in Poland was thus the result of government security policy, backed by army circles, rather than high-quality offers presented by private companies. The weak French government could only support some projects, which undermined its eastern policy.[53] As French Minister in Warsaw Hector de Panafieu lamented,

> What might they think about France's financial situation, if our banks are so cautious, that a consortium combining Creusot, Batignolles, and Hersent cannot get a 30 million loan? Can they trust these firms, [...] which cannot get such minor credit?[54]

4.3 The automobile

As in other countries of Central and Eastern Europe, the car was a rare visitor on Polish lands before the war. Little changed after the conflict, due to prohibitive tariffs, expensive maintenance, and costly petrol. After gradual growth in the 1920s, the Great Depression combined with fiscal policy targeting drivers cut the number of privately owned cars by a third between 1931 and 1933.[55] For the majority of the urban population, taking a taxi was the only reliable way of riding one. With such a limited civilian market, the military was a major force contributing to the spread of motorization, by placing orders, creating repair shops, and ultimately spearheading production.[56]

After independence, Poland found itself with a selection of foreign cars and no domestic production. With limited access to spare parts, local workshops were crucial for maintenance, which allowed them to gain significant experience. This included maintaining army vehicles, initially accounting for the majority of all Polish automobiles. The Central Car Workshops (Centralne Warsztaty Samochodowe) had their successes with manufacturing armoured and unarmoured automobiles. Together with other state-owned factories, in 1928 they became part of a newly formed company: the State Engineering Works (Państwowe Zakłady Inżynierii).

Polish authorities realized the limitations of existing workshops early and attempted to get domestic production started based on foreign capital and expertise.[57] Throughout the 1920s there were numerous abortive initiatives, such as the failed talks with the Franco–Polish Avation and Automobile Consortium (Consortium Franco–polonaise d'Aviation et d'Automobiles).

In 1923, Polish authorities put out a tender for military trucks. They were looking for a company to supply the products and know-how, and within three years move production to Poland. Initially, the Italian manufacturer Spa-Ansaldi defeated the competition: Renault, de Dion-Bouton, and Fiat, curiously all represented by the same company, Frankopol (which will return later in the story), as well as Berliet. A representative of the last company added that the contract would mean creating a serious competitor in Poland, and that French producers only took part in the tender due to "pure patriotism."[58]

As in the case of infrastructure, French authorities, including the Military Mission, quickly intervened, convincing the Poles to annul the result.[59] A new tender was put out, also in 1923, exclusively to Polish companies, for the delivery of trucks "from allied or friendly countries." Offers were to name a foreign partner willing to provide financing of at least 250,000 dollars to shift production to Poland by 1926.[60] Thus the Polish firm would gradually become a car manufacturer. It was a sensible approach to industrial policy. The three French companies again presented their offers. De Dion-Bouton won, but after Berliet made a counterproposal with much lower prices, the Poles thought they were being deceived, and annulled the results of the second tender as well, asking the companies to resubmit their offers.

The story is a troubling variation on the impact of French authorities on the actions of private companies. Three French firms returned with new offers: Berliet, de Dion-Bouton, and Renault. De Dion-Bouton met the technical criteria, but, as Christophe Laforest writes, its "only mistake was playing fair."[61] Berliet not only offered its products below cost, but it also hired the son of the French Military Mission's technical councillor responsible for cars, who in turn made sure that this manufacturer, rather than Dion-Bouton, got the contract. When General Dupont from the French Military Mission found out, he didn't find the matter very problematic. He argued unconvincingly that what the councillor's actions were improper, but the man had done his best to help all three French companies.[62] Despite calls to right the obvious wrong, Prime Minister Raymond Poincaré decided to let the matter go to protect the French position in Poland. The Polish company Ursus won the contract, split between Berliot (which was to supply most vehicles) and Spa-Ansaldi.[63]

In an amusing twist, the contract turned out problematic for Berliot. Not trusting the Polish currency, the company had insisted on fixing the prices of its trucks in francs, without a valorization mechanism. With prices rising in France, suddenly the company found itself losing money on each car, while the Poles profited from the depreciating franc. As a result, in 1926 the French company reneged on the agreement. Ursus never produced any Berliet trucks, focusing instead on Spa vehicles.[64] With the impact of the Great Depression, the company went under, and ended up as part of the State Engineering Works. Later, when French companies made another attempt at penetrating the Polish market, they were unable to match the offer of the Swiss producer Adolph Saurer AG, and the state company started producing trucks on a Swiss, rather than a French, licence.

This early attempt to kickstart local car production had the markings of good industrial policy, but the French torpedoed it. They caused delays, introduced nepotism, affected the tender, and ultimately cost their ally three years in launching car production. Ironically, by weakening the French ally, they also undermined Paris's own security goals in Eastern Europe. Finally, the case shows a weakness of French economic diplomacy. With no coordination, multiple French companies sabotaged each other's positions, and could count on no help with financing from their authorities. In contrast, Italian companies were willing to back each other, and could count on support from their government.[65]

The next major Polish attempt to kickstart car production came in 1928, at the initiative of President Ignacy Mościcki. Lacking resources, but wanting to keep control over the endeavour, Warsaw authorities hoped to create a mixed company with a Polish government majority, into which the French would bring capital, and the Poles – the newly formed State Engineering Works. In this, we see an evolution of thinking about such endeavours, from the state mobilizing private investors, to a mixed company. In 1928, based on research among European producers, the Poles approached Renault.[66] French authorities tried to "convince Louis Renault that the participation of his company in the organization of the Polish car industry held great interest for the French national defence."[67] Renault was reluctant, especially since Fiat proved a serious competitor, once again with strong financial backing from the Italian government.[68] Ultimately, French banks were uninterested, and despite engagement from the authorities, the French automaker decided to pull out, refusing to provide the Poles with more than a few engineers as consultants. Despite further attempts, including a plan to use a part of the 4th tranche of the 400 million francs military credit, the matter ended with no success.[69]

In 1930, Polish military authorities were willing to try once more–this time hoping to achieve an arrangement similar to the agreement with Saurer. André Citroën was willing to talk. His company had already considered building a factory in Poland in the early 1920s, and sold armoured cars to the Polish Army. It opened a Polish subsidiary, the Société polonaise des automobiles Citroën (or Polski Citroën), which since 1929 ran an assembly workshop to avoid exorbitant import tariffs. It was a relatively small operation, but as Tadeusz Łychowski testified sarcastically, Paris considered it a "French contribution to the Polish economy."[70] A leading seller on the market, Citroën was interested in starting full production in Poland, in line with the company's strategy of fast expansion. The Polish military, which conducted the talks, seemed to like the French company's initial proposal, which rested on the State Engineering Works starting production of licensed cars, and the French controlling their distribution. However, once the Poles got a better offer from Fiat, which included "fresh money," they ended the talks with the French without further negotiations. The French Military Mission protested, but its position in Poland was much weaker. Other French companies did not manage to convince Warsaw either.[71]

According to Ambassador Alfred Chłapowski, the blame for Fiat's victory lay on the side of the French, who were not willing to offer enough funding. Łychowski, who worked in the Polish Ministry of Industry and Trade, and had a particularly low opinion of military circles, argued that the military did not know how to negotiate with the French.[72] Be that as it may, based on the agreement, State Engineering Works started building Fiat-licenced cars and (after 1935) trucks. They controlled an 80–90 per cent share of the market thanks to prohibitively high tariffs. Unsurprisingly, Fiat cars were sold at higher prices than abroad, contributing to the drop in the number of automobiles in the country. The French got a much better deal in Czechoslovakia.[73]

As Christophe Laforest writes, "Renault could congratulate itself for not adopting a bold and expensive penetration strategy like Citroën did, whose investment in Warsaw was ultimately resulted in a complete loss."[74] Deprived of its market, the assembly workshop shut down (as did General Motors'), much to the French authorities' chagrin, as automobiles, like wines and perfumes, played a special role among French exports. Soon afterwards, Citröen overextended its resources. Despite the technical prowess of its products, such as the famous Traction Avant car, the company declared bankruptcy in late 1934, and was taken over by its largest creditor, Michelin.

Nonetheless, as the Poles realized the stifling influence of the monopoly granted to State Engineering Works-made Fiat cars, and the concurrent fall in the number of registered cars during the Great Depression, they moved to support more producers by granting new concessions. In 1936, despite experiences so far, both Renault and Citröen applied, fighting the Americans: Ford and General Motors, the latter represented by the Polish private industrial company Lilpop, Rau i Loewenstein SA from Warsaw. General Motors won, partially due to its wide range of models, which appeared on Polish roads by 1937.[75]

It was only at the end of the interwar period that the French managed to sign an agreement concerning production in Poland. The locomotive producer Fablok (Pierwsza Fabryka Lokomotyw w Polsce S.A. Zakłady w Chrzanowie), received a concession to import and build Renault cars in April 1939. The new assembly shop would be built in Nałęczów within the Central Industrial Basin. By this time, however, the French could no longer count on monopolizing the market. The Poles managed to avoid the control of their allies, and made sure that a domestic company would produce the machines – 16 years after the original tender. Still, war cut the efforts short.[76]

4.4 Aviation

The story of French forays into Polish aeroplane production is shorter than that of cars, yet it starts from a similar set of circumstances.[77] Initially, the Polish Army had little beyond a few captured aeroplanes. Fighting wars for its independence and borders, the quickly growing military needed a functioning air force, and so turned to buying planes abroad, including on French credit. As Wojciech Mazur writes, France had a preponderant influence over the Polish Air Force in 1919, when it supplied "planes, equipment, and the majority of personnel – pilots, observers, technical officers, mechanics, instructors, and commanders."[78] In later years, the Poles continued to organize their air force based on the French model, and buy French planes under changing governments and decision makers. They included the French general Armand Lévêque from the French Aviation Mission (a part of the wider Military Mission). In an exceptional level of connection between the two armies, he led the Department between 1923 and 1924. Later, general Włodzimierz Zagórski, who supported buying many planes, took the post.[79] Between 1923 and 1930, half of all military Polish orders placed in France (225 million francs) concerned aviation, with some three-quarters of their value coming between 1924 and 1926.[80]

Buying aeroplanes was expensive, and the Poles soon attempted domestic production, initially in cooperation with the French. I will focus on the two most spectacular examples.[81] In 1919, after an initial study of the French firm Avions Farman, the head of the Aeroplane Department of the French Military Mission organized an Aviation Consortium, representing major producers. Its actions were similar to those described in other investments throughout the chapter. The consortium, which soon evolved into the Franco–Polish Aviation and Automobile Consortium (mentioned above), sent Raymond Saulnier from the Société Anonyme des Aéroplanes Morane-Saulnier to talk to the Poles. Warsaw was happy to see the French invest, provided that any new companies stayed under Polish control.[82] As a result, in May 1921, the Franco–Polish Automobile and Aviation Works (Francusko–Polskie Zakłady Samochodowe i

Lotnicze S.A.) – or Frankopol, as it was commonly known – signed a ten-year contract for the delivery of over 2,500 planes and twice as many engines. The new company, which overcame Italian competition, was to open a factory by the end of 1922, and construct a growing proportion of its deliveries in Poland. The contract was decidedly one-sided, leaving the Poles with little room for manoeuvre.[83] Nonetheless, Polish military authorities attempted to shape the production of the company, using the French Military Mission to obtain licences for the plant.[84]

A double overestimation undermined the agreement. The Polish Army lacked the resources to purchase so many planes, and French aviation companies, which now turned their attention to the Romanian and Czechoslovak markets, did not have the capital required to open production. Moreover, as with cars, they were not interested in creating a competitor in Central Europe. Already in 1922, the company was starting to provoke Polish suspicions, and Lévêque, who sided with the Poles, found it difficult to improve the situation. As Mazur writes, Warsaw itself was partially to blame, since internal politics within the Polish Army delayed any decisions concerning the company. The situation was made worse by Polish officers, such as general Zagórski, who fostered connections with the Franco–Polish company. Ultimately, after a failed attempt to build an alternative to Frankopol in cooperation with Lorraine-Dietrich, Lévêque resigned.[85]

Despite a new agreement in December 1924, which brought the number of deliverable planes to 500, and engines on a Lorraine-Dietrich licence to 2,700, and despite funding from the Polish government, Frankopol did little to start production. A Polish commission quickly found evidence of fraud, although Zagórski continued to defend the company.[86] After an attempt at price blackmail from French producers, the Polish Ministry of Military Affairs reneged on the agreements, demanded the return of significant advance payments, and swore to stop matériel purchases from these companies.[87]

The scandal again points to the detrimental influence of Paris on Polish investments. It was the French Military Mission which helped kickstart the talks between the Poles and the consortium. As with car production, they were not the only competitor. The Italians tried to intervene, initially in Warsaw, and then in Paris. Italy's ambassador asked the French to make sure that General Henri Niessel, the head of the French Military Mission "did not oppose Italian firms from getting their part of Polish commands."[88] As correspondence between the MAÉ and the French military shows, Paris's officials were furious. Since the French had helped the Poles politically, now they felt entitled to due profits.[89]

Nonetheless, while Frankopol's fraudulent conduct helped fill the Consortium's coffers, ultimately it undermined French security policy in Poland. As the French Military Mission was the first to discover the "constant wrongdoings" of the company, soon, tensions arose between French authorities and private investors.[90] The French realized that between Frankopol, problems with car production, a failure of cooperation in the Starachowice factory (where Schneider and Vickers allegedly defrauded the Poles without starting production), Warsaw would not be pleased.[91]

Soon after Frankopol's fraud was discovered, the Poles changed policy in dramatic circumstances. With the May coup, General Ludomir Rayski took command over the Air Force and its acquisitions. In interwar Poland's most chilling political mystery, Zagórski, who opposed the coup, was arrested, then likely murdered by Piłsudski's supporters.[92] Rayski, a long-time opponent of Zagórski, shifted policy away from buying planes abroad to domestic production. Even with no additional purchases, the country had to cope with an overabundance of ageing aircraft.[93]

In June 1926, Polish military authorities started talks with a number of producers about the takeover of Frankopol (as nationalizing the company would require significant outlays).[94] They included the Czechoslovakian giant Škoda from Plzeň (then under the control of Schneider), the Italian firm Issota Fraschini, the French manufacturer Lorraine-Dietrich (which had licensed Frankopol its engine design), as well as Bristol, Hispano Suiza, and Rolls-Royce. The inclusion of Škoda surprised some officials in Paris, but as the company ultimately was French-controlled, it received ample support. As Mazur points out, this resulted in a peculiar arrangement, where the French pushed for a solution adopted by Warsaw, fighting against Polish representatives in Paris and Prague, who tried to torpedo the talks,

> spreading rumours of German control over Škoda. The French could not fathom the situation, and thus explained it through an intrigue of the Italians (annoyed at having lost their position), or perhaps the Germans, hoping to prevent a Polish–Czechoslovak rapprochement.[95]

Nonetheless, based on a personal intervention of Józef Piłsudski, by November 1926 the Polish Ministry for Military Affairs signed an agreement with the Czechs, transferring the assets of Frankopol to a newly formed Polish subsidiary, Polish Škoda Works Inc. in Warsaw (Polskie Zakłady Škody SA).[96] This change meant a continuity of French influence on Polish aviation, although through a different set of investors, which were to limit their production to engines (with the Poles taking over assets connected to aeroplane production). Moreover, the Czechoslovak company financed its operations through a bond issue in London.[97] This time the operation was more successful, and by 1927 the company manufactured aircraft engines based on French and American licences, with a further ten-year contract signed in 1929. However, as Škoda had little experience in engine production, its products, based on external designs, were often dated.[98] It diversified its production into cables and electrical equipment (creating a subsidiary: Warszawska Wytwórnia Kabli S.A. – Škodapol), and achieved significant success and international recognition. It became the largest private firm in the (as the industry styled itself) combustion engine, automobile, and aviation sector in the country, with the State Engineering Works its only major rival. By 1932 its share capital reached an impressive 15 million złoty.[99]

As Mariusz W. Majewski writes, the company had to contend with actions of the Polish military. By 1930, the Poles insisted that rather than import certain components, Škoda should buy them locally. This was good industrial policy, even if done for security reasons. Škoda attempted to comply with limited success, as producers were scarce and unwilling to learn. The problem would repeat itself with multiple companies, showing the difficulty of building a high-technology factory in a country without the necessary economic and technological environment. Moreover, Polish policy under Rayski was shifting against private producers in the sector. In 1927, the authorities created the State Aviation Workshops (Państwowe Zakłady Lotnicze, PZL). This state-owned company initially tried to build aircraft on foreign licences (including French), but soon moved to its own designs utilizing foreign engines.[100] As the Great Depression loomed over the sector, authorities moved to consolidate production. Failing (or even successful) private firms were transformed into new state-owned enterprises.[101] By 1934 this policy extended to the Polish Škoda Works.[102] Authorities saw the company as dangerous to the Polish aviation industry, especially due to growing Czechoslovak-Soviet cooperation. Officially, the Poles also falsely complained that the company failed to cooperate with domestic producers. In 1935, the government bought the factory and the accompanying rights from the Czechoslovaks, transferring them to PZL. A much smaller Škoda continued to manufacture electrical equipment. This meant, on the one hand, another failed Schneider incursion in the country, and on the other, the loss of any French influence in the aviation sector.[103]

The Polish development of aircraft production was an arduous, state-led process, in which central control sometimes undermined the vitality of domestic producers. As I discussed in Chapter 3, revolving doors between Polish authorities and the growing state sector created a systemic bias against private and foreign-owned companies. Moreover, as aviation (and cars) formed part of the military sector, the rising importance and independence of the army after 1926 strengthened such tendencies. Nonetheless, the final result was a qualified Polish success. Poland and Czechoslovakia alone in the region achieved "self-sufficiency in military aviation production and transformed into serious competitors as exporters of military aircraft in their own right."[104] Admittedly, these results owed much to earlier French help, the significant technical and personnel assistance, as well as the rather generous access to licences thanks to ample support from the government in Paris.[105]

4.5 Conclusions

In this chapter, I looked at potentially the most unambiguous French influence on Polish development: the Polish state guiding French firms towards narrowly focused investment. Its impact however was complex, and varied between the studied endeavours.

The two main types of investment held different meanings for the two countries. The Poles needed infrastructure for the basic safety and functioning of the state, but its creation would not change the Polish position in the global division of labour. The potential for development – beyond the obvious consequences of better infrastructure – depended on the shape of the contracts, such as the percentage of construction and materials allotted to Polish companies, or repayment rules. The Poles managed to improve their position in this regard in the 1930s. From the point of view of foreign investors, these were relatively safe endeavours, based on well-established technology, with profits guaranteed by the Polish government. Combined with pressure from the government and army in Paris, for which both projects were crucial for security reasons, this created a network of political and economic support which carried them to completion.

Aviation and the automobile held less obvious promises to French capital. They entailed direct investment in the Central European country, with no comparable safety net. Why put money in Poland, if French companies could continue to manufacture cars or planes in France and export them? On the other hand, arming France's ally was an ongoing security concern for Paris. It meant that the projects enjoyed ample support – at least when the French army held much sway in Warsaw. As its influence waned after 1926 – and especially after 1932 and the dissolution of the Military Mission, – the increasingly independent Polish Army had no interest of listening to the French. As a result, the projects had the greatest chance of success in the 1920s, but ran into problems from private investors. From the Polish point of view, these investments were primarily of a security nature, especially in the 1920s, and as a result, cooperation with foreign capital was a sensible way to get factories running faster. It was only in the 1930s that authorities in Warsaw made development a more important part of their thinking.

Notes

1 *Polskie Kopalnie Skarbowe na Górnym Śląsku. Spółka Dzierżawna. Spółka Akcyjna w Katowicach. Société Fermière des Mines Fiscales de l'Etat Polonais en Haute–Silésie. Sociéte Anonyme à Katowice* (Warszawa: Zakłady Graficzne B. Wierzbicki i Ska, 1929).
2 Marian Dąbrowski, ed., *20-lecie komunikacji w Polsce Odrodzonej, 1918–1939* (Kraków: Koncern Prasowy "Ilustrowany Kuryer Codzienny," 1939).
3 Janusz Żarnowski, *Polska 1918–1939: praca, technika, społeczeństwo*, 2nd ed (Warszawa: Książka i Wiedza, 1999), 200.
4 Carlota Perez, *Technological Revolutions and Financial Capital: The Dynamics of Bubbles and Golden Ages* (Cheltenham: Edward Elgar, 2002), 11, 14, 18.
5 Dominique Barjot, *La grande entreprise française de travaux publics (1883–1974)* (Paris: Economica, 2006); Grzegorz Piątek, *Miasto, modernizm, modernizacja 1920–1939* (Warszawa: Wydawnictwo WAB, 2022); Ryszard Mielczarek, *Budowa portu handlowego w Gdyni w latach 1924–1939* (Gdańsk: Instytut Kaszubski, 2001); Grzegorz Kotlarz, Henryk Dąbrowski, and Edward Wieczorek, *Magistrala węglowa: najciekawsze linie kolejowe Polski*, 2nd ed. (Rybnik: Eurosprinter, 2017).
6 Youssef Cassis, *Big Business: The European Experience in the Twentieth Century* (New York: Oxford University Press 2004), 55–57; Chris Freeman and Francisco Louçã, *As Time Goes by: From the Industrial Revolutions to the Information*

Revolution (Oxford: Oxford University Press, 2001), 286; Richard F. Kuisel, *Capitalism and the State in Modern France: Renovation and Economic Management in the Twentieth Century* (Cambridge: Cambridge University Press, 1981), 94.

7 Gołębiowski, *Przemysł*, 53.

8 Peter B. Evans, *Embedded Autonomy: States and Industrial Transformation* (Princeton: Princeton University Press, 1995), 85.

9 Evans, *Embedded Autonomy*, 91; Thomas David, *Nationalisme économique et industrialisation: l'expérience des pays d'Europe de l'Est (1789–1939)* (Genève: Librairie Droz, 2009), 280.

10 Luminiţa Gatejel and Jerzy Kochanowski, "Transport, Infrastructure and Communication," in *The Routledge History Handbook of Central and Eastern Europe in the Twentieth Century: Challenges of Modernity*, ed. Stanislav Holubec, Władysław Borodziej, and Joachim von Puttkamer (London and New York: Routledge, 2020), 129–82, 153.

11 This section is based on my earlier studies: Jerzy Łazor, "Kto ma budować Gdynię? Wpływ władz w Paryżu na kształt konsorcjum francusko-polskiego," *Dzieje Najnowsze* 54, no. 3 (2022): 5–26, https://doi.org/10.12775/DN.2022.3.01; Jerzy Łazor, "French Capital, Gdynia, and the Position of Polish Coal on International Markets in the Interwar Period," in *Fueling the World Economy: Seaports, Coal, and Oil Markets during the Early Globalization*, ed. Daniel Castillo Hidalgo and Cézar Honorato, Palgrave Studies in Maritime Economics (Cham: Palgrave Macmillan, 2023), 99–121, https://doi.org/10.1007/978-3-031-32565-6_6.

12 Leszek Jerzy Jasiński, *Bliżej centrum czy na peryferiach? Polskie kontakty gospodarcze z zagranicą w XX wieku* (Warszawa: Centrum Europejskie Natolin, Wydawnictwo Trio, 2011), 43; Zbigniew Landau, and Jerzy Tomaszewski, *Gospodarka Polski miedzywojennej 1918–1939. Vol. 1: W dobie inflacji 1918–1923* (Warszawa: Książka i Wiedza, 1967), 323–24.

13 Robert Mark Spaulding, *Osthandel and Ostpolitik: German Foreign Trade Policies in Eastern Europe from Bismarck to Adenauer* (Providence, RI: Berghahn Books, 1997), 158; Karol Józef Błahut, *Polsko–niemieckie stosunki gospodarcze w latach 1919–1939* (Wrocław: Zakład Narodowy im. Ossolińskich, 1975), 65–76.

14 Piotr Stefan Wandycz, *France and Her Eastern Allies 1919–1925: French–Czechoslovak–Polish Relations from the Paris Peace Conference to Locarno* (Minneapolis: The University of Minnesota Press, 1962), 163–64.

15 Mielczarek, *Budowa*.

16 Kotlarz, Dąbrowski, and Wieczorek, *Magistrala*, 10–11; Marcin Przegiętka, *Komunikacja i polityka: Transport kolejowy i drogowy w stosunkach polsko-niemieckich w latach 1918–1939* (Warszawa: Instytut Pamięci Narodowej, 2015), 214–16.

17 Archives Diplomatiques, La Courneuve [henceforth: AdC], Correspondance politique et commercial, 1918–1940, Pologne [henceforth: CPC PL], Gérardin to Poincaré, 10 August 1922, 2–4v.

18 AdC, CPC PL, 263, Poincaré to François-Marsal, 28 April 1924, 101v; AdC, CPC PL, 263, Note concernant les nouvelles lignes de chemins de fer en Pologne, 18 April 1924, 93; Zbigniew Landau, *Polskie zagraniczne pożyczki państwowe 1918–1926* (Warszawa: Książka i Wiedza, 1961); DzU RP 1924, nr 110, poz. 988.

19 AdC, CPC PL, 260, Jolivet to [FLW], 7 May 1923, 23; AdC, CPC PL, 260, Maginot to Bokanowski, 8 May 1924, 210.

20 AdC, CPC PL, 260, Délibération de la 3e Section de la Commission d'Études du Conseil Supérieur de la Défense Nationale dans sa séance du 18 avril 1924, 7 May 1924, 182–90; AdC, CPC PL, 260, Résumé des délibérations de la 3e Section de la Commission d'Études et avis formulés concernant la garantie financière demandée par le Consortium Franco–Polonais au sujet de la concession des travaux du port de Gdynia, 18 April 1924, 148–50.

21 Mielczarek, *Budowa*, 41; Dominique Barjot, "L'entreprise Hersent: ascension, prospérité et chute d'une famille d'entrepreneurs (1860–1982)," in *Le capitalisme familial. Logiques et trajectoires*, ed. Jean-Claude Daumas (Besançon: Presses universitaires de Franche-Comté, 2003), 133–66, 142; Dominique Barjot, "Une face méconnue du capitalisme français en Russie," in *La France et les Français en Russie*, ed. Annie Charon, Bruno Delmas, and Armelle Le Goff (Paris: École nationale des Chartes, 2011), 443–57, https://doi.org/10.4000/books.enc.1306.

22 AdC, CPC PL, 260, de Barante to Poincaré, 2 April 1923, 12v; Bolesław Kasprowicz, "Problemy ekonomiczne budowy i eksploatacji portu w Gdyni w latach 1920–1939," *Zapiski Historyczne* XXII, no. 1–3 (1956): 119–74, 132.

23 AdC, CPC PL, 260, Poincaré to Panafieu, 9 May 1923, 20–20v.

24 Tomasz Schramm, *Francuskie misje wojskowe w państwach Europy Środkowej: 1919–1939* (Poznań: Uniwersytet Adama Mickiewicza, 1987), 112.

25 AdC, CPC PL, 260, Charles to Raiberti, 24 October 1923, 103.

26 AdC, CPC PL, 260, Port de Gdynia, 21 January 1924, 119–19v.

27 Anne Burnel, *La société de construction des Batignolles de 1914 à 1939: histoire d'un déclin* (Genève: Librarie Droz, 1995); Agnès D'Angio, *Schneider & Cie et les travaux publics, 1895–1949* (Paris: École nationale des Chartes, 1995), 283; Julian Rummel, "U kolebki Gdyni (fragment pamiętnika)," *Rocznik Gdyński*, 1977, 197–207, 201; Kasprowicz, "Problemy," 133.

28 Georges-Henri Soutou, "L'impérialisme du pauvre: la politique économique du gouvernement français en Europe Centrale et Orientale de 1918 à 1929. Essai d'interprétation," *Relations internationales* 3, no. 7 (1976): 219–39; Barjot, *La grande entreprise*, 349, 354; Dominique Barjot, "Public Utilities and Private Initiative: The French Concession Model in Historical Perspective," *Business History* 53, no. 5 (2011): 782–800, https://doi.org/10.1080/00076791.2011.599590.

29 AdC, CPC PL, 260, Concession des travaux du port de Gdynia, 19 April 1924, 152–53v; AdC, CPC PL, 260, François-Marsal to Poincaré, 5 May 1924, 174–75v; AdC, CPC PL, 261, Chłapowski to Herriot, 18 October 1924, 19–20; AdC, CPC PL, 261, Consortium Franco–Polonais pour la Construction du Port de Gdynia to Briand, 16 February 1926, 121–22v.

30 AdC, CPC PL, 260, Contrat pour la construction du port de Gdynia (Pologne), 4 July 1924, 243–73.

31 AdC, CPC PL, 261, Briand to Caillaux, 8 July 1925, 83–84v; AdC, CPC PL, 261, Laroche to Briand, 11 February 1927, 194–97.

32 Mielczarek, *Budowa*, 47–49; AdC, CPC PL, 405, "Consortium Franco–Polonais pour la Construction du Port de Gdynia," 11 April 1932, 67–68.

33 AdC, CPC PL, 261, Tripier to Briand, 29 July 1927, 202–3; Christophe Laforest, "La stratégie française et la Pologne (1919–1939). Aspects économiques et implications politiques" (PhD, Université Paris 1 Panthéon-Sorbonne, 2001), 169–73.

34 Łazor, "French Capital."

35 The National Archives, Kew [henceforth: TNA], FO 371/10456, N8686/2172/55, Muller to MacDonald, 9 April 1924, 264–5.

36 This section is partially based on my earlier paper: Jerzy Łazor, "Pierwsza francusko–polska koncesja kolejowa z 1924 r. Przyczynek do relacji finansowo–gospodarczych Polski i Francji po pierwszej wojnie światowej," *Kwartalnik Historyczny* 128, no. 3 (2021): 785–812, http://doi.org/10.12775/KH.2021.128.3.03.

37 Zbigniew Landau, *Plan stabilizacyjny 1927–1930. Geneza, założenia, wyniki* (Warszawa: Książka i Wiedza, 1963), 59–88.

38 AdC, CPC PL, 408, Laroche to Brianda, 3 June 1930, 19–21.

39 AdC, CPC PL, 408, Note confidentielle au sujet de la voie ferée Silésie–Gdynia, 30 July 1930, 38–40.

40 AdC, CPC PL, 408, Laroche to Briand, 6 August 1930, 36.

41 AdC, CPC PL, 408, Internal MAÉ Memo, 23 June 1930, 32–32v.
42 AdC, CPC PL, 408, Jochaud du Plessix to Flandin, 31 May 1930, 25.
43 AdC, CPC PL, 408, Laroche to Briand, 25 August 1930, 44–45; AdC, CPC PL, 408, Emprunt du Silésie—Baltique, 30 October 1930, 54; AdC, CPC PL, 408, Reynaud to Briand, 8 November 1930, 55–55v; Przegiętka, *Transport*, 216–9; Dawid Keller, "Regulator, właściciel czy…? Dyskusje o roli państwa wobec kolei w okresie międzywojennym – wprowadzenie do zagadnienia," in *Państwo wobec kolei żelaznych w Polsce*, ed. Michał Kapias and Dawid Keller (Rybnik: Muzeum w Rybniku, 2017), 163–80, 170.
44 AdC, CPC PL, 408, Chłapowski to Briand, 31 March 1931, 207–8.
45 AdC, CPC PL, 408, MAÉ to Laroche, 23 April 1931, 239–42.
46 AdC, CPC PL, 409, Laroche to Paul-Boncour, 18 February 1933, 88–89; Archiwum Akt Nowych, Warsaw [henceforth: AAN], Ministerstwo Spraw Zagranicznych [henceforth: MSZ], 3766, Memo on Franco–Polish relations, 31 May 1932, 8–9.
47 AdC, CPC PL, 409, Chemin de Fer Silésie–Gdynia, 7 May 1935, 182–83; AdC, CPC PL, 409, Noël to MAÉ, 31 October 1935, 186–90; AdC, CPC PL, 409, Laval to MAÉ, 2 November 1935, 193.
48 AdC, Fonds Nominatifs, Léon Noël, Noël to MAÉ, 17 July 1936, n.p.; Mylène Mihout-Natar, "L'intervention des capitaux français dans la Pologne de la Seconde République (1918–1939): contribution à l'histoire de l'impérialisme économique français en Europe centrale" (PhD, Université Charles de Gaulle – Lille III, 2002), 752.
49 TNA, FO 371/17785, Notes on C210/210/55, 312.
50 Laforest, "La stratégie," 190–91; Mihout-Natar, "L'intervention," 752–54.
51 AdC, CPC PL, 405, Construction d'un métropolitain en Varsovie, 16 August 1934, 127–127v; Archives départamentales de Loire-Atlantique (Nantes), Fonds de la Compagnie des tramways de Nantes, 41 J 174, Points principaux des conditions de concession pour la construction et l'expoitation d'un métropolitain à Varsovie, n.p.
52 Czesław Madajczyk, "Spory wokół sprawy elektryfikacji Polski (1926–1930)," *Najnowsze Dzieje Polski: materiały i studia z okresu 1914–1939* 5 (1962): 153–220.
53 AdC, CPC PL, 263, Poincaré to François-Marsal, 30 May 1924, 105–8b.
54 AdC, CPC PL, 261, Panafieu to Herriot, 15 September 1924, 7v.
55 Żarnowski, *Polska*, 196; Zbigniew Landau and Jerzy Tomaszewski, *Gospodarka Polski miedzywojennej 1918–1939. Vol 3: Wielki kryzys 1930–1935* (Warszawa: Książka i Wiedza, 1982), 308; David, *Nationalisme*, 281; cf. Brian R. Mitchell, *International historical statistics: Europe 1750–1993* (Basingstoke: Macmillan Press, 1998), 735–48.
56 Teodor Wójcik, "Centralne Warsztaty Samochodowe w Warszawie w latach 1918–1928: Przyczynek do genezy polskiej motoryzacji," *Przegląd Historyczno-Wojskowy* 14(65), no. 2 (2013): 187–95.
57 This section is based on Laforest, "La stratégie," 134–54; Mariusz W. Majewski, "Rozwój motoryzacji w Polsce w latach 1919–1930," *Annales Universitatis Paedagogicae Cracoviensis. Studia Historica* 9, no. 78 (2010): 56–77; Mariusz W. Majewski, "Eksploatacja licencji motoryzacyjnych w Państwowych Zakładach Inżynierii (1930–1936)," *Annales Universitatis Paedagogicae Cracoviensis. Studia Historica* 10, no. 95 (2011): 82–98.
58 AAN, Prokuratoria Generalna [henceforth: PG], 2820, Galli-Commoretti to Bukowiecki, 13 August 1923, n.p.
59 AdC, CPC PL, 241, de Barante to Poincaré, 23 September 1923, 210–11.
60 AdC, CPC PL, 241, Convocation pour la déposition d'offres, 31 August 1923, 234–41.
61 Laforest, "La stratégie," 137.
62 AdC, CPC PL, 242, Dupont to Maginot, 7 May 1924, 140–43.

63 Majewski, "Rozwój," 66–67.
64 Ibid., 70–71.
65 Laforest, "La stratégie," 138.
66 Majewski, "Rozwój," 74–75; AdC, CDC PL, 252, Tripier to Briand, 27 November 1928, 188–188v.
67 Laforest, "La stratégie," 141.
68 AdC, CDC PL, 252, Laroche to MAÉ, 24 April 1929, 226.
69 Laforest, "La stratégie," 142; Mihout-Natar, "L'intervention," 289; AdC, CDC PL, 252, MAÉ to FEW, 18 May 1929, 228–28v.
70 Polish Institute and Sikorski Museum, London [henceforth: PISM], B.I. 116/48 Protokół przesłuchania dr Tadeusza Łychowskiego, 1 October 1941, 678; AdC, AdC, CPC PL, 276, MAÉ to AFV, 2 March 1928, 48; RISA 1930, 1462; RPPiH 1932, 503.
71 Laforest, "La stratégie," 144–47.
72 PISM, B.I. 116/48, Protokół przesłuchania dr Tadeusza Łychowskiego, 1 October 1941, 678–81.
73 Alice Teichova, *An Economic Background to Munich: International Business and Czechoslovakia 1918–1938* (London: Cambridge University Press, 1974), 263–65.
74 Laforest, "La stratégie," 148.
75 Mariusz Relich, "Załamanie motoryzacji w Polsce na skutek tzw. demotoryzacji kraju w latach 1931–1935 i próby jej odbudowy w drugiej połowie lat 30. XX wieku," in *Na lądzie, w wodzie i w powietrzu… Z dziejów transportu i komunikacji na ziemiach polskich na przestrzeni wieków*, ed. Tomasz Głowiński and Robert Klementowski (Wrocław: Gajt, 2014), 201–12, 209.
76 Jerzy Gołębiowski, *Przemysł wojenny w Polsce 1918–1939* (Kraków: Wydawnictwo Naukowe WSP, 1990), 286; Laforest, "La stratégie," 150–54.
77 This section's main narrative is based on: Wojciech Mazur, *Pod wiatr. Francja i lotnictwo wojskowe II Rzeczypospolitej (1921–1938)* (Ksiegarnia Kraków: Akademicka, 2015), https://doi.org/10.12797/9788376386577; Mariusz W. Majewski, "Początki produkcji silników lotniczych w II Rzeczypospolitej (1921–1926)," *Annales Universitatis Paedagogicae Cracoviensis. Studia Historica* 2, no. 17 (2003): 201–21; Mariusz W. Majewski, "Druga próba uruchomienia produkcji silników lotniczych Polskie Zakłady Škody (1926–1935)," *Annales Universitatis Paedagogicae Cracoviensis. Studia Historica* 4, no. 28 (2005): 148–65.
78 Mazur, "Pod wiatr," 13.
79 Jonathan A. Grant, *Between Depression and Disarmament: The International Armaments Business, 1919–1939* (Cambridge: Cambridge University Press, 2018), 117, https://doi.org/10.1017/9781108552721; AdC, CPC PL, 236, de Panafieu to Briand, 24 February 1926, 168–168v.
80 Mihout, "L'intervention," 805.
81 By 1926 the Poles had bought licences for 7 French aircraft and 2 aircraft engines; Mazur, *Pod wiatr*, 119, footnote 57.
82 AdC, CPC PL, 251, Henrys to Pralon, 22 September 1919, 138; AdC, CPC PL, 251, Saulnier to Główny Urząd Zaopatrywania Armii, 10 April 1920, 139; Mihout, "L'intervention," 232.
83 AAN, PG, 71, Agreement from 31 May 1921, 1–6; Majewski, "Początki produkcji," 205.
84 Centralne Archiwum Wojskowe, Rembertów [henceforth: CAW], Biuro Administracji Armii Ministerstwa Spraw Wojskowych [henceforth: BAA], I 300.54.124, Sosnkowski to Dupont, 15 November 1922, 3.
85 Mazur, *Pod wiatr*, 48, 58; Majewski, "Początki produkcji," 202–11.

86 CAW, BAA, I 300.54.123, Sikorski to Komitet Ekonomiczny Ministrów, 7 January 1925, 182–84v; and Krzemiński to Żeligowski, 3 March 1926, 567–74; CAW, Departament Sprawiedliwości Ministerstwa Spraw Wojskowych, I 300.58.160, Zagórski to Żeligowski, 19 February 1926, n.p.; Mihout-Natar, "l'intervention," 233; Jerzy Gołębiowski, *Sektor państwowy w gospodarce Polski międzywojennej* (Warszawa—Kraków: Państwowe Wydawnictwo Naukowe, 1985), 113–114; Mazur, *Pod wiatr*, 103–5.
87 Gołębiowski, *Sektor*, 114; Tadeusz Grabowski, *Rola państwa w gospodarce Polski (1918–1928)* (Warszawa: Państwowe Wydawnictwo Ekonomiczne, 1967), 186–87.
88 Quoted in Laforest, "La stratégie," 116.
89 Laforest, "La stratégie," 117.
90 Mihout, "L'intervention," 233.
91 Laforest, "La stratégie," 98–113.
92 Andrzej Garlicki, *Józef Piłsudski: 1867–1935*, 3rd ed. (Warszawa: Czytelnik, 1990), 446–47; Majewski, "Początki produkcji," 218–20.
93 Mazur, *Pod wiatr*, 115; Grzegorz Kulka, "Sprawy honorowe gen. Włodzimierza Ostoi-Zagórskiego w latach 1923–1928," *Dzieje Najnowsze* 48, no. 3 (2016): 107–27, 122, https://doi.org/10.12775/DN.2016.3.06.
94 CAW, BAA, I 300.54.123, Krzemiński to Żeligowski, 3 March 1926, 573; Majewski, "Początki produkcji," 214–17.
95 Mazur, *Pod wiatr*, 106.
96 Škoda also had an older subsidiary in Poland: Polskie Towarzystwo Zakładów Škody, Sp. z o.o., founded in 1925. It sold Škoda's products (cf. RISA 1930; RPPiH 1934).
97 Majewski, "Druga próba," 162.
98 Ibid., 152.
99 RPPiH 1934, no. 1440; Gołębiowski, *Przemysł*, 115–16; Grant, *Between Depression*, 118.
100 Gołębiowski, *Przemysł*, 117.
101 Jerzy Gołębiowski (ed.), *Kapitał państwowy w spółkach prawa handlowego u schyłku Drugiej Rzeczypospolitej. Szczegółowe sprawozdanie z działalności przedsiębiorstw o kapitale mieszanym za rok 1937 wzgl. 1937/1938* (Kraków: Wydawnictwo Naukowe Akademii Pedagogicznej, 2004), 28.
102 Majewski, *Druga próba*, 160–67.
103 Mihout, "L'intervention," 234.
104 Grant, *Between Depression*, 110.
105 Mazur, *Pod wiatr*, 269–72.

5 French capital in interwar Polish resource extraction

Coal, oil, and security policy

In October 1919, Charles Dauphin, who had served as an officer in the French-sanctioned First Polish Army Corps, asked the French diplomatic service whether he could keep his military uniform after demobilization. He had just got a job at a company in Sosnowice, and thought that wearing French regimentals would make dealing with the locals easier. Paris ultimately denied his request, but the story sheds light on how French private investors and their agents imagined their work in the newly independent Poland. Sosnowice (soon renamed to Sosnowiec), was a city in the Dąbrowa Basin, through which the French controlled the majority of coal production in old Russian Poland. Now they looked towards the contested Upper Silesia, since, as the author of a study on the province declared, "In economic terms, to take over a country's coal is to become its master."[1] As these words were written, in June 1920, the French had just won the majority of Poland's oil production in Eastern Galicia, another contested territory, this time located on the eastern borders of the new country. By the end of the decade some were supposedly referring to Polish oil as coming from "the colonies," although the story printed in a popular paper published in Cracow says more about Polish fears than Galician reality.[2]

In this chapter, I look at the two energy sectors, in which the French placed the majority of their capital in Poland. I argue that while Paris started the interwar period in a position of power, by the end of the 1930s the French were faced with increased government regulation, forced exports, and dwindling influence over the state of their affairs. This context allows a reconsideration of the asymmetric relationship between Warsaw and Paris. After being forced to sign unequal agreements guaranteeing French rents, the Poles gradually asserted their position, and introduced obligatory cartels which functioned in favour of domestic producers. Faced with waning influence, the French could do little, and by the 1930s abandoned major intervention in these sectors, stopping well short of forceful actions.

As I show, the entrance of French capital into the two energy sectors did not translate into higher production. Moreover, since Polish demand for oil and coal was smaller than output, companies in both sectors relied on exports and dumping. Any positive impact from French holdings on Polish development would

DOI: 10.4324/9781003375586-5

come only from reinvestment in the economy. Looking at Polish policy in energy resource production thus means asking whether Warsaw had any influence over such investment. The answer is mostly negative. Only in oil production did the French cooperate with the Poles to increase prospecting, but by 1931 Warsaw viewed foreign owners as exploiters rather than potential investors.

5.1 The oil sector[3]

Modern oil extraction in Galicia dates to the 1850s, with the first refinery created in Bóbrka near the Jasło Basin, the westernmost of the three oil-rich areas. The tri-city of Drohobycz, Truskawiec, and Borysław formed the most important Drohobycz Basin, while the Stanisławów Basin (near today's Ivanofrankivsk) marked the eastern extent of production at the time. Unlike other resources in the region, oil in Austrian Galicia belonged to whoever owned the land. Without state concessions, and with limited success of self-organization, extraction was chaotic. As production grew, towns such as Borysław ballooned out, with thousands living in squalid quarters, in a lunar landscape pocked by old digs and blackened by spills, earning the region the moniker "Galician Hell." During its biggest boom in 1909 it produced 2 million metric tons of oil, or 5 per cent of global output.[4]

After early investment in ozokerite, the French came to Galician oil just as the sector was experiencing the boom. In 1907 they created the Société de Naphte de Limanowa, which–via the Viennese Petroleum Licht–und Kraft Gesellschaft–built an important refinery in Limanowa. In 1913–1914 almost a dozen other French companies moved in, primarily based on financing from the north of France. The largest of these was the group controlled by Société des Pétroles de Dabrowa (Dąbrowa), created by the Georges Clairin et Cie firm from Lille. The total value of French investments, sometimes grouped with Belgian capital, was estimated at 73–155 million francs, or 14–20 per cent of the sector.[5]

Despite an early and short-lived Russian occupation during World War I, production in Galicia remained high, as it was the Central Powers' only domestic supply of the resource. Workers in the sector were exempt from military service, and the army controlled the distribution of oil. French-owned companies were sequestered, but still achieved high profits, which translated into high dividends after the end of hostilities. For Dąbrowa, this entailed payouts of 16 per cent a year. Nonetheless, a push to maximize production resulted in underinvestment, which forced some companies to import fresh capital after the Armistice.[6]

In 1918, the future of Galician oil fields was undecided. The majority of known deposits were in the eastern part of the province, claimed by both the Poles and the Ukrainians.[7] The conflict quickly deteriorated into a bloody war with Lwów and the oil basins particularly hotly contested.[8] By June 1919 Poland took both. French authorities and private lobbyists supported Warsaw, the latter grouped in the London-based International Committee appointed to protect British–French–Belgian and Allies' Oil Interests in Galicia. Finally, the border was confirmed in March 1923.[9] The region never received the promised local autonomy, and, like other lands with significant Ukrainian population, was partially colonized by the Poles.[10]

As hostilities raged, businessmen and politicians discussed what to do with the oil sector. Forced takeovers of companies with Austrian and German capital seemed likely, but would require financial compensation, for which the Poles had no money.[11] Like in Upper Silesia, this opened the door to foreign investors. In April 1919, the International Committee proposed to organize this dispossession through a mixed joint-stock company, in which the Poles would own 40 per cent of shares. Neither the Polish, nor the French authorities were interested, preferring to avoid sharing control over Galicia with others.[12]

When the Poles took possession of Eastern Galicia, they sequestered German- and Austrian-owned companies. At the same time, allied owners were slow to retake control over their investments.[13] As Stefan Bartoszewicz recounts, "torpor and idleness" took over the basin.[14] Combined with the prospect of forced takeovers in the coming peace treaty, and the poor state of the market in Vienna, this persuaded Austrian and German owners to sell their shares in oil companies. The buyers were French. In late 1919 and early 1920, the province experienced a fundamental "reshuffling" of its foreign investors.[15] When the initial wave of French investments stopped, they were valued in Paris at c. 650–800 million francs. The lower bound was close to what the Poles estimated them to be worth in 1930, giving the French 70 per cent of all joint-stock companies, and full control over private limited companies.[16]

Private investors overvalued Galicia's wealth, swayed by memories of the boom in 1907–1909, and reports of wartime profits. More broadly, World War I, and the ensuing wars for Polish eastern borders, resulted in an extreme asymmetry of information. The longer hostilities lasted on a territory, the longer French investors had to use unreliable, fragmentary, third-party produced evidence on the state of their companies and the usefulness of future investments. In a time of uncertainty, it seems that a few companies' decisions to invest pushed others, producing the large inflow of money.[17]

Requests from investors, wanting to finance their expansion in Galicia through the stock market, inundated the Ministry of Finance. The ministry would always consult the Quai d'Orsay and the Commissariat of Fuels.[18] These investments thus took place with consent of Paris, and with the support of its diplomats, hoping to secure oil for the French economy.[19] The French based their positions on opinions of their representatives in Warsaw, who were usually poorly informed.[20] It was only with Poland's setbacks in the war against Soviet Russia in 1920 that the ministry started refusing certain requests. The eagerness to gain control of Galician oil was influenced by the French wartime experience of almost running out of oil in 1917. It was a turning point for French energy security policy, now informed by the position: "he who has oil, has Empire."[21] By 1920, France and the United Kingdom divided between them influence in three oil-producing countries: Romania, Mesopotamia, and Galicia.[22]

Unlike other French companies in Poland, oil investments were mostly "two-headed," to use Mihou-Natar's phrase, comprising a French joint-stock company, which paid out dividends, and a Polish firm responsible for mining and refining oil (a joint-stock or private limited company). This structure carried over from the Habsburg days.[23] Bigger groups formed holdings. They were headed by an investment company in France, controlled by private and institutional shareholders. Such an enterprise then owned shares in many companies in Poland (and other countries of the region), sometimes directly, sometimes through further intermediaries. This structure makes accurate estimates of their worth difficult, particularly since the companies often changed. As an example, Figure 5.1 shows the evolution of the Silva Plana and Limanowa groups, illustrating their structural changes in the first years after 1918. It also demonstrates the growing consolidation of the sector. Initially, this translated into mergers between companies belonging to the same capital groups, and later by the latter's horizontal expansion. By the middle of the 1920s, only four companies represented the majority of French investments in Galicia: Société des Pétroles de Dąbrowa (200 million francs), Compagnie Franco-Polonaise des Pétroles (190 million francs), Société Française des Pétroles "Premier" (created from the British-owned Premier Oil Ltd; 125 million francs) and Société Française des Pétroles de Silva Plana (102 million francs). By the end of the 1930s only two major groups remained: Małopolska (which grew out of a merger of Dąbrowa, Premier and some smaller firms), controlling some 40–45 per cent of domestic production, and Silva Plana.[24]

Małopolska was connected to the largest financial crash associated with French investment in Poland. The holding was controlled by a financial group created by Michel Devilder through two companies: Crédit Général des Pétroles and Société des Pétroles de Małopolska. The group also included firms in the Polish energy sector and in other countries in the region. Figure 5.2 shows the complex structure of the Polish component of the group in 1931. A frenzy of speculation soon pushed Małopolska's market valuation in France to 2.5 billion francs, earning the Crédit Générale the moniker of "the biggest machine for absorbing French savings in Polish oil."[25] This position was untenable. Once the bubble burst, Devilder's group collapsed. However, Małopolska's situation in Poland was good, and soon negotiations started to salvage the functioning parts of the business.[26] Due to the size of the company, its restructuring saw extensive engagement of the Louvre, and the Quai d'Orsay and its diplomats in Central European capitals and in London. The new, downsized oil operation was spun off into a separate Société Française Industrielle et Commerciale des Pétroles, with a capital of only 200 million francs.[27] One of the major four French-controlled banks in interwar Poland, the Polish Industrial Bank (Polski Bank Przemysłowy) became an accidental victim of this crisis, as it also belonged to the Devilder group. Attempts to let the bank be taken over by another Polish firm collapsed.[28]

Returning to the 1920s, when the buying frenzy in Galicia stopped, and the (justified) fears of Polish intervention in the strategic sector made the French

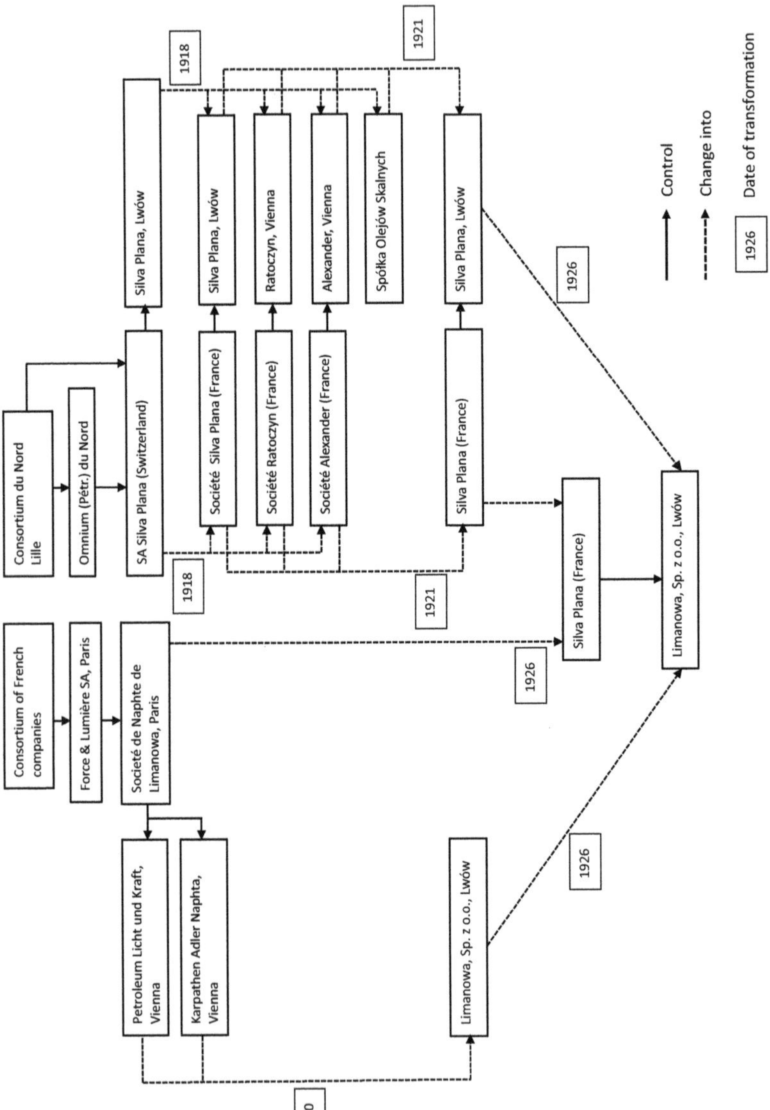

Figure 5.1 Organization of the Silva Plana and Limanowa Groups, 1918–1926.

Sources: Mihout-Natar, "L'intervention," 854.

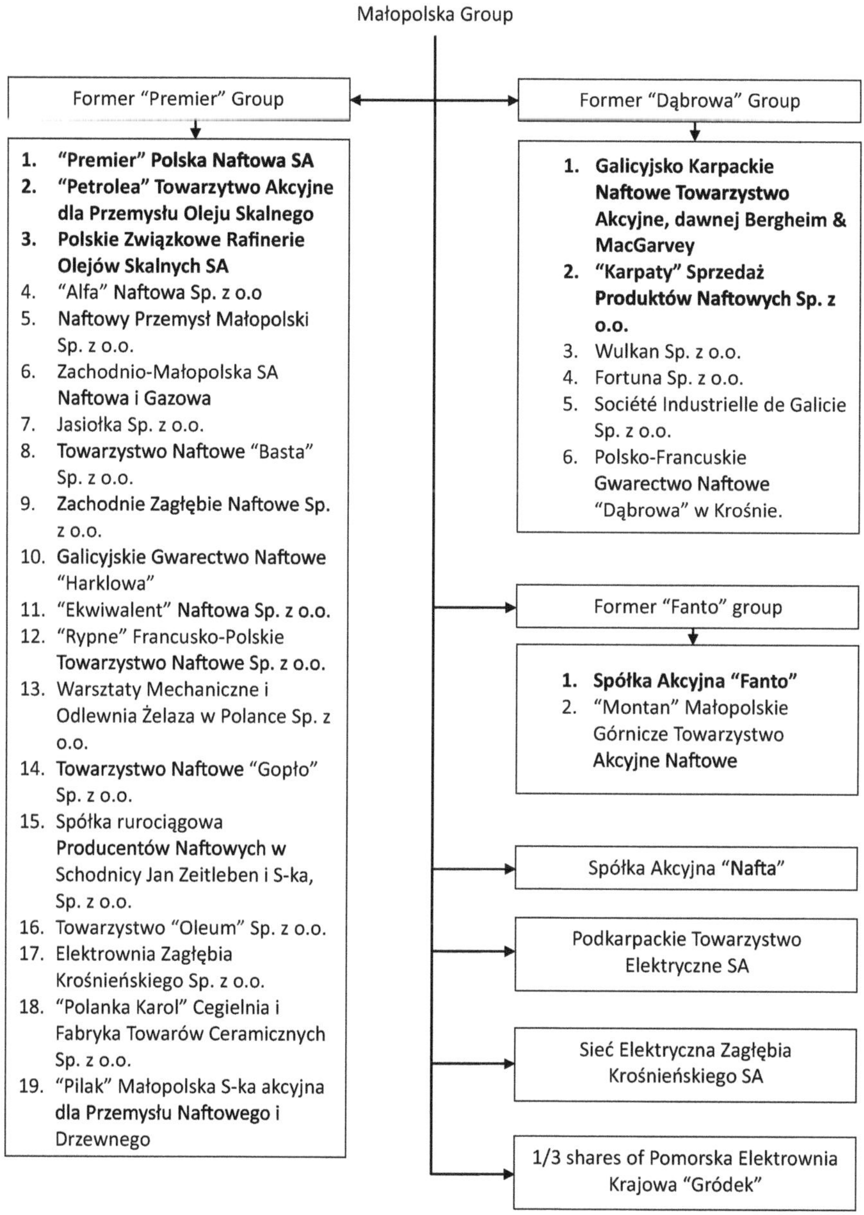

Figure 5.2 Structure of Małopolska Group in Poland in 1931.

Bolded companies were the most important

Sources: AAN, Akta Wincentego i Władysława Choroszewskich, 87, Referat w sprawie sanacji grupy "Małopolska," 6 July 1931, 2–3

worried, they decided to use their dominant position in Poland to win privileges for their companies. Between 1920 and 1924, the Quai d'Orsay together with the Commissariat of Fuels (Directorship of Fuels after 1921) tried to strengthen and stabilize the French position in Galicia, and secure oil supplies. They were lobbied and supported by the Comité des Pétroles Françaises de Pologne. The officials focused on three spheres: obtaining special status for French companies in the sector, making sure that they kept their national character, and taking over the state-owned refinery in Drohobycz.

Initially, officials in Paris hoped to shield French companies from Polish fiscal, monetary, and industrial policy. Negotiations started in July 1920 with the French offering bank loans in exchange for unilateral privileges. The Poles, starved for cash, and in the middle of a war with Soviet Russia, were willing to agree, but ultimately Władysław Grabski, ever the French opponent, torpedoed the deal by demanding 1 billion francs.[29] In February 1921, Aristide Briand succeeded in linking the passing of an oil treaty to the alliance, as I discussed in Chapter 2. With both sides hesitant, it took a year for the agreement to be signed on 6 February 1922.[30] Based on its provisions, any new French investments would be exempt from special levies, while established companies were granted the most favoured clause. Moreover, French firms could freely export their products beyond a certain minimum level of production earmarked for the domestic market. Crucially, they also got free access to foreign exchange for dividends, dues, and imports.[31]

Privileges stipulated in the agreement would only be accorded to firms which the government in Paris considered French, to protect from German influence. In practice, this meant that Warsaw and Paris had to agree on a list of such firms. The list became an unlikely tool for the Poles to defend from French demands, as it allowed Warsaw to delay the coming into force of the agreement. Initially, the French could only blame themselves, since the Senate in Paris would not ratify the treaty before July 1923. It was only then that the French government started working on the list. Quai d'Orsay notified the Poles on 28 November 1923.[32] Now Warsaw had to confirm the list, and this gave the Poles additional space to breathe. When Władysław Grabski became Prime Minister, his government long ignored French demands on the subject, and then stalled further by asking for details on some companies. The Poles only accepted the list in August 1924, 30 months after the agreement had been signed.[33] This delay allowed Grabski's government to introduce its financial reforms, which included a special tax on property.

Grabski's attitude also proved crucial to Poland's fight for the refinery in Drohobycz (and the connected topic of state-owned oil-bearing land). The refinery had been created before the Great War to stabilize the sector, undermined by an overproduction crisis, and to preemptively protect it from Standard Oil.[34] After the war, the refinery, now in the hands of Polish authorities, was guaranteed access to crude oil through compulsory purchases from small producers.[35] It played a huge role in the sector, as it accounted for a third of Galicia's capacity, allowing the authorities to stabilize the price of oil, and to limit competition between companies.

The French attempted to take over the refinery many times through various means (including proposals for a mixed company, like in Upper Silesia), but they only managed to secure preemption rights. Under Grabski, the Poles systematically protected the refinery. First, a series of bills passed by Parliament forbid its sale to balance the budget, and its use as security for French military credits. Second, Grabski went on the offensive, asking Paris to either lease the company for a large sum, or give up the right of preemption. The French were shocked – Grabski was acting unlike any other Polish politician before him. His tactics proved successful. Paris continued to protest, but as authorities could not find investors willing to engage in Poland without government guarantees, they had little to offer. Negotiations ended, and the refinery, owned by the state-owned company Polmin, remained in Polish hands.

For the French, Galicia proved an expensive mirage. The interwar period saw a fall in Polish oil production, from 800,000 tons in 1925 to 500,000 tons in 1938. The number of wells doubled and employment grew, but there was no concurrent increase of geological surveys.[36] Moreover, the sector's international position changed. In the early 1920s, thanks to the depreciating Polish mark, oil exports brought tidy profits. Once Poland stabilized its currency, the overvalued złoty multiplied the effect of expensive oil extraction (partially due to ageing technology), refineries operating under capacity, and costly freight. Even in the Free City of Danzig, Galician oil cost more than American imports. With exports hardly profitable, much of the oil agreement became pointless, and producers competed for the domestic market. Production was higher than demand, and producers had to choose between closing wells and not recuperating costs, or dumping.[37] Oil – a core input of the new economy of the fourth Kondratiev – was thus hardly a good bargain in Poland.[38]

As French companies controlled much of the sector, they were greatly affected by the fall in production. In 1922, the Dąbrowa group reported 12 million francs of profit based on its share capital of 50 million. In 1928 the same group claimed a capital of 200 million, but its profits fell to a mere 0.6 million francs. Małopolska, which did not spare money for investment in technology and management, reported good results, but these had little to do with its fantastic valuation. In 1928, its 29 million francs of profit, while impressive considering the sector's general slump, was dwarfed by its capital worth 450 million francs. When the Great Depression hit, the sector was undercapitalized, and companies consistently underinvested, causing shrinking through asset depreciation.[39] It was particularly true for large firms, with the biggest seven responsible for only two-thirds of investment outlays. The situation only improved in the last years before the war.

With the sector in trouble, Polish authorities reacted by pushing for the creation of a cartel, with the Polish Oil Industry Syndicate emerging in 1927, just as the government sought to encourage prospecting through tax breaks.[40] Małopolska and Polmin together controlled 60 per cent of votes in the Syndicate, which allowed them to force the creation of the Pionier Company, tasked with geological surveys. The same two companies, together with

Limanowa, created an export company in Gdańsk, which controlled some 80 per cent of Polish sales abroad.

In 1931, the Polish Minister of Industry and Trade created the Oil Commission to study possible solutions to the sector's woes. Despite earlier cooperation, now the Commission's deliberations spelled trouble for the French. The Poles did not consult any foreign owners, which the Commission's members saw as "exploiters of Polish assets," unlikely to contribute enough to prospecting.[41] Based on its reports, Polish authorities reorganized the sector, creating a new compulsory cartel in 1933, the Polish Oil Exports (Polski Eksport Naftowy).[42] As sales abroad were not profitable, the cartel managed a system of obligatory export quotas, forcing companies to sell a part of their production abroad below production costs.[43]

The result was paradoxical. In no other Polish sector, save the iron and steel industry, was the penetration of foreign capital greater than in oil production. Nonetheless, it was here, in the production of a strategic resource, that state interventionism was the most comprehensive, with a compulsory cartel, obligatory exports, and a state-owned refinery with the power to make or break the market. Both outside observers and domestic producers nonetheless saw this arrangement as sensible, due to the state of the sector.[44]

What about French goals? The authorities in Paris never achieved their objective of safeguarding their oil supply from Galicia. They came the closest in 1920, when an early version of the oil agreement guaranteed 40 per cent of Polish production for France.[45] By 1922, Paris abandoned this goal with a major upheaval of French energy policy. The government switched diplomatic and economic efforts from Poland and Romania – the position of both being too precarious in the case of a war with Germany – to overseas oil deposits, such as the fields of Mosul.[46] Quai d'Orsay thus lost much of its interest in Poland, abandoning projects such as the Franco–Polish oil transport company. The battle for Drohobycz in 1924 was the last instance when French authorities put appreciable efforts in Galicia apart from supporting Małopolska after the market crash. And when exports became unprofitable, even French owners focused on the Polish market.

The situation in Galicia finds a telling comparison in Romania, a country similarly under French influence, and endowed with significant oil reserves, at the time considered the biggest in Europe after Russia's.[47] Before World War I, foreign capital controlled most extraction. After the conflict, Romania tried to take over companies belonging to citizens of the Central Powers in a process called "nostrification." The French and the British contested these efforts and themselves took the place of Germans and Austrians. In Romania, oil played a much bigger role than in Poland. In the most difficult period between 1933 and 1935, it accounted for as much as half of all exports, and was crucial for supporting the country's precarious balance of payments. For comparison, coal, which was Poland's most important export item, was on average responsible for 17 per cent of the country's international sales. As Bogdan Murgescu writes, while Romania greatly increased exports of oil in the 1930s, it happened "as world prices reached a historic low. Thus, Romania reaped only a small part of the economic benefits that were potentially available during the interwar period."[48] Considering Poland's difficult economic position, if it weren't for the fall in production, Warsaw would likely pursue similar policies to those in Bucharest. With higher extraction and transportation costs, Polish exports would entail even greater dumping.

5.2 The coal sector[49]

Interwar Polish coal deposits were divided into three basins inherited from the three empires. The Dąbrowa Basin formed the most industrialized region of Russian Poland, the Cracow Basin to the south had operated within Austrian Galicia, and the Polish part of the richest Upper Silesian Basin had been German. This division had more to do with politics than with geography: today, a drive from the centre of Dąbrowa to Katowice takes but 15 minutes if traffic is light.

Politics also directed capital flows, with most French investment going to Dąbrowa between 1875 and 1897, mostly before the signing of the Franco-Russian Alliance (1891–1894). The total share capital of the five companies created then reached some 70 million francs germinal, and they produced over half of the coal in Dąbrowa.[50] Two of them formed part of a powerful French heavy industry group, headed by the ironworks Huta Bankowa (Société Anonyme des Forges et Aciéries de Huta Bankowa), and including holdings deeper in Russia.[51] The plant in Dąbrowa Górnicza had been central to the Poles' aborted industrialization push in the 1830s. In 1877 French investors from Lyon – Saint-Étienne leased the company (and later bought it) and rebuilt its ironworks from the ground up.[52] With a share capital amounting to 23 million francs, it controlled almost a third of the province's steel and iron production. French holdings in Austria and Germany were smaller. Three firms produced 1.5 million tons, including a quarter of Galician output, and merely 2 per cent of coal mined in Upper Silesia.

Among seven companies in Russia and Austria, only two had been founded based on local law, and had local headquarters. Four were based in Paris or in Belgium, one was founded under French and one under Silesian law. Management in Poland operated with little oversight from the boards.[53]

Profits in Russian Poland were significant, thanks to high import tariffs and lax labour laws, and the companies' shares did well, with their capitalization 4–5 times higher than the nominal value.[54] Without protection, German exports would have undercut domestic producers. Upper Silesian coalfields were richer, and had deposits of higher quality. Combined with better equipment and capital outlays, Germans achieved higher efficiency and lower prices. The Cracow Basin was not a threat. While its deposits were significant, they were of the lowest quality in the region.[55]

The Dąbrowa Basin fell to the Germans in the first weeks of World War I, and the Central Powers held it until 1918. Berlin ruled the northern part of the region, and Vienna the southern, taking French-owned companies under temporary administration. Throughout the period, forced requisitions, often little more than plunder, led to losses and significant decapitalization. For instance, Société Française & Italienne des Houillères de Dombrowa reported losing a third of its share capital's value. This was thus a very different experience than in Galician oil, where Austrian administration was often beneficial. In Dąbrowa production dropped, as did worker efficiency.[56]

Between 1913 and 1938, the total output of companies with French capital on Polish territories ostensibly tripled. Before the war, it amounted to about 8 per cent of the total production in the Upper Silesian Coal Basin (comprising coalfields in Poland, Czechoslovakia, and Germany). By 1938 it grew to about 25 per cent.[57] While this suggests extraordinary expansion, reality was more complicated.

After the war, owners of French coal mines in Poland faced difficult decisions. As I mentioned in Chapter 3, getting back to pre-war output required investment. New borders and the revolution in Russia shattered connections to both old markets and subsidiaries. Moreover, if Upper Silesia were allotted to Poland, the French in Dąbrowa would have to defend against German competitors without pre-war tariff protection. With Polish demand for coal (and steel or zinc) lower than supply, producers would need to rely on exports to sell their output.

The situation in Poland discouraged investors and diplomats, who had little understanding for the country's difficulties. Faced with a collapse of industrial production and a thirst for coal, Warsaw moved to sequester some failing companies.[58] It also required the owners of mines in Dąbrowa to provide food for workers below market prices, and pressured them to submit to labour demands. The basins in Dąbrowa and Cracow boiled with fervour after an aborted workers' revolt in 1918–1919, which further undermined French trust. As Alexis Bartet from Compagnie Galicienne (Francuska Spółka Akcyjna Galicyjska Kopalń) wrote to France in August 1919: "The workers do little work, their supervisors and foremen (organized into a separate union) provide no direction, and are the first to think of new demands. [...] The weakness of local authorities is difficult to imagine."[59] Others were dismayed by what they saw as rising xenophobia, threatening the small French community in the Dąbrowa Basin.[60] This was, again, quite different than in Eastern Galicia, where the fog of war and the asymmetry of information meant that the French did not have direct access to their companies until later.

Nonetheless, thanks to support from French diplomats and peers, the owners of coal mines in Dąbrowa and Cracow gradually regained control of their businesses in Poland, and decided to rebuild them. As this required new investment, many company representatives again asked the government in Paris to authorize capital transfers to Poland. Much more bullish than private investors, seeing in Poland a land of expansion and new opportunities, the government agreed. This decision was partially based on France's own demand for coal.[61] This informed both the attempts at economic rapprochement with

Germany which I discussed in the previous chapter, and production in Poland. Coal extraction in France's eastern partner was thus put back on its feet. In the process, Huta Bankowa came under the control of Schneider in 1919.

Having re-established their position in Russian Poland, the French now looked towards Upper Silesia. Superficially, the situation seemed like that in Galicia. Should it become Polish, its new rulers would expropriate private German companies. As a result, French investors in Dąbrowa soon asked the authorities in Paris for help in gaining a foothold in Upper Silesia. The same mood pervaded the halls of the Quai d'Orsay. Soon General Henri Le Rond, head of the Inter-Allied Administrative and Plebiscite Commission in Upper Silesia, and the Ambassador Charles Laurent in Berlin engaged in talks with German companies. Artur Benis, as representative of the Polish government, came to Paris to offer economic concessions and shares in Silesian company for support in decisions concerning the province's future.

As I describe in Chapter 6, the Silesian mirage never materialized. Despite years-long negotiations, multiple agreements, and significant loans in German marks to the Polish government, the French engagement in Upper Silesia ended with meagre results. It comprised 50 per cent shares in three mixed companies, with the other 50 per cent controlled by the Polish government, and a minor share in the German-owned Zakłady Hohenlohego (Hohenlohe Werke). Among the mixed companies, the only true success was the dominant French position in the giant Skarboferm, which leased coal mines from the Polish state, with a total production roughly equal to that of all pre-war French holdings.

While Skarboferm was profitable, it did not challenge the position of German capital. The Poles estimated that French holdings in this sector amounted to some 22 per cent of total share capital, behind Germany's 40 per cent.[62] Moreover, French investment in Dąbrowa partially wound down, with one firm closing down (in 1935) and two others changing ownership (in 1923 and 1932).[63] By the end of the interwar period, Poland's takeover of Zaolzie (or Cieszyn Silesia) brought the powerful Báňská a hutní within the country's borders.[64] Reorganized as a Polish company with a capital of some 60 million złoty (three times more than Skarboferm), it was under the control of Schneider. The tripling of French coal production between 1913 and 1938 was thus true mostly on paper. Pre-war investments kept their 8 per cent share in the total output of the Upper Silesian Coal Basin, but at the expense of significant new outlays. Skarboferm added a further 6 per cent, with the last 10 per cent coming from Schneider's subsidiary in Cieszyn Silesia. The last company would thus significantly bolster French holdings in the Polish coal sector – but the beginning of World War II made this inconsequential.

Poland produced over 34 million tons of coal a year. As with oil, the country's demand for the mineral was lower than production (and kept low with high prices). About a third found its way abroad, making it crucial for the Polish balance of payments.[65]

Initially, Poland sold most of its coal to other countries of Central Europe, especially to Germany, obliged to accept the mineral based on the rules governing the division of Upper Silesia. When this stipulation expired in 1925, Berlin launched a trade war, hoping to destabilize its eastern neighbour. Faced with a quickly deteriorating economy, the Poles found willing buyers in Scandinavia, and even in the United Kingdom, thanks to the 1926 general strike. By the 1930s, Poland survived the trade war, and now most of its coal found buyers overseas.[66] This radical reorientation of Polish coal exports was possible thanks to French capital, and its role in the construction of the port in Gdynia, and the coal trunk line, linking Silesia and Dąbrowa with the Baltic. I explored this topic in more detail in Chapter 4. French coal producers were also at the forefront of finding new markets, with companies from Upper Silesia and Dąbrowa exporting more than the Polish average. Due to the different way these two basins operated, this translated into different outcomes.

In Silesia coal was more calorific and mined more efficiently, with on average 2 tons mined per day per worker. Skarboferm in particular was among the most efficient companies. In Dąbrowa and Cracow the coal was worse and extraction more difficult, with only around 1.3–1.4 tons per day per worker.[67] There could be little understanding between such different firms, and Skarboferm was more likely to align with strategy with German-owned companies from Upper Silesia, than with those in Dąbrowa. Likewise, Huta Bankowa, with better coal deposits than other firms in its region, felt stifled by its peers.

After 1925, finding new markets was the biggest challenge for Polish coal producers. With the Great Depression, falling prices made it more difficult, especially after Britain's departure from gold in 1931. To compete internationally, the Poles had to keep pushing down the price in złoty, which quickly undercut the profitability of overseas sales.[68] This was a particular problem for French companies, since they exported more than the sector's average.[69] Sales depended on government subsidies, dumping, labour exploitation (as described in the novel *Czarne skrzydła* I discuss in Chapter 7), and keeping domestic prices high thanks to cartel arrangements. For instance, in 1932 Skarboferm exported to Central European states with comfortable profits, receiving pithead prices at around 80–105 per cent of what it got in Poland. Due to expensive transportation and fierce competition, the pithead price in overseas sales was, on average, only 28 per cent of the domestic price, generally under production costs.[70] A significant change for the sector was the opening of the Coal Trunk Railway, which allowed a large reduction in freight cost. In the case of Czeladź (Francuska Spółka Akcyjna Towarzystwo Bezimienne Kopalń Węgla Czeladź SA, a major producer in the Dąbrowa Basin), this single event meant an almost 40 per cent increase of pithead prices.[71]

The sector's wellbeing moved in line with the business cycle. French companies reported profits once Poland's borders stabilized, and paid large dividends (10–20 per cent) in the second half of the 1920s. They reported losses through much of the 1930s, as did the rest of the sector.[72] Based on its excellent coalfields, Skarboferm was a major outlier, continuing to pay 10 per cent dividends after 1926 (except in 1932). Poor results caused share prices of other French companies to collapse, with stocks falling in Paris by some 80–95 per cent to below their nominal value.[73] Some results, however, likely represented window dressing, with costs inflated through transfer prices and similar practices. Consequently, Huta Bankowa in France declared profits of 7 million francs in 1937/1938, whereas its Polish counterpart earned only 60,000 złoty and paid almost no taxes.[74]

As Poland needed to export coal, and producers could only compete on price, there was a danger of companies undercutting each other on foreign markets and at home. To avoid further depressing export prices, in 1925 coal producers created a nationwide cartel, or the so-called Polish Convention, modelled on the pre-war German Oberschlesische Kohlen-Konvention.[75] The organization set companies' production quotas, linked to voting power. Thus bigger companies could both produce more coal, and had a greater impact on decisions taken by the convention. Initially, it covered only Central European markets, but in the 1930s a reformed cartel extended to other countries.[76]

The agreement acknowledged the different positions of the major coal producing regions, protecting smaller firms in Dąbrowa and Cracow (mostly Polish- and French-owned) by requiring an 85 per cent majority for crucial decisions.[77] French firms in these basins could count on around 11 per cent votes, and if they worked together with Skarboferm and Zincs de Silésie (a Franco–Belgian company), they gained de facto veto power with over 20 per cent of votes.[78] However, as I mentioned, different economic interests bred little national unity. Skarboferm mined more calorific coal and enjoyed good relations with the Poles. On the other hand, Zincs de Silésie, nominally from Upper Silesia and with high quality coal, was more likely to vote with companies from Dąbrowa. Among the latter, some felt the cartel was too restrictive, and continued to resist it, resulting in conflicts in 1927, 1930–1931, and 1933–1934 between the Huta Bankowa group and other French companies.[79]

French authorities closely followed the conflicts, which generally involved Huta Bankowa demanding higher production and export quotas for itself at the expense of other firms, and with Skarboferm working with Upper Silesian firms wanting to lower the voting threshold.[80] Officials in Paris were afraid that if French companies were not united, breaking the convention would likely provoke Warsaw's retribution through forced cartelization.[81] This turn of events would then remove any influence weaker French companies had on the sector. As a result, as talks broke down, the French government intervened multiple times, pushing French owners and managers to return to the convention. In 1927, Huta Bankowa pushed back, arguing that private matters between foreign companies were not under the purview of the Quai d'Orsay. Aristide Briand would have none of it.[82] Three years later, the same process repeated itself, but this time Huta Bankowa's owners asked the Quai d'Orsay to tell the Poles about their decision to stay in the cartel, rather than do it themselves. Laroche felt awkward notifying August Zaleski about choices taken by a company registered in Poland vis-à-vis other Polish firms. However, officials in Paris saw it as their moral obligation.[83]

The final phase of the conflict began in 1933, when again Huta Bankowa rebelled against a new division of export quotas.[84] The Poles countered with government arbitration, which limited French exports to their home country. Now, firms in France – together with the Public Works Ministry – were pushing the Quai d'Orsay to intervene.[85] Ultimately, as in the case of oil, the Polish government took the initiative. Once the convention expired, the Minister of Industry and Trade decided to prolong it for six years as the Polish Coal Convention (Polska Konwencja Węglowa) and reduced the quotas of the two principal French companies in Dąbrowa: Huta Bankowa and Towarzystwo Kopalń i Zakładów Hutniczych Sosnowieckich.[86] The French could operate and profit in Poland, but, as in the oil sector, they would have little impact on the industry.

5.3 Conclusions

The French engagement in the Polish coal and oil sectors share similarities. In both cases, French capital had an important presence in production already before the Great War. Both saw a surge of interest in Paris when Poland regained independence due to increased French demand and insufficient domestic supply. Both resources were found on contested territories, which had belonged to the Austro-Hungarian and German empires, and French authorities were interested in increasing their control over them as part of their security policy. Investment would also serve to cement their power over the Polish economy. In both cases, diplomats discussed plans to create mixed companies with Polish and foreign capital, which would take over assets previously belonging to the Central Powers or to their citizens. In both, the changing dynamics of Franco–Polish relations shaped long negotiations. In both cases Polish production significantly exceeded domestic demand, making exports crucial, albeit costly. Coal in particular played a tremendous role in the Polish balance of payments. Ironically, investment in oil was originally done with exports in mind, but companies' profits depended on the domestic market, while in coal the opposite was true to some extent. The Poles increased government control over both sectors, leading to decreased influence of foreigner owners, despite the value of their holdings.

This, however, is where the similarities ended. With some exceptions, the coal sector did not see significantly more French investment, except for political ventures. Firms controlled by the French excelled in exports, making France a major importer of Polish coal. Oil saw much greater investment, with Poland's western ally coming to control the absolute majority of the sector. A frenzy of speculation saw these companies' stock surging in Paris, and when the bubble burst, hundreds of millions of francs were lost. The investment never brought what the French expected. Polish reserves, expensive to extract and dwindling, never contributed much to French consumption.

The Poles had a negative opinion of foreign investors in the oil sector, pointing out their insufficient outlays and the lack of understanding of the local environment.

The French correctly diagnosed the sector's problems, but failed to come up with a solution.[87] The Galician oil industry was declining, and would not recover without discovering new deposits – which only happened under Soviet rule. Moreover, the extraction of precious resources doesn't directly contribute to economic development unless profits from their sales abroad are reinvested in the economy. Other oil-producing developing nations discovered the same problem after World War II, resulting in a wave of nationalization. In the Polish case – both in oil and in coal – the authorities at least made sure that the controlled exports provided foreign exchange for the government, especially after the introduction of exchange control in 1936.

Ultimately, the two energy sectors show the changing dynamic of Franco–Polish relationship, and the power available to the weaker side once its existence stopped depending on France's support. They represented the greatest investments in Poland, yet ones which also yielded to domestic regulation, with Paris left with few instruments to further help its companies. As a result, with little potential for development in the sector, the Poles were able to mitigate some of the negative consequences of foreign investment.

Notes

1 Archives diplomatiques, La Courneuve [henceforth: AdC], Correspondance politique et commercial, 1918–1940, Pologne [henceforth: CPC PL], 212, La Haute Silésie. Étude économique, 26 June 1920, 29.

2 "Czy Polska jest kolonją francuską," *Ilustrowany Kurjer Codzienny*, 26 October 1929, 4.

3 This section draws from: Jerzy Łazor, "Francuskie inwestycje w polskim sektorze naftowym w okresie międzywojennym," in *Pieniądz, historia, polityka. Studia ofiarowane prof. dr. hab. Wojciechowi Morawskiemu w 70. rocznicę urodzin*, ed. Łukasz Dwilewicz and Jerzy Łazor (Warszawa: Oficyna Wydawnicza SGH, forthcoming in 2024).

4 Piotr Franaszek, "Galicyjski przemysł naftowy do 1914 r. w świetle najnowszych badań," *Rocznik Naukowo Dydaktyczny WSP w Krakowie. Prace Historyczne* 3, no. 126 (1992): 113–35, 113.

5 Alison Fleig Frank, *Oil Empire: Visions of Prosperity in Austrian Galicia* (Cambridge, Mass: Harvard University Press, 2005), 25, 171, 281; Stefan Bartoszewicz, *Wspomnienia z przemysłu naftowego 1897–1930* (Lwów: Piller-Neumann, 1934), 37, 41–42; Mylène Mihout-Natar, "L'intervention des capitaux français dans la Pologne de la Seconde République (1918–1939): contribution à l'histoire de l'impérialisme économique français en Europe centrale" (PhD, Université Charles de Gaulle – Lille III, 2002), 507, 510; Lubor Jílek, "Impasses d'une «politique nationale» d'approvisionnement: capitaux français dans les pétroles de Galicie 1918–1926," *Relations Internationales* 43 (1985): 323–41, 329; *Rapport fait au nom de la Commission des affaires étrangères et de politique générale des colonies et protectorats, chargée d'examiner le projet de lois adopté par la Chamber des Députés, portant approbation de la Convention conclue à Paris le 6 février 1922, entre la France et la Pologne, et relative au régime des industries du naphte, par M. Louis Dausset, Sénateur*, Sénat, 1923, no 627, 10 July 1923, 5.

6 Centre des archives économiques et financières, Savigny-le-Temple [henceforth: CAÉF], B 32.905, Historique succinct de la Société des Pétroles de Grabownica, 16 August 1939, n.p.

7 Jochen Böhler, *Civil War in Central Europe, 1918–1921. Reconstruction of Poland* (Oxford: Oxford University Press, 2018), 71–83.
8 Wojciech Morawski, "Galicyjskie zagłębia naftowe," in *Problemy energetyczne Polski. Część 1: Surowce*, ed. Anna Jarosz-Nojszewska and Wojciech Morawski (Warszawa: Oficyna Wydawnicza SGH, 2016), 33–50, 39.
9 Frank, *Oil Empire*, 22, 229; Piotr Stefan Wandycz, *France and Her Eastern Allies 1919–1925: French-Czechoslovak-Polish Relations from the Paris Peace Conference to Locarno* (Minneapolis: The University of Minnesota Press, 1962), 274.
10 Cf. Kathryn Ciancia, *On Civilization's Edge. A Polish Borderland in the Interwar World* (Oxford: Oxford University Press, 2020); Włodzimierz Mędrzecki, *Kresowy kalejdoskop: wędrówki przez ziemie wschodnie Drugiej Rzeczypospolitej 1918–1939* (Kraków: Wydawnictwo Literackie, 2018).
11 Mihout-Natar, "L'intervention," 507.
12 AdC, CPC PL, 254, Pralon to MAÉ, 19 September 1919, 120–21; AdC, CPC PL, 254, Pralon to Pichon, 1 December 1919, 135–37v; Leon Litwiński, "Nafta małopolska i jej kulisy," *Kultura*, no. 11 (1960): 113–31, 128–29; Leon Biliński, *Wspomnienia i dokumenty. Tom II, 1915–1922* (Warszawa: Księgarnia F. Hoesicka, 1925), 254–55; S. Bartoszewicz, *Wspomnienia*, s. 47.
13 Frank, *Oil Empire*, 219–20; Archiwum Akt Nowych, Warsaw [henceforth: AAN], Ministerstwo Spraw Zagranicznych [henceforth: MSZ], 3859, MPiH to MSZ, September 1936, 3.
14 Bartoszewicz, *Wspomnienia*, 46.
15 Wacław Bóbr, *Polski przemysł naftowy* (Warszawa: Przegląd Polityczny, 1928), 29.
16 French estimates: AdC, CPC PL, 255, Memo on French shares in Galicia, [August 1920], 2–4; Mihout-Natar, "L'intervention," 541. Polish estimates: Mieczysław Smerek, "Bilans płatniczy Polski za rok 1930," *Statystyka Polski* Seria B 17 (1933): 17–19. Cf. Bóbr, *Polski przemysł*, 26; Jan Fryc, *Przedsiębiorstwa i kapitał w polskim przemyśle naftowym* (Warszawa: Polska Gospodarcza, 1930).
17 Yair Arahoni, *The Foreign Investment Decision Process* (Boston: Harvard University, 1966).
18 The earliest document of this type I found came from October 1919 and concerned the issue of 12.5 million francs of stock by Société Générale des Pétroles (AdC, CPC PL, 254, Pichon to Pralon, 7 October 1919, 124–24v).
19 AdC, CPC PL, 254, Pralon to MAÉ, 13 January 1920, 156–57; AdC, CPC PL, 254, MAÉ to MF, 16 January 1920, 62–162v.
20 AdC, CPC PL, 254, Ordre de mission, 5 February 1919, 42; AdC, CPC PL, 254, Vicaire to Bérenger, 16 February 1919, 44; AdC, CPC PL, 254, Mougeot to Pichon, 7 December 1918, 3.
21 Jean-Marie Bouguen, *Le Pétrole En France. Genèse et Stratégies d'influence (1917–1924)* (Paris: Éditions L'Harmattan, 2013), 54.
22 Bouguen, *Le pétrole*, 30–35; Roberto Nayberg, "La politique française du pétrole à l'issue de la première guerre mondiale: perspectives et solutions," *Guerres mondiales et conflits contemporains* 4 (224) (2006): 111–33; Éric Boussière, "La France et les affaires pétrolières au lendemain de la Première Guerre Mondiale: la politique des groupes financiers à travers celle de la banque de l'Union Parisienne," *Histoire, économie et société* 1, no. 2 (1982): 313–28, https://doi.org/10.3406/hes.1982.1294.
23 Mihout-Natar, "L'intervention," 532.
24 Otto Wyszyński, "Francuskie kapitały w polskiej nafcie w świetle własnej oceny," *Nafta* 10, no. 10–11 (1931): 276–86, 277; Mihout-Natar, "L'intervention," 541; Bohdan Cywiński, *Przemysł Polski i nasze położenie gospodarcze. Uwagi na tle bilansów przemysłowych spółek akcyjnych z Lat 1928–1933* (Warszawa: Skład Główny w Domu Książki Polskiej, 1934), 29.
25 Laforest, "La stratégie," 252; Piotr Franaszek, "Kapitał francuski w procesie centralizacji kapitału w polskim przemyśle naftowym 1920–1939 (koncern naftowy 'Dąbrowa' i grupa 'Małopolska')," *Studia Historyczne* 29, no. 2 (1986): 229–43;

AAN, Akta Wincentego i Władysława. Choroszewskich, 87, Referat w sprawie sanacji grupy "Małopolska", 6 July 1931, 2–5, 7; Mihout-Natar, "L'intervention," 913–14.

26 AdC, CPC PL, 404, Note a.s. des pétroles de Pologne, 28 November 1930, 8; AdC, CPC PL, 404, FEW to MAÉ, 5 October 1931, 65–66.

27 AdC, CPC PL, 404, MAÉ to Laroche, 3 June 1931, 43; AAN, MSZ, 3853, Węcławowicz to MSZ, 3 August 1934, 28; Jílek, "Impasses," 323; Christophe Laforest, "La stratégie française et la Pologne (1919–1939). Aspects économiques et implications politiques" (PhD, Université Paris 1 Panthéon-Sorbonne, 2001), 252–64.

28 AdC, CPC PL, 404, MAÉ to Laroche, 3 June 1931, 43; Wojciech Morawski, *Słownik historyczny bankowości polskiej do 1939 roku* (Warszawa: Muza SA, 1998), 167.

29 Laforest, "La stratégie," 245–46; AdC, CPC PL, 229, Leygues to François-Marsal, 14 October 1920, 152–55.

30 Laforest, "La stratégie," 247.

31 DzU RP 1923, nr 106, poz. 832; Wandycz, *France*, 222.

32 AdC, CPC PL, 258, Poincaré to Zamoyski, 28 November 1923, 34–36.

33 CAÉF, B 31.947, Herriot to Clementel, 29 September 1924, n.p.

34 Franaszek, "Galicyjski przemysł," 119.

35 Mariusz W. Majewski, "Poszukiwania złóż ropy naftowej i gazu w Polsce (1919–1939)," *Annales Universitatis Paedagogicae Cracoviensis. Studia Historica* 8 (2009): 129–54, 138.

36 Morawski, *Galicyjskie zagłębia*, 40; Frank, *Oil Empire*, 238.

37 Bartoszewicz, *Wspomnienia*; Wyszyński, "Francuskie kapitały," 279.

38 Chris Freeman and Francisco Louçã, *As Time Goes by: From the Industrial Revolutions to the Information Revolution* (Oxford: Oxford University Press, 2001), 281–85.

39 Cywiński, *Przemysł Polski*, 29, 34–45, 62–63, Table A.

40 Franaszek, "Galicyjski przemysł," 114–19; Tadeusz Grabowski, *Rola państwa w gospodarce Polski (1918–1928)* (Warszawa: Państwowe Wydawnictwo Ekonomiczne, 1967), 137–38.

41 AAN, Akta Wincentego i Władysława Choroszewskich, 86, Protokół 1-go posiedzenia Komisji Naftowej, 8 May 1931, 2; and Protokół 5-go posiedzenia Komisji Naftowej, 23 May 1931, 29–30.

42 Iwona Kawalla, "Działalność Polskiego Eksportu Naftowego w latach 1933–1939," in *Kresy Wschodnie. Gospodarcze i społeczne znaczenie polityki kresów*, ed. Tomasz Głowiński (Wrocław: Gajt, 2015), 260.

43 The National Archives, Kew [henceforth: TNA], FO 371/20765, Taylor to Jerram, 8 March 1937, 137–47.

44 Kawalla, "Działalność," 269; Roman Masyk, "Zagadnienie czystych producentów ropy w II Rzeczypospolitej," in *Pieniądz, historia, polityka. Studia ofiarowane prof. dr. hab. Wojciechowi Morawskiemu w 70. rocznicę urodzin*, ed. Łukasz Dwilewicz and Jerzy Łazor (Warszawa: Oficyna Wydawnicza SGH, forthcoming in 2024); TNA, FO 371/20765, Taylor to Jerram, 8 March 1937, 137–47.

45 Jílek, "Impasses," 323; Laforest, "La stratégie," 242–45.

46 Bouguen, *Le pétrole*, 15.

47 This paragraph is mostly based on Bogdan Murgescu, "Anything but Simple: The Case of the Romanian Oil Industry," in *History and Culture of Economic Nationalism in East Central Europe*, ed. Helga Schultz and Eduard Kubů (Berlin: Berliner Wissenschafts-Verlag, 2006), 231–50.

48 Murgescu, *Anything*, 243.

49 This section is partially based on my earlier research: Jerzy Łazor, "French Capital, Gdynia, and the Position of Polish Coal on International Markets in the Interwar Period," in *Fueling the World Economy: Seaports, Coal, and Oil Markets during the Early Globalization*, ed. Daniel Castillo Hidalgo and Cézar Honorato, Palgrave Studies in Maritime Economics (Cham: Palgrave Macmillan, 2023), 99–121, https://doi.org/10.1007/978-3-031-32565-6_6.

50 A 6th company (Flora) was bought by the French in 1913 (Jerzy Jaros, *Historia górnictwa węglowego w Zagłębiu Górnośląskim w latach 1914–1945* (Katowice—Kraków: Państwowe Wydawnictwo Naukowe, 1969) 23; Wiesław Puś, *Przemysł Królestwa Polskiego w latach 1870–1914. Problemy struktury i koncentracji* (Łódź: Uniwersytet Łódzki, 1984), 263–64.
51 René Girault, *Emprunts russes et investissements francais en Russie, 1887–1914: recherches sur l'investissement international* (Paris: A. Colin, 1973), 282–83.
52 Jerzy Jedlicki, *Nieudana próba kapitalistycznej industralizacji: analiza państwowego gospodarstwa przemysłowego w Królestwie Polskim XIX w* (Warszawa: Książka i Wiedza, 1964); Puś, *Przemysł*, 265, 272; Irena Pietrzak-Pawłowska, "Zagłębie Dąbrowskie i Okręg Loary: penetracja kapitałów francuskich po 1870 r.," *Kwartalnik Historyczny* 72, no. 4 (1965): 793–807.
53 Ibid., 797.
54 Mihout-Natar, "L'intervention," 814.
55 AdC, CPC PL, 238, Conséquences économiques de l'annexion de la Haute Silésie à la Pologne, [May–July 1919], 84–98; Jaros, *Historia*, 25.
56 Jaros, *Historia*, 27–29; AdC, CPC PL, 253, État des mines de charbon et des hauts-fourneaux en Pologne russe, 9 December 1918, 35; AdC, CPC PL, 253, Société Française & Italienne des Houillères de Dombrowa to Pichon, 15 February 1919, 39–40.
57 Calculated based on data on individual companies taken from: Jaros, *Historia*.
58 AdC, CPC PL, 253, Pralon to Pichon, December 1919, 80–80v; AdC, CPC PL, 253, Pichon to Berthelot, 1 September 1919, 59–59v.
59 Family Archive of Bernard Bartet, Bartet to du Montcel, 19 August 1919, 2.
60 AdC, CPC PL, 253, FLW to Leygues, 17 December 1920, 85–86.
61 Marc Trachtenberg, *Reparation in World Politics: France and European Economic Diplomacy, 1916–1923* (New York: Columbia University Press, 1980), 110.
62 Mieczysław Grzyb, *Narodowościowo-polityczne aspekty przemian stosunków własnościowych i kadrowych w górnośląskim przemyśle w latach 1922–1939* (Katowice: Uniwersytet Śląski, 1978), 65; cf. a higher French estimate: AdC, CPC PL, 252, FCK to Briand, 15 March 1927, 12.
63 Jaros, *Historia*, 22–24.
64 Teichova, *An Economic Background*, 92, 95.
65 Łazor, "French Capital."
66 Robert Mark Spaulding, *Osthandel and Ostpolitik: German Foreign Trade Policies in Eastern Europe from Bismarck to Adenauer* (Providence, RI: Berghahn Books, 1997), 158; Karol Józef Błahut, *Polsko-niemieckie stosunki gospodarcze w latach 1919–1939* (Wrocław: Zakład Narodowy im. Ossolińskich, 1975), 65–76.
67 Mihout-Natar, "L'intervention," 879–80.
68 I explore this in detail in Łazor, "French capital"; Jaros, *Historia*, 55–56, 169; Cf. Archiwum Państwowe w Katowicach [henceforth: APK], Towarzystwo Bezimienne Kopalń Węgla "Czeladź" w Czeladzi - Piaskach [henceforth: Czeladź], 441, Statistiques générales 1925–1935, n.d., 1, 9, 14; Mihout-Natar, "L'intervention," 878.
69 Jaros, *Historia*, 169.
70 Jaros, *Historia*, 59.
71 Calculated from: APK, Czeladź, 441, Statistiques générales 1925–1935, n.d., 31.
72 Based on company-level data discussed in Chapter 3; Jaros, *Historia*, 71.
73 Mihout-Natar, "L'intervention," 868, 875, 882.
74 "Monitor Polski," 9 February 1939 (no. 32), 8; cf. Jaros, *Historia*, 73.
75 Christian Beyer, "Cartelization and Firm Performance in Upper Silesia 1880–1913," *European Review of Economic History*, 2021, 4, https://doi.org/10.1093/ereh/heab006.
76 APK, Konwencja Węglowa w Katowicach, 125, Projekt. Układ Uczestników PKW pod nazwą Konwencja Eksportowa, 8 April 1932, 1–20.

77 APK, Konwencja Węglowa w Katowicach, 1, Umowa Konwencji Ogólno-Polskiej (KOP), ważna od dnia 1 lipca 1926, n.d., 39–41; APK, Konwencja Węglowa w Katowicach, 5, Umowa Konwencji Węglowej Ogólno-Polskiej, ważna od dnia 1-go marca r. 1931, n.d., 48–50.
78 Mihout, "L'intervention," 874.
79 Zenon Szmidtke, *"Skarboferm" 1922–1939: związki polityki z gospodarką* (Opole: Państwowy Instytut Naukowy, 2005), 195.
80 AdC, CPC PL, 253, FCK to Briand, 25 January 1927, 217–8; APK, Skarboferm Spółka Dzierżawna, 385, Michel to de Peyerimhoff, 24 September 1930, 4–5.
81 AdC, CPC PL, 404, Laroche to Briand, 9 January 1931, 12–15.
82 AdC, CPC PL, 253, Terver to MAÉ, 12 July 1927, 239; AdC, CPC PL, 253, MAÉ to MTP, 26 August, 1927, 245 bis.
83 AdC, CPC PL, 404, Laroche to Briand, 14 March 1931, 49–50; APK, Konwencja Węglowa w Katowicach, 4, Three French companies to Williger, 21 February 1931, 6–23.
84 AdC, CPC PL, 404, Laroche to Paul-Bancour, 26 July 1933, 95–98.
85 AdC, CPC PL, 404, Laroche to MAÉ, 18 December 1933, 110–12.
86 APK, Konwencja Węglowa w Katowicach, 11, Statutes of the new convention, 26 April 1934; APK, Konwencja Węglowa w Katowicach, 182 and 183; AdC, CPC PL, 404, Lancial to Barthou, 11 July 1934, 117–18.
87 Zygmunt Bielski, "Rozwój techniki kopalnictwa naftowego za czasów polskich," *Nafta* 17, no. 4 (1938): 57–63, 60.

6 Politicizing investment

Private-public mixed companies with French capital in interwar Poland

On 8 July 1927, the impressively moustachioed French General Henri Le Rond stepped out of the special wagon provided for his trip from Cracow to Katowice by the Polish government. Welcomed by Silesian officials, he toured the region with the deputy voivode Zygmunt Żurawski, expressing satisfaction at its development. In the following days, he had dinner with the Polish politician Wojciech Korfanty and Henri de Peyerimhoff de Fontenelle, president of Comité Central des Houillères de France, inaugurated a new bridge in Goczałkowice, and was feted by the speaker of the Silesian Diet, other local dignitaries, and members of the clergy. With such a reception, one could imagine that Le Rond, the former head of the Inter-Allied Administrative and Plebiscite Commission in Upper Silesia, was a politician coming to Poland on official state business, especially since in Warsaw he met with Józef Piłsudski and Foreign Minister August Zaleski. The truth was more mundane. Le Rond was a newly elected board member of Skarboferm, the Polish State Mines in Upper Silesia Leaseholding Company Inc., and the board was meeting in Katowice.[1] The enterprise was a major coal producer, accounting for one in every 10 tons of the fuel mined in Poland. It was also the most prominent among a group of mixed companies, owned in half by the state, and in half by private French investors.

Mixed Franco–Polish companies arose soon after the Upper Silesian plebiscite in 1921. They counted among their directors and board members notable Polish and French businessmen and politicians such as Le Rond, Korfanty, and de Peyerimhoff. Secret international agreements regulated their creation, statutes, the division of capital between the Polish and French groups, and even the nationality of their presidents. They remained secret to avoid suggestions that France had sold its support in Upper Silesia to Poland for economic concessions. These investments were the most visible examples of connections between the economic and political spheres in relations between the two countries. They were also mostly unsuccessful. Two firms, including a bank in Katowice, went bankrupt within a decade, while a third, a great Franco–Polish holding, never materialized despite years of heated negotiations. Skarboferm's success was an exception: the company continued to report significant profits, bring dividends to its owners, while investing in its facilities in Poland, and improving efficiency significantly more than other firms in the sector.[2]

DOI: 10.4324/9781003375586-6

Private-public companies, combining private and public capital, were common in the interwar Polish economy, with its considerable public sector.[3] They mostly came from state-led modernization efforts, such as the creation of shipping companies, or from government intervention, when the authorities or a state-owned bank stepped in to save failing enterprises.[4] With rare exceptions, they did not include foreign capital.[5] Together with the Silesian firms' strictly political origins, tied to the Polish–German conflict in the province, this made them unique in the interwar Polish economy.

In this chapter, I chart the origins and functioning of these firms, and the various ways in which politics and policy influenced them. I show how a geopolitical problem – the Polish–German border conflict – resulted in competing projects for Silesian companies. Paris authorities, based on their political goals, tried to corral private businessmen into investing in Upper Silesia, but the latter resisted due to the perceived risk of the endeavour. Both groups also clashed with Warsaw. The Poles initially focused on clear political goals, but as negotiations progressed, they started giving more importance to economic issues. The political origin of these companies impacted their functioning, affecting the shape of the boards, actions taken by their managers, and the process of decision-making.

The Silesian project shows the dangers of public-private cooperation with foreign capital. Due to its weaker position, as well as political goals, Warsaw was not able to negotiate agreements that supported its long-term economic plans. Moreover, no other French investment in interwar Poland saw among its board members and managers so many recognizable names of politicians and industrialists. This close network of connections gave Skarboferm a clear edge, with impressive lobbying results. It also promoted rent-seeking from said politicians, and provided corruption opportunities. With highly placed board members profiting from high salaries and free holidays in France, it was unlikely that the situation would easily change.

6.1 Political and economic origins

After November 1918, Germany had to contend with a Polish state, eager to establish new borders in the west.[6] The conflict concerned the entire length of the Polish–German border. After long discussions during the Paris peace conference results were mixed. An early insurrection allowed the Poles to seize the Province of Posen, but Danzig, despite French support for Polish claims, became a Free City, in a solution which satisfied neither party. The Germans also won a plebiscite in East Prussia (save for a few hamlets). By late 1920, Upper Silesia remained the only unresolved conflict, and with a planned plebiscite looming, both sides were hoping to improve their position.

Before the Great War, Upper Silesia formed the second major industrial basin of the German Empire, having belonged to Prussia since the middle of the 18th century. As such, it did not form part of Poland's partitions from the late 18th century, which Warsaw tried to reverse after 1918. Nonetheless, the region had been under Polish rule in the Middle Ages. With a large population of Polish speakers, it seemed ripe for the taking based on Wilsonian rules. For France, depriving Germany of its second industrial basin would be a major boon, while Britain preferred to see the province remain with Berlin, with London afraid that otherwise the Poles would turn into a competitor of British coal on international markets. During the peace conference, a committee under General Le Rond recommended giving Upper Silesia to Poland, but with British pressure the French relented. In June 1919, the Allies decided that the fate of the territory would depend on a plebiscite, and until then a commission headed by Le Rond would administer the province.[7]

In October 1920, during a conference at the Ministry of Foreign Affairs in Warsaw, the Poles decided to "generate interest of big foreign capital in Silesian industry."[8] They would send diplomatic missions to allied powers, offering economic concessions, such as income from state properties in the province, should Upper Silesia be awarded to Poland. Based on the Versailles Treaty, the Poles indeed had something to offer – and something to gain. They would take over the property of the German state, and could – for compensation – also take that of German citizens. Considering the size of the Silesian industry, Polish authorities could thus promise significant concessions in the province, including the so-called Treasury Mines, a complex of rich, state-owned coal mines.[9] The Poles were not interested in taking over too many companies, fearing that this could cause mass emigration of skilled technical personnel, but the threat was a useful tool in talks with German owners and the Allies.[10] With empty coffers in Warsaw, it was also unlikely that the Poles could provide enough current capital to the state-owned mines, or support Silesia's money supply. The last point opened another opportunity for foreign investors, as there seemed to be a niche for a significant new bank in the province.

The Polish decision had roots in the story of Cieszyn Silesia. A small district to the south-west of Cracow and Katowice, it had belonged to Austria before the war. Now, due to its significant coal deposits, industry, and wealth, both Poland and Czechoslovakia vied for the territory. In Paris, the two countries used different arguments: Warsaw based its claims on ethnicity, while Prague emphasized the economic importance of Cieszyn for the nascent Czechoslovakia. In the following months, this part of Silesia saw an influx of French capital, with Schneider et Compagnie as the most important investor. The armaments and heavy industry giant had shown interest in the new country since the moment Paris recognized its independence. Now, in spring of 1920, it bought the controlling interest in the important heavy industry company Báňská a hutní in Třinec (the pre-war Österreichische Berg- und Hüttenwerke with headquarters in Vienna).[11] Schneider's experience in Czechoslovakia was positive. It was also different to that in Poland, where the Schneider-controlled Huta Bankowa group suffered from "Polish *étatisme*."[12] The company's management complained about requisitions of buildings by the local administration, government control over the coal market, or obligatory provisions of cheap food for workers. Despite a lack of archival traces of this connection in France, Wandycz and Teichova argue that the industry's attitude must have influenced the governments' position on Cieszyn.[13] In 1920, the connection seemed obvious to Polish authorities, which were also generally worried about the lukewarm French position during the Spa conference, and Paris's unwillingness to support Poland as Soviet forces were approaching Warsaw.[14] Now, rather than focus on ethnic arguments, the Poles thought that in order to win Upper Silesia, they needed to "get the English and the French interested, almost like a bribe."[15] Warsaw also considered approaching Rome and Washington.[16]

The authorities decided to send Artur Benis, a lawyer and economist from the Jagiellonian University in Cracow, who had been a technical adviser of the Polish delegation during the peace conference.[17] He left for Paris in early December 1920, and presented his case before the ever-powerful Philippe Berthelot at the Quai d'Orsay. The Poles offered concessions, including the creation of an international bank, as well as linking the income from German sate property in Upper Silesia with the payment of reparations. The English Minister in Warsaw also received these proposals. It quickly turned out that only the French were interested, but their reaction was mixed. Benis's proposal seemed needlessly complicated, expensive, and included investment from other great powers – something Paris authorities did not want. On the other hand, the French knew the worth of the Treasury Mines–with industrial circles wanting to claim them for themselves, or keep them out of the hands of the Polish state.[18] Some, such as the French ambassador in Germany's capital, Charles Laurent, worried about finances, arguing that the Polish scheme might consume funds better used elsewhere. This was a powerful argument, as Benis soon realized that his offer had not been the first. Direct talks between the French and German industrialists had begun long before the Polish mission.[19]

In June 1920, both Le Rond and Laurent contacted French industrialists, suggesting they could use the conflict in Silesia to buy shares in German companies. French producers had already been considering some form of cooperation with their eastern neighbours due to insufficient domestic coal.[20] In October, Laurent discussed the matter with the Germans, offering protection from Polish takeovers in return for German companies allowing the French to buy their shares. Since the Germans were interested (and indeed, had been considering it since 1919), Laurent suggested Colonel Ernest Weyl from Schneider as a representative of French companies in further negotiations.[21] An old classmate of Le Rond, Weyl would not raise suspicions and "combined all qualities needed for such an important and delicate mission," according to the ambassador.[22] While Le Rond suggested talking to each company separately, and using his position in Oppeln to put pressure on their owners, Laurent preferred centralized talks with a single representative in Berlin. Ultimately, Laurent's proposal won.[23] Beyond Schneider, the group also included the major lobby groups Comité des Houillères de France, and Comité des Forges, as well as Banque de Paris et des Pays-Bas, and Union Parisienne. By the end of November 1920, Weyl had already arranged the broad lines of a future agreement with German firms, including the purchase of their shares and guaranteed board membership for the French.

Comparing Benis's and Weyl's missions is instructive. The Pole came to Paris to talk to diplomats, rather than to industrialists. His proposals were broad and not connected to specific enterprises. This made sense if his goal were to get the diplomats interested, but could hardly convince investors, without whom the deal would be difficult to imagine. This made him a poor "initiating force" of investment.[24] Weyl's actions were different. He approached specific enterprises in Germany, used networking extensively, and was much more familiar with the sector. Moreover, French efforts were part of a wider striving, dating to the peace conference, to find a "reasonable settlement of economic issues" with Germany, which "climaxed in the Seydoux Plan negotiations at the end of 1920," named after Jacques Seydoux, the principal economic expert at the Quai d'Orsay.[25] Their "overtures…were rejected due essentially to the opposition of the Ruhr magnates."[26]

Once Benis learned about Franco-German talks, he asked Paris to include Poland in them as well.[27] More importantly, however, he pursued the problem of finance. If the project in Silesia were to be a joint effort, the Poles needed to provide their share of the capital. In this context, Benis suggested reusing the secret Klotz–Olszowski convention. It had been signed in January 1920 between the French minister of finance, Louis-Lucien Klotz and Kazimierz Olszowski, a department head at the Polish Ministry of Foreign Affairs.[28] It stipulated that Paris would lend up to 1 billion German marks (acquired in Alsace and Lorraine) to the Polish government at 5 per cent per annum.[29] The money would finance Franco–Polish takeovers of German companies in Poland and Danzig. The French would take 51 per cent, and the Poles – 49 per cent of their shares, with a French commissioner, paid by Warsaw, overseeing the execution of these purchases. By the end of 1920, nothing happened beyond naming the commissioner: Maxime Vicaire. A former representative of French companies in Poland and the Commercial Attaché in Warsaw, he continued to receive a considerable salary for nothing.[30] The Poles saw little interest in taking out public loans if this resulted in even more French control over Polish companies. Benis's proposal allowed them to recycle a costly mistake.[31]

In early February, French authorities agreed to Polish proposals, including the joint takeover of the Treasury Mines and the creation of an Upper Silesian bank, both financed through the Klotz–Olszowski agreement.[32] By this time, the Poles had distanced themselves from any connection between the project and reparations. What remained, was hammering out the details. After untypically fast negotiations, on February 20 a codicil was signed to the Klotz–Olszowski agreement, based on an equal division of shares between the French and Polish groups.[33] Then, on 1 March 1921, another agreement laid out the rules for the lease of the Treasury Mines and the creation of Skarboferm – a decent result for Warsaw, stemming from French expectations of Polish victory in the plebiscite.[34]

Further talks were connected to a breakthrough in Weyl's negotiations.[35] On 16 February 1921, seven major companies from Upper Silesia declared readiness to allow the French to buy their shares. The French in turn hoped to sell some to the Poles in return for privileges.[36] Initially, Benis was not impressed, but soon, together with representatives of French ministries and private companies (including Laroche, de Peyerimoff and Weyl), the Poles consented to an agreement. Despite some pressure from Wilhemstrasse and a temporary halt to negotiations, it finally happened on the day of the plebiscite, 22 March 1921.[37] The agreement stipulated that a group of French capitalists "headed by Schneider Creusot and its financial and political friends"[38] would buy minority shares in German companies, and divide them between themselves and Polish investors. Such companies would then be protected from a Polish takeover, and enjoy significant privileges (such as an exemption from taxes on assets and from forced loans). In return, they would guarantee places on the board for both the Poles and the French. The capital needed for the Polish part would again come based on the Klotz–Olszowski agreement. This *participations* (or shares) agreement proved the most controversial part of Franco–Polish negotiations.

The plebiscite, the Polish insurrection, and the ensuing chaos in Upper Silesia made further talks–concerning the planned bank, or implementing the other agreements–impracticable. However, earlier decisions impacted the flow of politics. Both Jules Laroche (who led the negotiations with Benis) and Le Rond worked in the commission which divided Upper Silesia into industrial regions to be later distributed between Poland and Germany. Zenon Szmidtke convincingly argues that the French gerrymandered the borders of these regions to make it more likely for holdings of the future Skarboferm to be allotted to Poland.[39] This proved useful once Aristide Briand decided to pursue further talks both with the Poles and with the Germans, as he thought that getting French capital into Upper Silesia could lessen German influence on companies remaining on the Polish side.[40] The Poles also wanted to continue to talk, even though the initial reason – getting Upper Silesia – was no longer on the table. As Benis returned to Paris, on November 17 a new agreement was signed on the Treasury Mines, regulating the lease and the functioning of the company.[41] Finally, after even further delays, this set of talks ended with a general agreement on the creation of the Bank of Silesia (27 December, 1921).[42] Such a flurry of negotiations was connected to the forthcoming talks between Germany and Poland, aimed at forging out the specifics of Silesia's division. Wanting to finalize the bank deal, and thus improve the Polish negotiating position, Briand decided to sign the agreement even before finding a suitable French private investor.

At roughly the same time (early 1922), Benis proposed to the Polish government an extension of the system to a new company: a German state-owned lead factory in Friedrichshütte (Strzebnica) and the associated rights to purchase the mineral. It was a large enterprise, producing some 40,000 tons of lead and 10,000 tons of silver a year. Le Rond found a French group which was willing to enter a Skarboferm-like agreement.[43] The talks continued throughout 1922, resulting in a treaty on November 20 of that year, the last in the scope of Benis's mission, and signed just before the formal French deadline.[44] The enterprise would informally be known as Tarnoferm. With this, the Silesian project almost took its final shape. Only the matter of private German shares remained.

French authorities considered the matter important, and worried about the British taking their place, or the Poles signing a direct agreement with the Germans.[45] However, as on 20 October 1921 the Council of Ambassadors postponed forced takeovers in the province for 15 years, the Germans were becoming uninterested. As French investors wavered, and asked the government for a statement of intent, in early 1922 both Aristide Briand and his successor Raymond Poincaré confirmed that the Silesian matter was of high national interest.[46] Nonetheless, talks in Warsaw went slowly (a bout of flu among diplomats in the city did not help).[47] On the German side, Hohenlohe Werke became the first (and only) company to allow the purchase of its stock, with an agreement signed on 1 March 1922. A few months later, the Poles started getting cold feet as well. They complained that "cooperation with French capital turned out to be theoretical," and hoped to be able to discuss the matter directly with either Upper Silesian Germans or other investors.[48]

Nonetheless, for reasons even the Poles later found difficult to understand, in October and November 1922 Poland and France signed two codicils to the original agreement on *participations*. The first one guaranteed significant benefits to companies which sold stock to the French, including the freedom from any exchange controls, and the protection of German managers and employees (which clashed with Poland's goal of Polonizing the province).[49] The second agreement stipulated the creation of a joint-stock Franco–Polish holding company, with a capital of 1.2 billion German marks. It would hold shares sold by German companies to the French. The holding and such companies would profit from further advantages, including tax exemptions. The Poles got nothing in return, and it is difficult to understand Korfanty's and Benis's further interest in the project, and Polish ministries' positive reactions to it in 1923.[50] In the scope of privileges afforded to French companies, which we discussed in Chapter 3, these would be among the most far-reaching.

Nonetheless, the Germans would not sell. As the mark continued to lose its value and talks progressed slowly, Paris became increasingly worried about its losses (which were estimated at 80 million francs in November 1922, almost seven times more than the real value of the loans granted to the Poles, shown in Table 6.1).[51] In early 1924 Raymond Poincaré decided to withdraw his support, ostensibly due to disagreements with private investors.[52] The Poles had also decided to pull out from the project. Minister Antoni Olszewski, who had studied the matters in Upper Silesia, argued for a radical change of Polish policy in the province, and the idea of giving big companies exemptions from property taxes was unlikely to succeed under Władysław Grabski.[53]

Table 6.1 The value of loans given by the French government for investment in Upper Silesia

Company	*Date of agreement*	*Date of loan*	*Value in million current German marks*	*Value in million current French francs*
Skarboferm	1921.03.01	1921.12.19	150	9.06
Franco–Polish holding company	1921.03.22	1922.11.19	390	1.04
Banque de Silésie	1921.12.29	1922.08.14	115	2.37
Tarnoferm	1922.11.15	1922.11.22	25	0.06

Sources: Archives diplomatiques, La Courneuve, Correspondance politique et commercial, 1918–1940, Pologne, 370, Avances à la Pologne autre que la dette de guerre proprement dite, Avances de sommes en Marks à la Pologne, 28 February 1931, 17; Centre des archives économiques et financières, Savigny-le-Temple, B 31.942, Pologne II. Participation française à des entreprises polonaises, n.d., n.p.

No-one was satisfied. The Polish Prime Minister resented the Silesian agreements and considered Benis's and Korfanty's efforts detrimental to Polish interests. The French felt that they missed an important opportunity to improve relations with German industrial circles, seen as crucial by many officials.[54]

6.2 The system of mixed companies

Artur Benis's mission resulted in the creation of three companies: Skarboferm, Tarnoferm, and the Bank of Silesia. Additionally, a Franco–Polish group bought shares in Hohenlohe Werke. The first three were rooted in public international law, sprouting from secret agreements between Poland and France. Diplomats quarrelled over the future firms' statutes, often in considerable detail. For the French, this was a way of extending and solidifying their interests in Poland, for the Poles – of mitigating French control.

While the French authorities themselves used mixed private–public companies "to operate commercial properties confiscated by the Germans," their emergence in Polish Silesia surprised Paris.[55] It had its roots in Benis's suggestion to the Polish government concerning Skarboferm. He proposed giving its shares to the state-owned Bank Krajowy, a predecessor of the Bank of the National Economy (Bank Gospodarstwa Krajowego, BGK), interwar Poland's most important state-owned bank. The reasoning for this decision was complex. Some of it came from Benis's misguided claim that the French government would itself at first take over the French part of Skarboferm. Warsaw was also unlikely to find private investors with enough capital to purchase the Polish part of the company's shares. People engaged in the negotiations were worried that French-owned companies in Poland would buy some of the nominally Polish stock, giving the control of Skarboferm over to French capital.[56] Whatever the reason, despite diplomatic interventions, negotiating further agreements with private groups in mind, organizing such groups, and even arguing that the agreements prevented "etatization," the Poles applied the same model to all mixed companies in Silesia, with Polish shares owned by the state.[57] This course of events broadly follows wider Polish policy in the early 1920s, when, despite declarations to the contrary, the share of the state in the economy consistently increased, as authorities replaced failing private capital.[58]

A single entity with full backing of the government thus controlled the Polish shares in each company. Likewise, the Polish halves of their boards included mostly government officials from the Ministries of Industry and Trade, and Treasury, which further increased the direct influence of Warsaw.[59] In contrast, French shareholders were fragmented, and could only count on indirect support from their authorities.

The equal roles of the French and the Poles were guaranteed in multiple stipulations within the companies' statutes, which were the topic of long intergovernmental negotiations. The revised Klotz–Olszowski agreement set the share of the French and Polish groups to 50 per cent each. Further rules guaranteed that the parity would not change due to the sale and transfer of shares. Boards of directors were likewise split equally between representatives of the French and the Poles, and the companies' presidents and vice-presidents would come from different countries, with the roles alternating every few years. This arrangement guaranteed that major decisions, such as liquidation, needed agreement from both groups of shareholders.[60]

The system was cumbersome. With board members and other officials equally split between two countries, meetings proved difficult to organize, especially since the boards were large.[61] To counter this, Bank Śląski reduced the number of its board members. However, large boards allowed more officials to profit. In the 1930s, meetings in Paris were scheduled in such a way as to allow board members to enjoy good weather in Paris, giving the Poles some company-sponsored holidays.[62]

Some French shareholders felt stifled by Polish government control. In Skarboferm they transferred their shares to a holding company (Société de Gestion d'Intérêts Miniers et Industriels Français à l'Étranger, founded in 1923), with the goal of protecting French control over the company.[63] Henri de Peyerimhoff was its president. On the other hand, after the coup in May 1926, the Poles started asserting their position–and de facto took control of the failing Bank Śląski. Based on these experiences, when in 1931 Paris and Warsaw negotiated the creation of a new mixed company to build the Coal Trunk Line, Paris insisted on an 8/15th majority for the French group.

Skarboferm's experience is instructive, as its French owners worked together with the government in Paris to ensure almost complete French control over the company, despite very few French citizens working there.[64] Using conditionality, they were able to make sure that the general director remained French between 1922 and 1939 (with François Reumaux followed by François Michel), as did the heads of accounting and the technical directors. This also meant that many of Skarboferm's investments were carried out by French rather than Polish (and thus potentially cheaper) companies. The Poles managed to gain some guarantees of future influence on the company after 1937, when Polish board members started voting together more consistently.[65]

There is some parallel here to the position of Škoda in Czechoslovakia, where the French kept complete control over the company, including accounting and other key positions, despite a sizeable portion of the shares being kept by the government in Prague. Moreover, by regularly hiring former ministers (and letting them know in secret that they would be hired when they were still in office), Schneider's representatives were able to effectively lobby for the company. On the other hand, since the Prague government was the primary buyer of Škoda's products, the influences ran in both directions.[66]

Despite its influence, the French government did not directly take part in the running of the companies. Nonetheless, the Quai d'Orsay set up certain mechanisms of supervision. As Finance Minister Charles de Lasteyrie explained, the government needed financial and political control to safeguard its funds used to kickstart these firms, and to protect France's security interests; for instance, by blocking cooperation with the Germans.[67] These mechanisms took different forms of varying severity, starting with the timid declaration in Tarnoferm's statutes that the company would act loyally. In Skarboferm, two external commissioners, with no access to board meetings, represented the Ministry of Public Works and the powerful Mouvement général des Fonds.[68] In Hohenlohe, a consulting engineer (*engineur conseil*) played a similar role, although the company was able to de facto bribe Jules Simon to not take the position.[69] In Bank Śląski control was stricter, as both governments picked their representatives among board members, tasked with reporting on the firm's position, and had the right to vet new members.[70]

A major conflict erupted when the French government attempted to force the vetting of new board members for the future holding company. The authorities' position was understandable, as the project entailed talking to the enemy, potentially resulting in German influence on French companies. Nonetheless, Henri de Peyerimnoff de Fontenelle and Louis Mercier – the leaders of the French group – strongly protested, arguing that their only reason for engaging in Silesia was the government's insistence. "You have before you the oldest, the most stable, the most exclusive national industry of this country. The people who run it are known not only to your officials, but to the entire national economy,"[71] they chastised the Prime Minister, offering the option to name government commissioners instead.

The argument about the government's insistence was true. Early on, authorities turned to the powerful Central Committee of French Coal Mines (Comité Central des Houillères de France), and over multiple meetings tried to convince its leaders to invest in Silesian coal.[72] This effort included leading figures at the Quai d'Orsay: the general secretary Philippe Berthelot himself, and the head of Commercial Relations, Jacques Seydoux.[73] Later, subsequent prime ministers restated the national interest tied to the Silesian project. It is therefore not surprising that investors were disappointed when Poincaré pulled out of the project, ostensibly over the conflict described above. On the other hand, de Peyerimnoff's and Mercier's vicious attack was extraordinary, showing the limits of private–public cooperation in France. They accused the Prime Minister of destroying the policies of his predecessors for political reasons.

De Peyerimnoff and Mercier also pointed out another consequence of the companies' political character. The complex protocols of international negotiations and the government's glacial decision-making were too slow for business. Calls for faster action regularly came from both governments, but with the matters falling under the purview of multiple ministries, each with its institutional structure and dynamics, they were rarely heeded. As a result, French investors blamed their government, Paris blamed Warsaw, and the Poles were frustrated by what they saw as French changes of position.[74]

Moving on to the three companies, they were different enough to make direct comparisons difficult. The Treasury Mines were the crown jewel of Polish holdings in the province. A set of rich coalfields with the accompanying collieries, they produced 4 million tons of coal in 1938, or 11 per cent of Poland's entire output.[75] Among Benis's proposals, they offered the safest investment, and there was little hesitation on the French side. The company – known as Skarboferm – was founded in 1922, with a capital of 300 million German marks, later converted to 8.2 million 1924 złoty, and after some changes, set at 17.63 million 1927 złoty in 1935.[76] A separate contract regulated the lease of the mines for 36 years, which allowed the Polish government to quickly pay back its loan.[77] The French group consisted of mining companies from Nord-Pas-de-Calais, representing the majority of production from the French basin. French firms from the Polish Dąbrowa Basin also bought minor shares. Beyond coal mines, the company had a coking plant, a few coal-related factories, and other assets, including stakes in many firms.[78] Like the other two mixed companies, Skarboferm enjoyed freedom from exchange control – a goal sought by other French firms in Poland, and only achieved in the oil sector. Since the mid-1920s, the company reported healthy profits, and apart from 1932 paid out respectable, 10 per cent dividends.[79]

From the outset, the firm was destined to play a role in politics, with the shape of the board and its place within the complex of French investment in the country. Its political importance is apparent as it continued to appear on the margins all major Franco–Polish loan negotiations, especially during the Great Depression. Paris considered the firm a crucial endeavour in Poland, meaning that bigger conflicts concerning the company were tackled by government officials in intergovernmental talks.[80] Moreover, the company saw very effective lobbying at the hands of Polish officials sitting on its board (including Korfanty and Czesław Klarner), while French diplomats made sure it was also treated well abroad.[81]

This position came at a cost. In the early years, the company subsidized some Polish national expenses, from Korfanty's role as the government's delegate, to various costs of General Le Rond's visit to Poland (including his honorary doctorate). Skarboferm also took part in the purchase of the Polish legation building in Riga in the 1930s, and in the 1920s it limited its sales to

Germany to make the French occupation of the Ruhr Basin more effective. When the Poles introduced the złoty in 1924, Skarboferm's board decided to subscribe 1.5 million gold shares of the new Bank Polski to bolster its position, using Korfanty to lobby their cause. Generally, however, the cost of engagement in politics was low, and the returns high.[82]

Tarnowskie Góry Leaseholding Company (Spółka Dzierżawna Tarnowskie Góry or Société Fermière de Tarnowitz, generally known as Tarnoferm) was Skarboferm's smaller, poorer, and ultimately unsuccessful cousin.[83] It was created in 1923, based on a 25-year lease of a Polish Treasury-owned lead and silver works in Strzybnica (Friedrichshütte). The factory also enjoyed historical "fiscal rights" to obligatory lead deliveries in Upper Silesia.[84] The French group, which remained active in the company's management, consisted of Société Minerais et Métaux and Association Minière. Although de Peyerimhoff showed interest in the factory in late 1921, the company were ultimately separate from other French investors in Upper Silesia.[85]

Politics played a smaller role in the company, and its failure had more to do with business. Its initial capital amounted to 50 million German marks, but with hyperinflation in 1923 it evaporated, requiring further investment to get it up to 5 million złoty. Moreover, the richest deposits of the pre-war company remained on the German side, with only about a sixth of the mineral making it into the factory. Finally, the "fiscal" privileges of the company lost value, while producers attempted to avoid them altogether.[86] The firm had to purchase expensive minerals abroad: almost two-thirds of all the lead it used (most from Germany, some from as far away as Australia). Some 90 per cent of the company's production was exported, so when lead prices and demand collapsed during the Great Depression, so did profits. The Poles insisted on keeping the company afloat, but after the general assembly voted to shut it down in April 1933, they relented, with the process finishing in 1937.[87]

The Bank of Silesia (Bank Śląski or Banque de Silésie) was founded in August 1922 as a new enterprise, unlike the other mixed companies. Initially conceived as simply another concession to allied capital, its creation quickly morphed into a Polish demand, an easy way to set up an issue bank in Upper Silesia and help in the forced takeovers of German companies.[88] The French understood it to be a condition for the other agreements, a way to support Skarboferm with funds and block investors from other countries from investing in the project.[89] While the Quai d'Orsay was willing to back the bank, private investors were reluctant. As the value of the German mark declined, the bank's responsibility for Upper Silesian money hardly promised great returns. The meagre capital it would have at its disposal seemed unlikely to impact the province's financial sector. Nonetheless, after multiple attempts the French government found investors in the form of a diverse group led by Crédit Industriel et Commercial under the helm of Albert de Monplanet.

Crucially, the bank was supposed to serve as the representative of Polska Krajowa Kasa Pożyczkowa and other Polish state banks for 15 years. The PKKP was a bank of issue, which the Poles inherited from the German occupation. The French were excited about the prospect of this privilege. French Minister in Warsaw Hector de Panafieu saw it as a way to "take economic control over Upper Silesia, and thus all of Poland for a mere few million francs."[90] However, after hyperinflation the Poles decided to ignore this part of the agreement. Despite multiple interventions, they never budged, and with the creation of the new Bank Polski, which issued the new Polish złoty, also in Silesia, the matter became moot.

The Bank of Silesia was a commercial failure. High inflation made its initial capital worthless, and later, bad management rendered repair efforts ineffective. Korfanty seemingly used the company to finance his business endeavours, and the bank wasted its resources on bad industrial loans. Due to competition from the much more robust Banque Franco-Polonaise, the company never took over significant French clients.[91] By the late 1920s, the Poles pushed for liquidation, which was finalized in 1937.

To summarize this overview, the Polish government did not directly engage in how these companies functioned. In Skarboferm specifically, the French managed the firm, and the authorities in Warsaw were content with oversight provided by their board members, and with the profits the company reported. However, as other firms ran into problems, the authorities stepped in, with Polish officials managing their liquidation.

The political origins of these companies hampered their development through overly complex organizational arrangements, or the influence of politicians. Still, such connections fostered successful lobbying, as can be seen in Skarboferm. Mixed companies thus seemed to face similar challenges to those of state-run companies, with the added caveat that their private co-owners expected profits and dividends. As a result, while many fully state-owned firms would have continued to bleed money and subsist on subsidies, two mixed companies closed down.

6.3 Irregular networks

In August 1924, Władysław Grabski's government decided to verify rumours of tax fraud by Upper Silesian companies. Former minister of industry and trade Antoni Olszewski was sent to the province, and in his secret reports dug deep into the mixed companies. He was appalled by the results of Benis's negotiations, by what he saw as collusion between different actors in the province, and by the atmosphere in which the talks had taken place. He was surprised to find that only three people had shaped most of the Polish policy. Apart from Benis, they included Jerzy Michalski, director of Bank Krajowy, and Wacław Olszewicz from the Ministry of Foreign Affairs. All three became board members of the mixed companies, as did Korfanty, who joined the project later. Moreover, Olszewski observed that the decision to keep the agreements secret, understandable from the geopolitical context, had been taken surprisingly far. Officials in the relevant ministries were not notified of Benis's talks, and the agreements, which needed parliamentary approval, were never put before the legislature.[92] And yet, as Olszewicz was shocked to discover in the documents of Hohenlohe Werke, the company had received an early copy of the holding agreement, when members of the Polish government remained ignorant of the talks.[93]

Some problems reported by Olszewicz stemmed from the informal Polish practice of state-owned companies hiring officials who helped found them – even when they were still in office. Public servants would often earn more from such positions that they did from their principal post in a ministry or in the military.[94] It was a destructive practice, since it fuelled corruption and weakened the private sector on a systemic level, as hiring a private firm was less beneficial to officials than creating a state-owned enterprise.

The French approach was ostensibly different, with officials at the Quai d'Orsay declaring that the very idea of government employees receiving remuneration from private companies was "shocking."[95] The Silesian negotiations even made some of them uneasy. As an internal note stated, their "anormal character…raises particularly delicate financial and political issues."[96] Nonetheless, these rules did not extend to former officials taking up posts, and both Le Rond and Vicaire also ended up in the Silesian companies. Even Ambassador Jules Laroche found his way to the board of Skarboferm after leaving his post.[97] Obviously, so did private negotiators, such as de Peyerimnoff de Fontenelle and Mercier.[98]

There was thus little practical difference between France and Poland in handling the creation of the mixed companies. It serves as the best example of the variety of goals and interests in the two countries – both in their governments, and among private companies – which influenced official state behaviour, investment decisions, and the structure of the new firms. Behind these institutions stood individuals, and ultimately, as Pieter Judson writes, "it is they, not abstract national communities (or data sets), who find opportunities to create commercial, cultural, or social networks, often for highly idiosyncratic reasons."[99] Let us, then, take a look at the connections of four important people active in the creation of these companies, with extensive connections to many French endeavours. Their stories illustrate the bottom-up processes which informed the functioning of French investments.

Wojciech Korfanty was the most prominent Polish representative in the mixed companies. A complex political figure from Upper Silesia, he was born near Katowice, then known as Katowitz, in 1873. Before the Great War he had served as a member of the Reichstag and the Prussian Landtag, and remained an important supporter of the Polish cause. After the war he emerged as the leader of the Polish movement and "dictator" of the Third Silesian Uprising. In independent Poland, he served in Parliament throughout the 1920s as a leading voice among Christian Democrats. Blocked from forming his cabinet in 1922 by Józef Piłsudski and the Polish Socialist Party, he became Deputy Prime Minister in the right-wing government of Wincenty Witos in the following year. He opposed Piłsudski's coup in 1926, and became a vocal member of the opposition against his rule. Arrested in 1930, and harassed in the following years, he emigrated in 1935. In exile, he co-founded the opposition movement Front Morges. As he lived in Prague in March 1939, Nazi occupation forced him to return to Poland, where he was arrested, and died in August, soon after regaining his freedom.

Korfanty sat on the boards of a dozen Silesian companies. For his position in Skarboferm alone he received on average some 3,600 Polish złoty a month (which made for a very high salary) and the use of a company car. In 1923, he bought a lavish house in Katowice, followed by minor properties in other parts of Poland.[100] Korfanty used his connections and money from big industry to build a newspaper empire, based on two dailies: "Rzeczpospolita," purchased from the pianist and politician Ignacy Paderewski, and "Polonia." In 1925, he also attempted to acquire the failing Bank dla Handlu i Przemysłu in Warsaw, becoming its president for a few months, before the institution almost shut down. Korfanty asked Prime Minister Grabski to help save the bank, but he declined, which negatively affected the Christian Democrats' relations with the government, already strained by attacks in "Polonia." It was also Grabski's cabinet which let BGK know about Korfanty's actions in Bank Śląski.[101]

Closely connected to the French, Korfanty was seen as a useful asset in Poland in the early 1920s. In 1922, General Le Rond himself argued against nominating the Polish politician president of the Bank of Silesia. He wrote that "France exerts influence over him greater than over any other" elected official, and so it was unwise to jeopardize his position with yet another post.[102] A year later a secret Quai d'Orsay note noted that the "Upper Silesian Tribune" was "eaten through by political ambition and a thirst for money,"[103] but saw him as a representative of German industrial interests in Poland.[104]

In early 1922, Korfanty complained to Le Rond that the Poles had not informed him of talks concerning the mixed companies.[105] Soon afterwards, he started coordinating actions with Benis. He became president of both Skarboferm and the bank, and, together with Benis, the "default" board member in any negotiated enterprise, including Hohenlohe. He was particularly interested in the holding company, and himself led negotiations with some private German owners. As he entered Silesian businesses, he promoted his Polish collaborators, resulting in a large number of Poles taking up important posts in Upper Silesia. It was part of a wider programme of Polonizing Silesian industry, but at the same time helped his associates gain lucrative positions.[106]

Korfanty's mixing of politics and business caught up with him. First, under Władysław Grabski, he was accused of facilitating tax fraud by German companies (based on Olszewski's report), but was ultimately cleared of the charges. When Piłsudski came to power, his people quickly moved against their political rivals, and passed a bill forbidding MPs from sitting on the boards of state-owned companies. Korfanty lost his positions in Skarboferm and Bank Śląski, yet continued to seek outstanding remuneration.[107] In the case of Skarboferm, where Korfanty was replaced as president by de Peyerimhoff, the Pole's rivals proved that the company had been paying the salary of his private gardener.[108] After Korfanty accused another MP of libel, a Parliamentary Tribunal (Sąd Marszałkowski) was convened in 1927 to assess the veracity of the claims against the Silesian politician. Of these, two were crucial. First, the Tribunal recognized that Korfanty had received over two million złoty – an extraordinary sum – from a lobby organization of Upper Silesian big industry (Berg- und Hütten-Verein) for his media empire, which was "morally disgraceful" for a Member of Parliament and publicist (this money was the locus of long litigation in the late 1930s).[109] Secondly, the Tribunal acknowledged that as President of the Board of Bank of Silesia, Korfanty had broken the law as well as good commercial practices. Apparently, he had abused his influence to help finance his endeavours, although his actions had not seemingly broken the specific laws in Upper Silesia.[110] The Tribunal did not, however, find any evidence of tax fraud.[111]

Korfanty is a difficult character to assess. Both his business acumen and questionable actions are clear. He was acquitted from the most serious fraud accusations, and later attacks by Sanacja were political. He clearly used his political connections for pecuniary goals, and reinvested the money into politics. His contacts with the French were but part of his wider connections in Upper Silesia.[112] Just like private French investors, he was willing to talk to all sides, provided it was profitable. And while he was removed from his posts by his Sanacja opponents and accused of wrongdoing, this did not prevent those in turn to put their people in lucrative positions in Skarboferm and other state-owned companies.[113]

Compared to Korfanty, Artur Benis was a minor figure. Born in 1865 in Cracow, he practised law and worked at the local Chamber of Industry and Commerce, while publishing legal and historical works. After the war, he was professor of economics at the Jagiellonian University, worked for the Polish delegation in Paris, and later for the Office d'Achat de l'État Polonais in the same city.[114] Not the first choice for a negotiator in Silesian matters, he agreed to take the job, but kept complaining about its difficulty.[115]

After negotiating the deals on the mixed companies, he sat on their boards (plus that of the zinc and coal giant Giesche) together with Wojciech Korfanty. In Skarboferm he became the executive director (*administrateur delegué*).[116] As Antoni Olszewski complained, the officials at the Ministry of Treasury and of Foreign Affairs, with whom Benis cooperated during the negotiations, also got well-paid jobs in the companies. Moreover, when Benis negotiated in Paris, his son was the secretary of the Polish Legation in the city, which coordinated the talks (he was later replaced by a close friend). Olszewski wrote, mixing metaphors:

> One gets the impression that our authorities are trapped in a spider's web. Its intricate threads meet at the nodes, or offices, with "the right people in the right places," and at the centre all converge on one man. He remains in the shadows, but directs the entire operation with a steady hand.[117]

While the evidence was at best circumstantial, the former minister suggested that Benis had knowingly facilitated fraud and his negotiations were detrimental to state interests. Olszewski wanted to see both Benis and Korfanty investigated and perhaps tried, but appreciated that such a procedure would further undermine Poland's international standing.[118] Nonetheless, Benis lost his position in the companies. The French likewise did not like him, remembering his support for the Central Powers during the Great War. When de Peyerimhoff suggested awarding him with a Chevalier Cross of the Legion of Honour – a common practice for negotiators engaged in the creation of such major companies – Le Rond and de Panafieu blocked the effort. The latter complained that Benis was difficult to work with, and made all negotiations longer. Likewise, Skarboferm's French board members and negotiators of the Tarnoferm deal complained about this bad will.[119] Ultimately, Benis was a political operative who managed to land a few prestigious positions, and had significant, arguably unconstitutional influence over policy which shaped Polish holdings in Upper Silesia.

Moving on to French actors, General Henri Louis Édouard Le Rond, born in 1864, is fondly remembered in Poland. After a successful military career, he emerged during the peace conference in Paris as one of France's experts on its future ally. He chaired the committee on Silesia, where his counterparts from other countries soon realized that he supported Poland's position "as much as any Frenchmen."[120] As he became head of the Inter-Allied Commission in Upper Silesia with headquarters in Oppeln (disliked by his colleagues from other countries for his often "authoritarian methods," earning him the moniker "King of Upper Silesia"), he supported talks with German firms. He exerted a powerful influence in Silesia, and his torrent of telegrams from Oppeln affected French foreign policy. In 1921 he received the Grand Officer Cross of the Legion of Honour, and five years later – the Grand Cross. In Poland, he was seen as a friend of the country. As a result, Le Rond was decorated with both the White Eagle and the Virtuti Militari crosses, while the Jagiellonian University awarded him an honorary doctorate. However, as a close associate of Philippe Pétain, he remained in service in Vichy France. After his death in 1949, he was buried without military honours.[121]

Le Rond's actions in Poland earned him a position on Skarboferm's board in 1927 (where he replaced Louis Mercier), which he kept until the end of the interwar period.[122] It was far from his only engagement in the Polish economy. Le Rond was among French investors headed by Marcel Boussac in his takeover of Żyrardów, and his most important role took him to Danzig. In the 1922 the old Danziger Werft, combined with a local rail equipment factory, was reconstituted as the International Shipbuilding & Engineering Co., Ltd. It was a mixed company, with the French and the British holding 30 per cent of the shares each, and the rest split equally between the Danzigers and the Polish state.[123] Le Rond became its chairman as part of a French effort to overcome British and German domination in the company. When this firm became the majority shareholder of the new shipbuilding company in Gdynia, he took the same position in the new company as well, seen by the French as an important security investment.[124] Combining these positions allowed Le Rond to ensure Skarboferm got some custom design train wagons from the Danzig company.[125]

No evidence suggests foul play on Le Rond's part. On the one hand, he used his international post to push French private economic interests with high-political goals on mind. On the other, his activities resulted in his posts–cementing French influence, but also beneficial to the general.

Not all French diplomats and politicians were equally able to translate their service into a success in business. Maxime Vicaire offers perhaps the best example. He started his career in Poland thanks to a recommendation from Joseph Noulens.[126] His initial job was to estimate the value of war indemnities for French companies, but by May 1919 he became the investors' permanent representative and lobbyist. His brother André worked in Huta Bankowa.[127] Highly regarded by both investors and minister Pralon, Vicaire took the new post of French Commercial Attaché in Warsaw.[128] In parallel developments, he became the commissioner stipulated in the Klotz–Olszowski agreement from 17 January 1920, and by the end of the year, represented the French Ministry of Finance in talks with Warsaw.[129]

In 1922, Vicaire was named the director of Bank of Silesia. What at first seemed a promising promotion to an important post (enough for him to unsuccessfully ask for a diplomatic passport), soon proved to be less glamorous.[130] As the bank never became an ersatz central bank of Polish Upper Silesia, and other French designs for the province crumbled, Vicaire found himself running a small company in dire financial straits. Influenced by the charismatic Korfanty, he succumbed, and was let go together with him in 1926. Evidently, Korfanty was a much more skilled politician and businessman, and used his networks among the French (and the Germans) for his benefit.

Today, Wojciech Korfanty remains a celebrated Polish interwar politician, with hagiographies and a wide avenue in Katowice named after him – one of a hundred in Poland. Henri Le Rond is also occasionally remembered, if less celebrated, with only one street named after him – also located in Katowice. Benis and Vicaire are relegated to the works of professional historians.[131] Together, they represent but a small portion of important actors who similarly functioned around Skarboferm and other mixed companies.[132] The networks they created are nothing extraordinary: they exist everywhere in business. Nonetheless, they testify to the powerful attraction of the border between public and private ownership, which offered private investors easier access to politicians, while supplying state representatives and former officials with impressive remuneration.

6.4 Conclusions

The Franco–Polish mixed companies were born out of a curious political endeavour. As interwar politicians and post-war historians agreed, France had already been in favour of giving Upper Silesia to Poland (although the French were not so sure, and had to reassure themselves that they had not been bribed).[133] This made Benis's mission ostensibly pointless, or even detrimental to Polish interests.[134] Later efforts allowed for some damage control: the refusal to honour the special privileges of Bank of Silesia, pulling out of the deal on participations, or assuming control of the companies' shares by Warsaw. Arguably, however, Benis's mission also helped prevent a more sinister possibility: that the French would come to terms with the Germans with no Polish input.

From Paris's point of view, the lack of a Franco–German agreement made the Silesian matter a partial failure. Certainly, the new borders weakened Germany, and French companies managed to gain important concessions in Silesia, but the main prizes – the takeover of German private companies or a serious economic rapprochement – never materialized. Prolonged negotiations coupled with inflation did little beyond causing significant losses. Much of the problem seemed to lay with the refusal of private French companies to take part in government-led projects. Mihout-Natar claims that this was not a question of diverging goals between the public and private spheres, but rather the "inability of authorities to mobilize others around the message of national interest."[135]

Benis argued that the talks made some investors in France friendlier towards Poland, and created ties between Warsaw and "the French government's technical and financial counsellors, which proved very helpful with time."[136] In other words, the usefulness of the Silesian project lay in forging a network of contacts, useful both in getting the French public interested in Silesia, and in other talks within the wider scope of Franco–Polish relations.

The voyage of Le Rond with which I opened this chapter is a good example of how the existence of Skarboferm created such political and personal connections, with highly placed businessmen and politicians now interested in the Polish economy. Nonetheless, these networks also had a potentially destructive character, as they fostered corruption and the creation of informal connections. Moreover, from a developmental point of view, the Silesian project was dubious. It allowed France to take control over important coalfields, and siphon away money from a company which would have otherwise been Polish.

Notes

1 Skarboferm (or Skarboferme in French) is a portmanteau of *skarbo*, from *Kopalnie Skarbowe* or Fiscal Mines, and *ferm*, from *fermière*, or leaseholding. The company adopted the name formally in 1938, but it had been used informally before. Archives diplomatiques, Nantes [henceforth: AdN], Consulat de France à Katowice [henceforth: CFK], 5, Terver to Briand, 12 July 1927, n.p.; Archiwum Państwowe w Katowicach [henceforth: APK], Skarboferm Spółka Dzierżawna [henceforth: Skarboferm], 2.6/184, Protokół posiedzenia Rady Nadzorczej, 9 July 1927, 1–14; Zenon Szmidtke, *"Skarboferm" 1922–1939: związki polityki z gospodarką* (Opole: Państwowy Instytut Naukowy, 2005), 31, 181; Mariusz Patelski, "Henry Le Rond – generał (prawie) nieznany," *Indeks*, no. 9–10 (2004/2003): 59.

2 Szmidtke, "*Skarboferm*," 156, 310.

3 Jerzy Gołębiowski, *Kapitał państwowy w spółkach prawa handlowego u schyłku Drugiej Rzeczypospolitej. Szczegółowe sprawozdanie z działalności przedsiębiorstw o kapitale mieszanym za rok 1937 wzgl. 1937/1938* (Kraków: Wydawnictwo Naukowe Akademii Pedagogicznej, 2004), 29.

4 Zbigniew Landau, *Bank Gospodarstwa Krajowego* (Warszawa: Oficyna Wydawnicza SGH, 1998).
5 For a list of such mixed companies, see Tadeusz Bernadzikiewicz, *Udział państwa w spółkach handlowych* (Warszawa: Towarzystwo Wydawnicze Młodych Prawników i Ekonomistów, 1938); Gołębiowski, *Kapitał*.
6 Jochen Böhler, *Civil War in Central Europe, 1918–1921. Reconstruction of Poland* (Oxford: Oxford University Press, 2018), 95–115.
7 T. Hunt Tooley, *National Identity and Weimar Germany: Upper Silesia and the Eastern Border, 1918–1922* (Lincoln: University of Nebraska Press, 1997), 201; Frédéric Dessberg, "Enjeux et rivalités politiques franco-britanniques: le plébiscite de haute-Silésie (1921)," *Revue historique des armées* 254 (2009): 53–66; Archives diplomatiques, La Courneuve [henceforth: AdC], Correspondance politique et commercial, 1918–1940, Pologne [henceforth: CPC PL], 212, La Haute-Silésie. Étude économique, 26 June 1920, 26.
8 Zbigniew Landau, Jerzy Tomaszewski, "*Misja prof. A. Benisa*," *Teki Archiwalne* 6 (1959): 29–225, 36.
9 Landau and Tomaszewski, "Misja," 50–51.
10 Landau and Tomaszewski, "Misja," 36.
11 Alice Teichova, *An Economic Background to Munich: International Business and Czechoslovakia 1918–1938* (London: Cambridge University Press, 1974), 99–101; Cf. Agnès D'Angio, "Schneider et Cie face aux risques géopolitiques en Europe centrale et orientale (1918–1939)," *Les cahiers Irice* 2, no. 6 (2010): 35–59, https://doi.org/10.3917/lci.006.0035.
12 AdC, CPC PL, 253, de Barante to Pichon, 23 August 1919, 60–64; Szmidtke, "*Skarboferm*," 26.
13 Piotr Stefan Wandycz, *France and Her Eastern Allies 1919–1925: French–Czechoslovak–Polish Relations from the Paris Peace Conference to Locarno* (Minneapolis: The University of Minnesota Press, 1962), 91, 149–150; Teichova, *An Economic Background*, 79, 100–101; Mylène Mihout-Natar, "L'intervention des capitaux français dans la Pologne de la Seconde République (1918–1939): contribution à l'histoire de l'impérialisme économique français en Europe centrale" (PhD, Université Charles de Gaulle – Lille III, 2002), 23–28.
14 Marc Trachtenberg, *Reparation in World Politics: France and European Economic Diplomacy, 1916–1923* (New York: Columbia University Press, 1980), 152–54.
15 Landau and Tomaszewski, "Misja," 36.
16 Landau and Tomaszewski, "Misja," 56–57, 170–71.
17 Szmidtke, "*Skarboferm*," 30.
18 AdC, CPC PL, 238, Conséquences économiques de l'annexion de la Haute-Silésie à la Pologne, [May–July 1919], 87; Wandycz, *France*, 227; Szmidtke, "*Skarboferm*," 36.
19 Landau and Tomaszewski, "Misja," 39, 60–62, 102, 176; AdC, CPC PL, 212, Mémoire de M. Arthur Benis, Délégué Plénipotentiaire du Gouvernement polonais pour les affaires économiques de la Haute-Silésie, 17 December 1920, 47–49.
20 Trachtenberg, *Reparation*, 112; Szmidtke, "*Skarboferm*," 24–25.
21 Tooley, *National Identity*, 203–5; AdC, CPC PL, 251, Haguenin to Pichon, 13 December 1919, 134.
22 AdC, CPC PL, 216, Laurent to Berthelot, 25 October 1920, 6; Szmidtke, "*Skarboferm,*" 22.
23 Szmidtke, "*Skarboferm*," 27.
24 Yair Arahoni, *The Foreign Investment Decision Process* (Boston: Harvard University, 1966), 54–55.
25 Trachtenberg, *Reparation*, viii.
26 Trachtenberg, *Reparation*, 114.
27 Landau and Tomaszewski, "Misja," 107.

28 Text of the convention: Landau and Tomaszewski, "Misja," 163–68.
29 Szmidtke, "*Skarboferm*," 34.
30 Anna Maria Cienciała and Titus Komarnicki, *From Versailles to Locarno: Keys to Polish Foreign Policy, 1919–25* (Lawrence: Kansas University Press, 1984), 17.
31 AdC, CPC PL, 212, Vicaire to François-Marsal, 11 January 1921, 58–63 and 28 April 1920, 90–91; Centre des archives économiques et financières, Savigny-le-Temple [henceforth: CAÉF], B 31.942, [Doumer] to Panafieu, [January 1922], n.p.; Landau and Tomaszewski, "Misja," 46.
32 Landau and Tomaszewski, "Misja," 63; Wandycz, *France*, 228.
33 Landau and Tomaszewski, "Misja," 64–66; AdC, CPC PL, 212, Participation française aux affaires de Haute-Silésie, 5 February 1921, 104–6.
34 Landau and Tomaszewski, "Misja," 72–75; Szmidtke, "*Skarboferm*," 40–41.
35 AdC, CPC PL, 212, Haute-Silésie. Tractations avec les entreprises allemandes, 2 February 1921, 14–14v and Note pour le Président du Conseil. Participations francaises dans les affaires industrielles de Haute-Silésie, 18 January 1922, 223–25.
36 AdC, CPC PL, 212, Laurent to Briand, 21 February 1921, 160–61.
37 Tooley, *National Identity*, 205–206 AdC, CPC PL, 216, FEB to Briand, 4 March 1921, 58–59; Szmidtke, "*Skarboferm*," 27–28.
38 Landau and Tomaszewski, "Misja," 107.
39 Szmidtke, "*Skarboferm*," 50–51. Cf. The National Archives, Kew, FO 371/7496, Stuart to Curzon, 26 January 1922, 45.
40 AdC, CPC PL, 216, Briand to Le Rond, Laurent, 10 June 1921, 109–9v.
41 AdC, CPC PL, 212, Convention entre la Pologne et la France relative aux mines fiscales de Haute-Silésie, 16 November 1921, 212–15.
42 AdC, CPC PL, 212, Convention entre la France et la Pologne au sujet de la consitution de la Banque de Haute-Silésie, 29 December 1921, 218–22.
43 AdC, CPC PL, 212, Charbonnel to Poincaré, 17 March 1922, 236–37.
44 AdC, CPC PL, 212, Raymond Poincaré to FLW, 31 May 1922, 260; AdC, CPC PL, 249, Accord franco-polonais réglant l'amodiation de l'usine à plomb et argent de Strzebnica (Friedrischütte), 20 November 1922, 45–49.
45 Landau and Tomaszewski, "Misja," 108–9; AdC, CPC PL, 212, Note pour monsieur Laroche, 25 February 1922, 232–32b; AdC, CPC PL, 216, Poincaré to de Panafieu, 27 January 1922, 224–26.
46 AdC, CPC PL, 216, Réunion à la Présidence de la République, 10 November 1921, 123–24; AdC, CPC PL, 216, Briand to de Peyerimhoff de Fontenelle, 7 January 1922, 193–94; AdC, CPC PL, 216, [MAÉ] to Laurent, 18 January 1922, 204
47 AdC, CPC PL, 216, Poincaré to de Panafieu, 27 January 1922, 224–6; AdC, CPC PL, 216, de Lasteyrie to Poincaré, 22 February 1922, 244; AdC, CPC PL, 216, Pinot to Poincaré, 22 February 1922, 245–47.
48 Landau and Tomaszewski, "Misja," 120.
49 Landau and Tomaszewski, "Misja," 181; Mieczysław Grzyb, *Narodowościowo-polityczne aspekty przemian stosunków własnościowych i kadrowych w górnośląskim przemyśle w latach 1922–1939* (Katowice: Uniwersytet Śląski, 1978).
50 Landau and Tomaszewski, "Misja," 152–58.
51 AdC, CPC PL, 217, Poincaré to FLW, 4 November 1922, 169.
52 AdC, CPC PL, 218, Poincaré to de Lasteyrie, 4 March 1924, 57–57v.
53 Landau and Tomaszewski, "Misja," 173.
54 AdC, CPC PL, 218, Intérêts miniers français en Haute-Silésie, 11 December 1924, 88–89v; AdC, CPC PL, 218, Simon to Seydoux, 20 December 1924, 103; AdC, CPC PL, 217, Le Rond to MAÉ, 8 June 1922, 68–70.
55 Richard F. Kuisel, *Capitalism and the State in Modern France: Renovation and Economic Management in the Twentieth Century* (Cambridge: Cambridge University Press, 1981), 67.
56 Landau and Tomaszewski, "Misja," 89–91; Szmidtke, "*Skarboferm*," 48–49.

57 Landau and Tomaszewski, "Misja," 104; AdC, CPC PL, 220, Banque de Silésie. Souscription de la part polonaise, 192; AdC, CPC PL, 278, de Panafieu to Blachet, 9 May 1925, 171.
58 Jacek Luszniewicz, "Etatism of the Economy of the Second Polish Republic in the Period of Parliamentary Democracy: Conditions, Stages, Evaluation (Part 1: 1918–1923)," *Studia i Prace KES* 9, no. 3(35) (2018): 35–60; Jacek Luszniewicz, "Etatism of the Economy of the Second Polish Republic in the Period of Parliamentary Democracy: Conditions, Stages, Evaluation (Part 2: 1923–1926)," *Studia i Prace KES* 9, no. 4(36) (2018): 65–84. Cf. Wojciech Roszkowski, "The Growth of the State Sector in the Polish Economy in the Years 1918–1926," *Journal of European Economic History* 18, no. 1 (1989): 105–26, 108.
59 AdC, CPC PL, 218, Contestation entre la Gouvernment Polonais et la Société Fermière de Tarnowitz, 22 January 1925, 109.
60 Cf. Tadeusz Bernadzikiewicz, *Koncern państwowy w Polsce* (Warszawa: Towarzystwo Wydawnicze Młodych Prawników i Ekonomistów, 1938), 22–23.
61 APK, Skarboferm, 2.11/377, Protokół w przedmiocie dochodzeń co do wymiaru podatku dochodowego dla posła Wojciecha Korfantego na rok 1928, 21 October 1929, 2.
62 APK, Skarboferm, 2.11/373, Michel to Klarner, 20 October 1936, 34–35.
63 Szmidtke, "*Skarboferm*," 84–85.
64 APK, Skarboferm, 2.13/439, Liste de citoyens français, 22 January 1936, 4.
65 Szmidtke, "*Skarboferm*," 155, 249–50.
66 Teichova, *An Economic Background*, 204–6, 211.
67 AdC, CPC PL, 218, de Lasteyrie to Poincaré, 28 February 1924, 55–56.
68 Landau and Tomaszewski, "Misja," 127.
69 AdC, CPC PL, 218, Simon to Herriot, 3 March 1925, 125–26.
70 Landau and Tomaszewski, "Misja," 131.
71 AdC, CPC PL, 218, de Peyerimhoff de Fontenelle and Mercier to Poincaré, 8 December 1923, 36.
72 Szmidtke, "*Skarboferm*," 27.
73 AdC, CPC PL, 212, Leygues to Darcy, 31 December 1920, 52.
74 AdC, CPC PL, 216, Poincaré to Laurent, 21 January 1922, 218; AdC, CPC PL, 217, Poincaré to FLW, 4 November 1922, 169–69v.
75 Jerzy Jaros, *Historia górnictwa węglowego w Zagłębiu Górnośląskim w latach 1914–1945* (Katowice–Kraków: Państwowe Wydawnictwo Naukowe, 1969), 161.
76 Szmidtke, "*Skarboferm*," 77–78, 80, 86, 97–98.
77 Landau and Tomaszewski, "Misja," 136–52.
78 Szmidtke, "*Skarboferm*," 63–5, 78–9; Gołębiowski, *Kapitał*, 203.
79 RPPiH 1938, 1261.
80 Szmidtke, "*Skarboferm*," 12, 242.
81 AdC, CPC PL, 409, Charles-Roux to MAÉ, 3 February 1932, 13; APK, Skarboferm, 2.11/373, Michel to Klarner, 1 October 1936, 39.
82 Szmidtke, "*Skarboferm*," 66–73, 92–93, 114, 166–67, 309.
83 History of the company based on: Archiwum Akt Nowych, Warsaw [henceforth: AAN], Ministerstwo Spraw Zagranicznych [henceforth: MSZ], 3856, Note sure la Société Fermière de Tarnowitz (Tarnoferme) et sur la position du groupe français de cette société, November 1936, 222–28; APK, Polska Huta Skarbowa Ołowiu i Srebra w Strzybnicy, 54, Państwowa Huta Ołowiu i Srebra w Strzybnicy, [1937], 1–14. Cf. Szmidtke, "*Skarboferm*," 93.
84 AdC, CPC PL, 218, Contestation entre la Gouvernment Polonais et la Société Fermière de Tarnowitz, 22 January 1925, 106.
85 AdC, CPC PL, 216, Peyerimhoff to Simon, 28 December 1921, 168; AdC, CPC PL, 217, Liste des administrateurs français designés pour faire partie du conseil de suriveillance de la Société Fermière de Tarnowitz, 16 January 1923, 224.

86 AdC, CPC PL, 218, Contestation entre la Gouvernment Polonais et la Société Fermière de Tarnowitz, 22 January 1925, 106–9.
87 AAN, Akta Wincentego i Władysława Choroszewskich, 52, Świętochowski to Ministerstwo Przemysłu i Handlu, 19 June 1934, np; AAN, MSZ, 3856, Kwiatkowski to Minerais et Métaux, 8 July 1930, 228–9. Cf. Władysław Marian Zawadzki, "Polityka finansowa w okresie 1931–1935," ed. Zbigniew Landau and Jerzy Tomaszewski, *Kwartalnik Historyczny* 6, no. 1 (1965): 127–51.
88 I explore this topic in Jerzy Łazor, "'Broń dyplomatyczna pierwszej rangi'? Powstanie polsko-francuskiego Banku Śląskiego SA po I wojnie światowej," *Roczniki Dziejów Społecznych i Gospodarczych* 81 (2020): 289–320, http://doi.org/10.12775/RDSG.2020.10.
89 Wojciech Morawski, *Słownik historyczny bankowości polskiej do 1939 roku* (Warszawa: Muza SA, 1998), 137–38.
90 AD, CPC PL, 220, de Panafieu to MAÉ, 8 January 1922, 102.
91 Wacław Konderski, *Z działalności banków polskich w latach 1928–1935: Wspomnienia*, (Warszawa: Książka i Wiedza, 1962), 71–74.
92 Landau and Tomaszewski, "Misja," 169–210; Szmidtke, *"Skarboferm,"* 104.
93 And indeed, the project is still among the company's files: APK, Zakłady Hohenlohego SA Wełnowiec, 1567, Projet d'Avenant à la Convention Franco-Polonaise du 22 Mars 1921, n.d., 35–37.
94 Polish Institute and Sikorski Museum, London, B.I. 116/50, Zeznania Inż. L. Małeckiego, 14 February 1940, 705.
95 AdC, CPC PL, 218, Entreprises privées en Haute-Silésie, 17 December 1923, 43.
96 AdC, CPC PL, 212, Note pour Monsieur Laroche. Conventions franco-polonaises à la Haute-Silésie, 27 May 1922, 259–59b.
97 *Polskie Kopalnie Skarbowe na Górnym Śląsku Spółka Dzierżawna – Spółka Akcyjna w Katowicach. Sprawozdanie Zarządu oraz Rady Nadzorczej z Działalności Spółki za rok operacyjny 1937*, Katowice 1938, 3.
98 Landau and Tomaszewski, "Misja," 122; Szmidtke, "*Skarboferm*," 105.
99 Pieter M. Judson, "Seeing the Habsburg Monarchy as a Global Empire in an Age of Self-Styled Nation-States," *Geschichte Und Region/Storia e Regione* 30, no. 1 (2021): 223–29, 225.
100 APK, Skarboferm, 2.11/377, Decision of Najwyższy Trybunał Administracyjny, 2467/27 and 2468/27, 5 June 1928, 30; APK, Skarboferm, 2.11/374, Korfanty's Office to Skarboferm, 28 May 1925, 23; Przewłocki, *Wojciech Korfanty*, 80–81.
101 Morawski, *Słownik*, 110–11, 179.
102 AdC, CPC PL, 220, Le Rond to MAÉ, 24 March 1922, 169.
103 AdC, CPC PL, 218, Konfanty, 28 February 1925, 116.
104 Jan Przewłocki, *Wojciech Korfanty: polityka, wzloty i niepowodzenia* (Kielce: Szumacher, 1993), 78, 83.
105 AdC, CPC PL, 216, Le Rond to MAÉ, 19 January 1922, 205–9.
106 Szmidtke, "*Skarboferm*," 161–66.
107 Przewłocki, *Wojciech Korfanty*, 89; APK, Skarboferm, 2.11/377, Korfanty to Skarboferm, 27 February 1929, 23.
108 APK, Skarboferm, 2.11/377, Korfanty to Skarboferm, 23 September 1927, 48.
109 APK, Skarboferm, 2.11/376, Orzeczenie buchaltera Kazimierza Motylewskiego, 20 March 1937, 11–27.
110 Grzegorz Bębnik, Sebastian Rosenbaum, and Bartosz Węcki, *Wojciech Korfanty: 1873–1939*, 2nd ed. (Warszawa, Instytut Pamięci Narodowej, 2023), 57.
111 Zbigniew Landau and Bronisława Skrzeszewska, eds., *Wojciech Korfanty przed Sądem Marszałkowskim: Dokumenty* (Katowice: Wydawnictwo "Śląsk," 1964), VI, 165–68; Adam Pragier, *Czas przeszły dokonany*, edited by Andrzej Friszke and Ewa Pejaś (Warszawa: Muzeum Historii Polski, 2018), 67–82; Szmidtke, "*Skarboferm*," 70.

112 Bębnik, Rosenbaum, and Węcki, *Wojciech Korfanty*, 53–56.
113 Szmidtke, "*Skarboferm*," 168–70.
114 Szmidke, *"Skarboferm,"* 30–31.
115 Landau and Tomaszewski, "Misja," 44.
116 Grzyb, *Narodowościowo polityczne aspekty*, 32, 69; Szmidke, *"Skarboferm,"* 59.
117 Landau and Tomaszewski, "Misja," 202.
118 Landau and Tomaszewski, "Misja," 206.
119 AdC, CPC PL, 217, de Panafieu to MAÉ, 3 June 1922, 66. AdC, CPC PL, 217, MAÉ to Ministère des Finances and Ministère des Travaux publics, 29 June 1922, 82–82v; AdC, CPC PL, 217, Conversation avec M. de Peyerimhoff, 9 August 1922, 100–100v.
120 Tooley, *National Identity*, 141.
121 Wandycz, *France*, 212; Patelski, "Henry Le Rond," 58; Tooley, *National Identity*, 206–207; Szmidtke, "*Skarboferm*," 47, 168.
122 Szmidtke, "*Skarboferm*," 180.
123 Mihout-Natar, "L'intervention," 732–739; Zbigniew Landau and Jerzy Tomaszewski, *Sprawa żyrardowska. Przyczynek do dziejów kapitałów obcych w Polsce międzywojennej* (Warszawa: Książka i Wiedza, 1983), 83–84; Gołębiowski, *Kapitał*, 249.
124 AdC, CPC PL, 261, Laroche to Brianda, 4 IV 1928 r., 221–21v.
125 Szmidtke, "*Skarboferm*," 182.
126 AdC, CPC PL, 238, Noulens to Sergent, 3 February 1919, 14–14v; AdC, CPC PL, 251, Noulens to Pichon, 7 June 1919, 117.
127 Georges-Henri Soutou, "La politique économique de la France en Pologne (1920–1924)," *Revue historique* 251, no. 1 (1974): 85–116, 96; AdC, CPC PL, 238, Note pour le ministre des Affaires étrangères "Groupement des industriels Français en Pologne," 25 [May] 1919, 18–19.
128 AdC, CPC PL, 238, Eugène Pralon to MAÉ, 27 February 1920, 45–46.
129 Landau and Tomaszewski, "Misja," 120.
130 CAÉF, B 31.942, Poincaré to de Lasteyrie, 30 November 1922, n.p.
131 Rejestr TERYT, Główny Urząd Statystyczny, https://eteryt.stat.gov.pl/eTeryt/rejestr_teryt/aktualnosci/aktualnosci.aspx, access: 30 July 2023.
132 Szmidtke, "*Skarboferm*," 155, 177–78.
133 "None of our agreements suggest that we sold Poland our support in Upper Silesia. It was the Polish government that asked us for help keeping the Treasury Mines running, and if it did so early, that's because it wanted to avoid any interruptions in their functioning" (AdC, CPC PL, 212, Note sur les accords franco-polonais relatifs aux exploitations minières de Haute-Silésie, 5 August 1921, 191).
134 Zbigniew Landau, *Polskie zagraniczne pożyczki państwowe 1918–1926* (Warszawa: Książka i Wiedza, 1961); Landau and Tomaszewski, "Misja," 171–82, 225.
135 Mihout-Natar, "L'intervention," 733.
136 Landau and Tomaszewski, "Misja," 108.

7 Foreign investment and domestic politics in interwar Poland

The case of French capital in Żyrardów

Ignacy Matuszewski fell. His shot had just missed Wacław Lednicki from the agreed upon distance of 20 paces and the younger man had better aim. Two weeks earlier, on 8 August 1934, Matuszewski published an article in the government daily *Gazeta Polska* (of which he was editor-in-chief), attacking an agreement between Polish shareholders of the linen factory Zakłady Żyrardowskie and its French owner, Marcel Boussac. The ensuing press campaign attacked Lednicki's father Aleksander for facilitating the agreement, driving him to suicide. To protect his father's honour, Wacław challenged Matuszewski to a widely publicized duel. In later years, which saw Wacław become a professor of Slavic literature at Harvard and Berkeley, he described the duel as one of his life's happiest moments. Yet Matuszewski was lucky. The bullet bounced off his fly button, and the politician fell from pain rather than injury.[1]

The duel was part of the most important conflict concerning foreign capital in interwar Poland, centred around a linen factory. Founded in 1833, it became the seed of Żyrardów, a new town named after the French engineer and inventor Philippe de Girard. While he had worked for the company and contributed his inventions to the industrial process, the French otherwise had little to do with the factory until after World War I. Since 1857, it belonged to two Austrian traders, Karl Hielle and Karl August Dittrich, with their families remaining major shareholders once it became a joint-stock company in 1885. It grew fast, gaining near-monopoly in linen production in Russian Poland. It employed some 9,000 workers, bringing shareholders tidy dividends (8 per cent in 1913). By 1931, Żyrardów, known as the Red City for its distinctive brick architecture (for which it is seeking UNESCO recognition today), reached some 25,000 inhabitants, dependent on the factory for jobs.[2]

The conflict surrounding Żyrardów started with the French takeover of the factory in 1923, and continued with varying intensity until the Poles took it back in 1936. Together with the similar, if less dramatic plight of the Warsaw power plant (Compagnie d'Électricité de Varsovie), it dominated Polish discussions on French capital in the 1920s and 1930s. It captured the imagination of the press-reading public, and engaged diplomats and politicians in a seemingly unending cycle of interventions, as evidenced by thousands of pages left in French and Polish archives.

DOI: 10.4324/9781003375586-7

As I show, while the two companies represented only 1/30th of all French capital directly invested in Poland, politicians in Warsaw used both for domestic goals.[3] In 1924, the fate of Żyrardów served the Polish centre-left to attack the right, in 1932, after a murder of the company's managing director, it fuelled the struggle between the opposition and the ruling Sanacja. By 1934, its future depended on internal conflicts within the ruling Polish camp, resulting in the duel with which we started this chapter. Ultimately, it is impossible to understand the fate of the company without resorting to domestic politics. At the same time, it informed the changing Polish attitudes towards foreign capital.

While this chapter deals with a single company, its story illustrates wider trends in Franco–Polish relations. On the one hand, it shows the excesses of foreign capital functioning within an asymmetrical relationship – and this angle was the topic of most Polish research into the company. On other hand, is underlines the precariousness of foreign property rights – especially of companies such as Żyrardów, which did not form part of a complex value chain. Moreover, it shows the limits of Paris's intervention in the mid-1930s, as the Franco–Polish relationship deteriorated.[4]

7.1 The Żyrardów Panama

During World War I, the plant in Żyrardów shared the fate of other industrial sites in Russian Poland. The retreating Russians either evacuated or destroyed many machines in 1915, and the occupying German forces subsequently requisitioned much of what remained. By autumn 1918, the number of workers fell to only 525, and the losses were estimated at 20 million roubles, or over 50 million francs germinal.[5] With Russian shareholders cut off by the revolution, the Hielle and Ditrich group, now in Czechoslovakia, regained a de facto controlling interest in the company.[6] Unwilling to commit resources to rebuilding the factory, the board shut down its operations in May 1919. In response, Polish authorities temporarily took over management of the company, and over the next four years rebuilt much of the factory, based on government loans equalling some 47 million Polish marks, or 2.6 million francs germinal. In 1923 production was back to 70 per cent of its pre-war level.

After the Poles sequestered the factory, the Hielle and Dittrich group decided to sell their shares. In late 1919 they found an interested party in a financial group led by Marcel Boussac, a French businessman who had amassed significant wealth during World War I, and whose extensive textile empire had notable political backing.[7] The group, headed by Boussac's two companies (Société des Manufactures de Senones and Société de Comptoir de l'Industrie Cotonnière), included the Generals Edmund Ferry and Henri Le Rond. The French then contacted Warsaw to ask whether the authorities would lift sequestration if the purchase proceeded. Their representative General Ferry proposed, among other things, an equal division of shares between French and Polish owners, and reportedly suggested a link between the takeover and French military supplies.[8] The Poles were apprehensive about the proposal, but could do little due to the presence of Le Rond, and Boussac's political backing. Finally, in April 1920, the French group purchased the shares for well under their market value.[9]

Warsaw long resisted pressure to transfer control to Boussac's group, with negotiations lasting into 1923.[10] The Poles feared that the group represented little more than speculative capital, and would not continue rebuilding the factory. In consequence, they wanted the French to pledge themselves to repay government loans, regain pre-war levels of production, and Polonize the company by letting Polish investors acquire 50 per cent of its shares; up from 19 per cent.[11] The loans remained the most difficult problem. Due to inflation and (in 1923) hyperinflation their real value fell. The Poles insisted on valorization, while Boussac's group argued that the loans had been given without such clauses, and thus the company should only pay the nominal value. For a long time, no agreement seemed possible.

The situation changed when the right-wing cabinet of Wincenty Witos took office in 1923. Władysław Kucharski, its Minister of Industry and Trade (and later of Treasury), lobbied by big Polish capital and the French, soon agreed to the takeover. The minister demanded the French pay back 22 billion Polish marks (later reduced to 20 billion), the same amount which the Poles asked for in April 1923. Back then this was roughly equal to the original 2.6 million francs germinal, but by August 1923, when Kucharski finalized the agreement, the value dropped to less than a fifth of that amount.[12] Boussac's group assumed control of the company on 2 November 1923, at the height of hyperinflation.[13]

Arguably, the government had no legal basis for insisting on valorization. The agreement was a compromise, which allowed the resolution of a long-festering conflict. However, the Ministry of Industry and Trade then allowed the French to borrow the money they were required to pay from the state-owned bank Pocztowa Kasa Oszczędności, once again without a valorization clause. The company would finance repayment of this new loan by issuing stock. With raging inflation, it was easy for Boussac to pay back the nominal amount, ultimately equal to some 24 thousand gold francs. The Poles thus effectively gave up on trying to recuperate the rebuilding costs of the factory. It was a shockingly one-sided solution, with no gains for Warsaw.

Few government decisions provoked comparable fury. The agreement was brought to light in April 1924 in Parliament. A group of over a hundred MPs, mostly from the Polish Socialist Party (Polska Partia Socjalistyczna, PPS), wanted to put Władysław Kucharski on trial before the State Tribunal. Jędrzej Moraczewski, the first Polish prime minister in 1918, led the group, attacking Kucharski in a long speech. The composition of the attacking side, which included Kazimierz Bartel, the future Prime Minister under Piłsudski, underlined the motion's political character. The clash over Żyrardów was part of a wide-ranging power struggle between the right-wing National Democracy (or Endecja), and the forces grouped around Marshall Józef Piłsudski, then in self-imposed exile in suburban Sulejówek.

The first phase of the Żyrardów Affair was thus a matter of internal Polish politics. It was the "Monstrous crime of Mr Kucharski committed upon the State Treasury" (as a popular newspaper from Cracow dubbed it), which was under scrutiny, rather than whatever the French had done or would do.[14] Positions were divided along party lines. The right defend Kucharski, and the left attacked him, coining the term "Żyrardów Panama."[15] After the first bitter debate, the Sejm decided to investigate the charges against Kucharski via a special parliamentary committee (which included both Moraczewski and Bartel). As the MPs studied the issue of Żyrardów in April, May, and July 1924, discussions adopted a distinctly sectarian air. Finally, on 16 December 1924, the matter returned before the Sejm, where Moraczewski presented the committee's position, reiterating the motion to put Kucharski on trial before the State Tribunal. Despite convincing evidence against the former minister, the centre-left did not control enough votes: with 175 MPs voting for, 138 against, and 33 abstaining, the motion fell short of the required 60 per cent majority. As a result, Kucharski never got a trial.

When the motion appeared in Parliament, Kucharski would not comment on it, arguing that it was "political and personal in character."[16] It is easy to argue that this was at least partially true. Due to the scarcity of capital in Poland after the war and the extent of destruction suffered by its industry, state loans with no valorization clauses were used to support struggling companies during inflation.[17] The loan to Boussac's group in 1923 was more surprising, if not truly exceptional in Polish practice. The untypical element of Żyrardów's situation was the group which profited from these state funds: new foreign investors rather than pre-war owners.

The case also saw multiple, ultimately unproven allegations of corruption or self-serving decisions from Kurcharski and other important Polish figures. The latter included Andrzej Wierzbicki, the head of the big industry lobby group Lewiatan (Centralny Związek Polskiego Przemysłu, Górnictwa, Handlu i Finansów). He first advised the minister to let the French assume control of the company, and later sat on its board.[18] While historians remain unconvinced that corruption had taken place, Żyrardów certainly tried to improve its position in Poland by hiring prominent political figures, including former Prime Minister Leopold Skulski in 1924.

The political conflict did not affect the situation in the company. Żyrardów issued new stock, which Boussac's group purchased for itself via intermediaries. This included shares which, according to the agreement from 1923, should have been reserved for the Poles, but the company denied this had been the case.[19] The new owners repaid the nominal value of the loans, and to add insult to injury, their representatives complained that no-one had paid them indemnities for war damages.[20] This issue was the object of litigation in Poland, ending up in the Supreme Court in 1929. Żyrardów lost, but its owners refused to comply, protected by French diplomats (who, as ever, relied on conditionality, linking the matter to, for instance, the Silesia-Gdynia railway bond issue). The matter ended in a one-sided agreement in August 1932 between the two governments. Paris forced it by linking Żyrardów to a new commercial treaty.[21]

7.2 The Żyrardów tragedy[22]

The agreement did not end the Żyrardów Affair. By the time it was signed, the focus of the conflict had already shifted towards the new owners' management. The Poles accused Boussac of exploiting workers and underreporting profits, and thus avoiding taxes and paying dividends to Polish shareholders. According to documents from the 1930s, the company transferred abroad some 23 million złoty before sequestration in 1934.[23] Among other schemes, Żyrardów's foreign managers purchased weaving patters and materials from France at exorbitant prices. When accused of such tricks, the French reacted by asking diplomats for help.[24] In 1926 workers in Żyrardów went on strike, and the tide of public opinion turned against the company after 1927, when Żyrardów's municipal authorities published a memorandum attacking the French.[25] Jules Laroche observed in 1928 that "there are few Polish services today, where you can utter the name Żyrardów without having to hear disagreeable things about French attitudes in Poland."[26] The company's policies turned even worse as the Great Depression hit. Mass layoffs in the one-factory town, coupled with reductions to the company's social spending, deeply affected the municipality and the worker community.[27] By late 1931, the press violently attacked both Żyrardów and the French-owned power plant in Warsaw, similarly mired in long litigation.[28]

The problem with the power plant, ran by Compagnie d'Électricité de Varsovie, also dates to the consequences of the war. The firm had been sequestered and plundered by German occupiers. After the war, the owners were reluctant to take it back without significant compensation, which the new Polish administrators were unwilling to pay. The French returned only once the Poles had put the plant back on its feet and stabilized their currency, which brought electricity prices back up. At the same time, the owners asked for their concession to be prolonged by 20 years, and for further guarantees concerning electricity prices based on the goods, rights, and shares convention discussed in Chapter 3.[29] Since the Poles did not agree, the French resorted to international arbitration. Throughout the 1930s, the Compagnie would win, but the Poles refused to accept the arbiter's decisions, arguing instead that the French had committed fraud. The result were many aggressive articles by the Warsaw press.

Attacks on French companies were nothing new. Throughout the 1920s, anger at the French slowly bubbled up throughout Poland, with the most widely-commented reaction to their companies' policies in the form of Juliusz Kaden-Bandrowski's 1928–1929 novel *Black Wings* (*Czarne skrzydła*).[30] The author – Piłsudski's former *aide-de-camp* – described a fictional French-owned coal mine in the Dąbrowa Basin as a system of violence (with sexual undercurrents), which permeated all strata of the local society. It started with the stripping of Polish resources by foreign cartels, and continued with the sadism of the company's French director towards local managers. The managers were in turn cruel to physical workers, over whom they held the power of life and death due to rampant unemployment. The cycle was completed when the workers lynched the director by throwing him down a burning mineshaft. Kaden-Bandrowski showed that the system debased the "natives" (as the French called the Poles in the novel), weakened social ties, and eroded institutions. The novel, loosely based on events in the mine Reden, mirrored the more radical anti-French press articles from the Dąbrowa Basin, where journalists focused on colonial-like exploitation, writing that French directors "play the role of pioneers of civilization, believing that they are in Cameroon and that the Poles are black slaves."[31]

Kaden-Bandrowski's literally vision proved prescient in 1932. On 26 April 1932, Julian Blachowski, a former clerk at the company, shot his old boss, Żyrardów's managing director Gaston Koehler-Badin. Within two days, almost every newspaper in the country reported on the tragedy, and soon dozens of authors found "excellent reasons to excuse the killer," before turning their attention to French policies in the factory.[32] In Żyrardów, reporters discovered a "city of the living dead," "the capital of penury and unemployment," brought to its knees by the owners of the factory.[33] The press frenzy subsided somewhat after a fortnight, only to return in October, when, after short court proceedings, Blachowski was sentenced to five years in prison. Newspapers described the trial in detail, and continued to report on the factory. Short news notes appeared next to well-researched takedowns, high quality reportage, and poetry, including an early poem by future Nobel prize winner Czesław Miłosz.[34]

The murder heralded a new phase of the Żyrardów Affair. The number and character of articles on the company shocked the French. For Jules Laroche the coverage was "francophobic" and "abominable," for representatives of the company: "false," "violent," and "perverse."[35] It quickly warranted interventions by the French Ambassador at the Polish Ministry for Foreign Affairs. Laroche met with both minister August Zaleski, and the deputy minister Józef Beck, aiming to limit press discussions on the plant.[36] The Poles preventively censored some articles (notably, two in the left-wing *Robotnik*), but the press continued its attacks. This should not be surprising. As I discussed in Chapter 2, 1932 was close to the nadir of interwar Franco–Polish relations. Warsaw did not consult Paris before signing the non-aggression treaty with the USSR on July 25, and Beck replaced the pro-French Zaleski on November 2, directly after Blachowski's sentencing.

The great abundance of press commentaries on the murder allows a reconstruction of how the conflict interacted with Polish politics, and of the evolving discourse on foreign capital. It also provides a glimpse into Polish semi-peripheral identity within the global capitalist order.[37] Within days of the murder, the press linked the tragedy to Żyrardów's plight. This interpretation raised questions about the Polish state. Was the situation in the factory the result of the authorities' incompetence, or was something more fundamental at play here? Why did such exploitation occur at the hands of investors from Poland's most important ally? Finally – what did it say about Poland's position in the world?

Asking questions about responsibility for the murder allowed various parties to attack their opponents. Similarly to the parliamentary scandal, foreign capital was incorporated into broader domestic conflicts and used as a weapon. However, in 1932 the Polish political scene was different, producing surprisingly alliances. The right, with the dominant position of the National Democrats, still struggled against the left, but after 1926 both groups were in opposition to the ruling Sanacja. Józef Piłsudski had started his career in the underground Polish Socialist Party, and enjoyed the support of the socialists during the 1926 coup. Nonetheless, he soon distanced himself from his erstwhile comrades. Both the socialists and the National Democrats became a vocal if powerless opposition in the increasingly authoritarian state.[38] Both thus used the opportunity provided by Blachowski's deed to accuse the government of mismanagement. This is why newspapers of the two parties, usually strongly opposed to each other, published very similar articles, underlining the failure of the authorities in the town. With the government's neglect, "big business" and "anonymous capital" (from the French *société anonyme* or joint-stock company) dominated Żyrardów, enslaving the town, and exploiting workers.[39] For the ruling Sanacja, the situation was more dire, as it was difficult to argue that authorities had not failed at least to some extent. As a result, government-leaning papers focused on attacking the factory's owners, which, by reference to the 1923 takeover of the company, allowed a jab at the right.[40]

While some commentators treated Żyrardów as an outlier, radical voices offered a more systemic diagnosis. Stanisław Piasecki from the National Democratic daily *ABC* saw the situation in Żyrardów as an element of the global economic system, the "monstrous factory under the sign that reads, 'standardization, rationalization, Taylorization,'"[41] built on the domination of big capital, which ignored borders and national interests. To counter this all-consuming behemoth, nations should create a new capitalism of small, local companies, which would contribute to domestic interests and remain loyal. In this Piasecki showed influences of nationalist writing and Catholic corporatism. The writer Paweł Hulka-Laskowski, known for his charming translation of *The Good Soldier Švejk*, expressed surprisingly similar sentiments. One of the leading voices on Żyrardów, Hulka-Laskowski argued that the town was under attack from "super capitalism," a system where capital dominates labour. In such a world, profits from production are concentrated in the richest countries, while losses from restructuring, unemployment, and worker poverty disproportionately affect the poor.[42] Laskowski also referred to Catholic social teaching, and suggested that a revolution might be necessary. Both writers, coming from very different political backgrounds and otherwise unlikely to agree in any debate, were finding ways to voice their objections to the global economic system. While Laskowski published some of his articles in pro-government newspapers, these discussions did not yet herald a significant change of policy towards foreign capital.[43]

To understand the situation in Żyrardów–and the role of its French owners–the Poles needed a way to conceptualize it. Commentators turned to what they knew. For some, the relationship between France and Poland seemed feudal. Almost immediately, however, Boussac's policies were interpreted through the lens of colonialism. "Enslaved by alien capital," declared the title of an article in the left-wing daily *Robotnik*, while another from the popular press called for the end of French slavery.[44] Other editors protested that "foreign mercenaries" ruled "over a piece of Polish land like over a conquered country, like over African soil," treating Polish workers "like natives from Tonkin and Madagascar."[45] The outbursts again shocked the French. Amusingly, the Commercial Attaché in Warsaw felt compelled to add in his memo, after rejecting all attacks on the company: "everyone knows that France has the most beautiful colonial empire in Africa."[46]

Commentators linked French actions to colonialism and slavery not because they rejected the colonial system or racial hierarchies; the Poles treated them as natural, and aspired to their own colonial holdings.[47] With the global economic hierarchy closely linked to colonialism, Polish protests reflected the wider semi-peripheral position of their country. As Kathryn Ciancia observed, the Poles were aware "of their intermediate position on the European civilizational hierarchy."[48] They felt that the French in Żyrardów treated them badly, because Boussac's managers used methods reserved for the colonies and "natives" that lived in them.

The murder of Żyrardów's director thus served as a conduit for a reassessment of the Polish elites' global identity. All their rationalization and explanation strategies led to the same conclusion: they were modern, European, and white, and the French had failed to observe Poland's place in the world. It also suggested a failure of the government's modernization project. In 1932, these interpretations were observable in public discourse, but the authorities still abstained from engaging in the conflict.

7.3 The international conflict

The final phase of the Żyrardów Affair saw Polish authorities gradually move in. A year after the murder, the Poles started a new press campaign against Żyrardów. *Gazeta Polska*, as ever, led the way, printing a de facto declaration of the government's changing approach to foreign capital.[49] Its author acknowledged the country's need for foreign investment and argued:

> no-one places capital in Poland because of our beautiful eyes, but because it's more advantageous. And since our geographic situation makes us seem less safe, we need to compensate for this with a slightly higher return on investment. Foreign credit will always be more expensive for us than for our western neighbours.

But if the country provided such advantages, it had the right to demand fair play. Investors should not "treat Poland like a newly discovered and savagely exploited colony at the end of the world." Polish society needed to profit from FDI, something which had not happened in Żyrardów.

The campaign, organized by parts of the ruling regime, caught the Polish Ministry of Foreign Affairs by surprise, as did the repeated French interventions in favour of the company. The Deputy Minister Jan Szembek sent a letter to the Ministry of Industry and Trade, asking for an explanation for the attacks.[50] After reaching an agreement with Boussac in 1932, the Ministry of Foreign Affairs would have preferred to work the matter out with Laroche, rather than hurt Franco–Polish relations.[51] Now the outcome of the Żyrardów Affair would increasingly depend on internal politics within the Sanacja group. Nonetheless, by early 1934 public opinion was so anti-French, that a minor technical incident in one of Skarboferm's mines caused by a French-produced cog provoked a xenophobic barrage against products, production methods, and technicians coming from Poland's Western ally.[52] There was political capital to be made from attacks on France.

The Poles coordinated their next attack on Żyrardów well, using minority Polish shareholders, who resented their negligible impact on the company, and the lack of dividends since the French takeover.[53] The Polish economist and government official Feliks Młynarski managed their actions, which culminated in an attack on Boussac during a general assembly of the company on 22 January 1934. Using a legal ruse, the Poles forced a formal condemnation of Boussac's methods, but with the French majority firmly entrenched, the confrontation ended in a stalemate. Then came the press campaign, led by an article in *Gazeta Polska*, an extension of the declaration quoted above. Heralding a new approach to foreign capital, its author declared that Żyrardów was no longer a symbol of foreign exploitation, but an "anachronism."[54] Foreign owners would either learn how to work legally or lose their businesses, no matter the international repercussions. In a jab at international finance and money doctors, the author added: "The time when the opinion or this or that financial magician could influence a State's financial situation is done…Now you don't need to give two hoots about their views – provided you observe your commitments." Five days later, during a discussion in the Financial Commission in Parliament, one of the key Sanacja officials (and leading member of the so-called Colonel faction) Bogusław Miedziński repeated these arguments, singling out French capitalists, who first "poached," then hid behind their ambassador.[55] Finally, a court in Warsaw recognized both the plight of minority shareholders, and the problems with the company's books. On 8 March 1934, it ordered judicial sequestration of the company until the end of legal action concerning the general assembly on January 22.

The French were angry and confused. It did not escape them that parallel to the attacks on Żyrardów, the Poles signed a non-aggression treaty with Nazi Germany. Some thought that perhaps Warsaw's economic talks with London had succeeded, making the Poles less susceptible to French arguments. Soon, however, they witnessed a reformulation of Polish policy. After the sequestration of Żyrardów, another press campaign followed, with an article in *Gazeta Polska* restating the new approach to foreign capital. Foreigners were welcome, but malfeasance would be punished, no matter the geopolitical context.

At roughly the same time, the Poles moved against other companies. They sequestered the Warsaw power plant, and the German-controlled heavy industry giant Wspólnota Interesów (Interessen Gemeinschaft) in Upper Silesia. Soon afterwards the government took over the aviation works of Škoda's subsidiary in Warsaw, which we discussed in Chapter 4. Jules Laroche saw these attacks, and the support they received from the public, as self-serving. As the change of policy "resulted in letting go of foreign managers, it met the aspirations of Poles, who covet such well-paid jobs."[56] Nonetheless, the move against Wspólnota Interesów, despite German-Polish relations being at their interwar zenith, surprised him.

Boussac and the Poles then exchanged blows. The French businessman challenged the Warsaw court's decision in Poland, and his company sued the compulsory administration in a court in Paris. The Poles did not show up and Boussac won, but this was little more than a symbolic victory. The French deluged their authorities with demands for help, while the Poles tried to limit the access of French shareholders to a planned general assembly. Polish-sponsored posters attacking Boussac appeared on walls in Paris. The French hired Price Waterhouse & Co to look into the company's books, but the state administrators refused to hand them over, as the Poles started hinting at a criminal trial of Żyrardów's managers.[57]

So far, Polish authorities steered and shaped the conflict, even if the severity of some press reactions caught them by surprise. It provided a way to channel social discontent caused by the Great Depression. But during the summer of 1934, the French took the initiative with the surprising help of Polish minority shareholders. The latter were seeking compensation rather than conflict, and gladly accepted settling out of court.[58] Negotiations took place in July 1934 in a surprisingly friendly atmosphere. The respected liberal political activist and lawyer Aleksander Lednicki represented Boussac, who later came to Poland and concluded a preliminary agreement, signed on 3 August 1934 in Biskupice. The French were willing to compromise, so the result was favourable to the Poles, and initial Polish press reactions were positive. The press declared victory, and gave credit to the Minister of Industry and Trade, Henryk Floyar-Rajchman.

The celebrations were premature. The agreement deprived the Polish authorities of a powerful political weapon–and they fought back. On 7 August 1934, three pro-government newspapers attacked the agreement. On the following day Ignacy Matuszewski published an article of "unprecedented violence," bringing the press campaign "to a paroxysm" (and the author to the duel with which I opened the chapter).[59] The piece was a broadside attack on Boussac and the agreement, which he likened to an unwelcome pre-emptive amnesty granted to the French owner. "The Żyrardów Affair is a matter of foreign capital's ethical norms in Poland." It needed to be a demonstration of acceptable and punishable behaviour, and its outcome would determine the state of the Polish industry: either healthy and dependable, or "speculative, thieving, plundering." Laroche protested with little success. Józef Beck declared that he agreed with the editor-in-chief that the agreement represented, "a manoeuvre of Boussac aimed at embarrassing the Polish government before the public opinion."[60]

Żyrardów's management was justifiably worried about the sudden attacks and a potential criminal investigation. And indeed, within days the Poles launched one, arresting two foreign managers – commercial director Lucien Caen and general secretary Jean Vermeersch – and charging them with acting against the interests of their employer. Once Laroche intervened on their behalf, the ambassador himself became a target of press attacks. *Gazeta Polska* chastised him for "intervening in the judicial procedure."[61] The official press agency Iskra published a similar takedown, declaring "that certain French actors, based on their colonial experience, would like to treat allied Poland like a new European Morocco."[62] It was a clear signal that the Poles wished to consider Żyrardów an internal affair.

The reversal of policy attests to rising tensions within the Sanacja camp. They erupted into a broader struggle for power once Piłsudski died nine months later. Matuszewski represented the dominant group of the so-called Colonels (Pułkownicy), formed by military circles, generally with roots in the World War I Legionnaire movement. Młynarski – a recognized expert on international finance – was disliked by Piłsudski, and after 1935 tried to reestablish his contacts with the Polish opposition.[63] Laroche pointed out that Matuszewski's outrage was partially due to voices from the opposition pointing out the Sanacja's hypocrisy. After all, the group had come to power in the 1926 bloody coup under the banners of "cleansing" Poland – or draining the swamp to use the modern American parlance. Now its members were supposedly taking money from foreigners to protect their ill-gotten gains.[64]

"There is the making of a good quarrel here," the British Foreign Office surmised.[65] The arrests stood out in the 20 years of Poland's policy towards foreign capital, and were likely to provoke the French. Laroche thought that both policy and domestic politics informed Polish actions.[66] They were a step towards Polonizing the industry, in line with the country's rising economic nationalism. At the same time, an attack on Żyrardów allowed the authorities to "give satisfaction to passions of a large part of the public opinion." Moreover, government circles saw the Biskupice agreement as a political attack against them. Hence the ensuing purge: the persecution of Poles somehow linked to the company, including the arrest of its former president Henryk Potocki.[67]

The French were stunned. In a long series of telegrams, Laroche noted the change in tone of the government press and asked for instructions.[68] Officials at the Quai d'Orsay were convinced of the Poles' bad faith, but nonetheless asked the Ministry of Finance to help them judge the veracity of accusations against the company.[69] At the same time, they chastised Ambassador Chłapowski in Paris, and instructed Laroche to intervene "officially and directly" in Warsaw.[70] During his meetings with Beck, Laroche learned that the Polish government was already censoring the most vicious attacks against the French, and it would make sure that the press did not hurt Franco–Polish relations.[71] Nonetheless, milder attacks continued, and the Poles entrenched themselves in accusations against the Żyrardów company, despite multiple interventions, including talks between Beck and Louis Barthou in Geneva in early September.[72] Boussac himself could do little in Poland. As he continued to be a target of attacks, he used his connections to get multiple articles presenting his position published in French newspapers and in *Financial News*.[73] Finally, On October 6, a Polish court decided to prolong the sequestration, thereby formally annulling the Biskupice agreement.[74]

Whatever the truth about Żyrardów, the Poles won few friends and influenced no Frenchmen by incarcerating two managers. The matter reached the French Parliament, where letters from the managers' families made a tremendous impression.[75] Initially, the most important goal of French diplomats was getting the managers free. This proved difficult, as the bail for the seriously ill Vermeersch was posted at 5 million złoty, higher than the share capital of many French companies in Poland, and at 0.3 million for Caen.[76] No matter how understanding Beck seemed of Laroche's arguments, and how much he promised to find a just solution, it still took many months.[77] As the French told their Polish peers in secret, both the government in Paris, and the families of the arrested were fruitlessly trying to get Boussac to pay the bail. Finally, after dozens of interventions, including that of a human rights organization, the bail was lowered, the managers were let free on Christmas Eve 1934, and soon allowed to leave the country.[78] The Quai d'Orsay promptly sent out notifications of the fact to 16 deputies, former ministers, and other notables who had lobbied for Caen and Vermeersch. No other Franco–Polish conflict produced a similar reaction.

With the managers out of prison, the most contentious element of the Żyrardów conflict disappeared. Laroche thought that the Poles' position signalled a will to de-escalate. He tried to convince the Quai d'Orsay to follow the same road, rather than deliver an aggressive note suggested by Boussac, who again tried to leverage his political position.[79] The situation stalled with a series of important changes in Franco–Polish relations: the visit of French Minister Pierre Laval, the nomination of Léon Noël as the new ambassador in Warsaw, and finally the death of Piłsudski.[80] Once normal relations resumed, Noël took the same position as Laroche, resisting his instructions to deliver the note. His meetings with Beck confirmed that both sides wanted to keep the matter calm, without litigation or press campaigns.[81] After a further government reshuffle in Warsaw, by November 1935 the Poles decided to end the issue (of "nationwide importance") by buying Żyrardów from Boussac.[82] With a dearth of private investors, the state would do it through intermediaries. Thus the Poles (ostensibly representing private buyers) went to Paris to talk with Boussac's organization. The latter quickly agreed to sell the factory and drop any financial claims. However, it took almost a year and multiple rounds of talks to settle the final price.[83]

The negotiations in 1935 and 1936 showed a curious mix of international and domestic politics. Polish representatives complained that the constant barrage of sensationalist articles in their press made the talks difficult. At the same time, Warsaw authorities, having become hostages to the public perception of the conflict, could not show themselves as too conciliatory, and wanted the French press to avoid the topic.[84] As Noël explained, "With rare exceptions, everyone in Poland is sincerely convinced that the Polish shareholders of Żyrardów were robbed by Mr Boussac and his collaborators."[85] The French pushed Boussac to settle, while continuing to leverage all other negotiations to pressure Warsaw to do the same, and the problems of the factory were among the most important topics discussed by the two capitals.[86] French pressure included threats to cut financial aid supporting the Polish monetary system. Minister Eugeniusz Kwiatkowski suggested that should the French persevere, Warsaw would make the blackmail public.[87]

The final talks saw Żyrardów linked to the Rambouillet agreement.[88] Warsaw attempted to use them as leverage in its talks on financing the construction of the Silesia-Gdynia railway. The French hinted that ending the dispute, either through an agreement or international arbitrage, would help with the military loan.[89] By October 1936 Paris even offered helpful suggestions to the Polish Embassy in Paris on how to "sell" the agreement to the Polish public.[90] After long talks, the final nominal value of the buyback price amounted to 11.1 million złoty; close to the Polish negotiation goals.[91] The final text of the agreement was accepted on 27 November 1936, 13 years after the French assumed control of the factory.[92]

Punishing Boussac directly for his company's actions in Poland was more difficult. What remained as a possible Polish tool, were criminal cases against Potocki, Vermeersch, and Caen. In November 1935, an internal Ministry of Trade and Industry note declared that "due to prestige," the matter could not be let go, but should bring to light all the crimes of "the true perpetrator, Boussac."[93] There was thus a moral dimension to the trial, the idea that evil should meet punishment–again to some degree linked to public reception of the conflict. Nonetheless, as an unofficial part of the final agreement on the buyback, the Poles also dropped the criminal case.[94] Unsurprisingly, both countries suppressed further press coverage.[95]

The minority shareholders of Żyrardów, despite the role they played in the conflict, never got adequate attention after the attacks on the Biskupice agreement. They received symbolic compensation for their losses in August 1937 and April 1938. No-one in Poland was satisfied, but the Żyrardów Affair finally left the political scene. In France, Boussac was able to add 11.1 million złoty to the estimated 22.5 million he had earned from the factory.[96]

7.4 Conclusions

The Żyrardów Affair spanned most of the interwar period, flaring up in dramatic circumstances in 1924, 1932, and 1934. Ostensibly, it concerned a single private company operating in a minor town between Warsaw and Łódź, but its importance was much greater. On the one hand, its position in public discourse remained a function of domestic Polish politics. In 1924, it provided the liberal opposition with a handy tool to attack their right-wing opponents. In the 1930s, it first served as a conduit for attacks on the Sanacja authorities, used by both the left- and right-wing opposition, and by 1934 became a tool in internal Sanacja struggles. On the other hand, the state of the Affair also depended on the changing Franco–Polish relationship. Unsurprisingly, at first the conflict was mostly an internal Polish matter. Only once the relationship between Warsaw and Paris soured did Żyrardów become a tool against the French – which it then ceased to be with the rapprochement in 1936.

But the importance of the conflict goes beyond domestic and international politics. Waldemar Michowicz wrote, quoting government materials, that Polish actions in 1934 were "'a firm and loud protest against the detrimental actions of foreign capital in Polish industry,' which the authorities chose to pursue only when they achieved a temporary increase of freedom in relation to its ally."[97] Żyrardów, together with the Warsaw power plant, thus informed policy changes relating to foreign capital. Their stories found an interested audience among the press-reading public because they provided a mirror in which the Poles could see their relationship with France and their position in the global division of labour. And the scale of public reaction stemmed from the fact that neither the public, nor Polish politicians liked what they saw.

Notes

1 Przemysław Dąbrowski, "'Panama żyrardowska' w okresie dwudziestolecia międzywojennego," *Studia Iuridica Lublinensia* 21(2014): 11–31, 24.
2 The history of the company in Polish is well-researched. I base the essential narrative in this chapter on Zbigniew Landau and Jerzy Tomaszewski (*Sprawa żyrardowska. Przyczynek do dziejów kapitałów obcych w Polsce międzywojennej* (Warszawa: Książka i Wiedza, 1983), and improve upon it using French archival sources and Mylène Mihout-Natar's and Christophe Laforest's works (Mylène Mihout-Natar, "L'intervention des capitaux français dans la Pologne de la Seconde République (1918–1939): contribution à l'histoire de l'impérialisme économique français en Europe centrale" (PhD, Université Charles de Gaulle – Lille III, 2002); Christophe Laforest, "La stratégie française et la Pologne (1919–1939). Aspects économiques et implications politiques" (PhD, Université Paris 1 Panthéon-Sorbonne, 2001).
3 Archives diplomatiques, La Courneuve [henceforth: AdC], Fonds Nominatifs, Léon Noël, Noël to MAÉ, 17 July 1936, n.p.
4 Jeffry A. Frieden, "International Investment and Colonial Control: A New Interpretation," *International Organization* 48, no. 4 (1994): 559–93, https://doi.org/10.1017/S0020818300028319.
5 Landau and Tomaszewski, *Sprawa*, 71–72.
6 Archiwum Akt Nowych [henceforth: AAN], Ministerstwo Przemysłu i Handlu [henceforth: MPiH], 142, Zakłady Żyrardowskie. Uzupełnienie, 12 November 1935, 7.
7 Laforest, "La stratégie," 390–91; Marie-France Pochna, *Bonjour, monsieur Boussac*, 1 vols. (Paris: R. Laffont Opera mundi, 1980); Christian Staphe, *Ma vie avec Boussac le "Vosgien"* (Haroué: Gérard Louis, 2017); Patrick Lamm, *Enquête sur l'affaire Boussac* (Paris: Éditions Robert Laffront, 1985).

8 This claim proved difficult to verify; cf. Mihout-Natar, "L'intervention," 450; Julian Konar, "Spór o Żyrardów," *Sprawy Międzynarodowe* 16, no. 2 (1963): 76–85, 79 footnote 8.
9 Polish sources suggest the sum of 17 thousand USD, while French data point to a much higher valuation of about 12 million marks (L'I'intervention," 390).
10 AAN, MPiH, 142, Zakłady Żyrardowskie. Uzupełnienie, 12 November 1935, 5.
11 Zbigniew Landau and Jerzy Tomaszewski, *Kapitały obce w Polsce 1918–1939: materiały i dokumenty* (Warszawa: Książka i Wiedza, 1964), 117; Landau and Tomaszewski, *Sprawa*, 95–96.
12 Landau and Tomaszewski, *Sprawa*, 101–2.
13 AAN, MPiH, 142, Zakłady Żyrardowskie. Uzupełnienie, 12 November 1935, 6.
14 *Ilustrowany Kuryer Codzienny*, 26 April 1924, 11.
15 *Robotnik*, 4 April 1924, 2; *Ilustrowany Kuryer Codzienny*, 5 April 1924, 11.
16 *Kurjer Polski*, 3 April 1924, 2.
17 Cecylia Leszczyńska, *Polska polityka pieniężna i walutowa w latach 1924–1936: w systemie Gold Exchange Standard* (Warszawa: Wydawnictwo Uniwersytetu Warszawskiego, 2013), 81–82; Zbigniew Landau and Jerzy Tomaszewski, *Gospodarka Polski miedzywojennej 1918–1939. Vol. 1: W dobie inflacji 1918–1923* (Warszawa: Książka i Wiedza, 1967).
18 *Kurjer Polski*, 8 April 1924; Zbigniew Landau, "Oligarchia finansowa Drugiej Rzeczypospolitej," *Przegląd Historyczny* 62, no. 1 (1971): 75–92, 80, 86.
19 Landau and Tomaszewski, *Sprawa*, 113.
20 AdC, Correspondance politique et commercial, 1918–1940, Pologne [henceforth: CPC PL], 400, Zakłady Żyrardowskie, 4 April 1934, 186–88.
21 AAN, Ministerstwo Spraw Zagranicznych [henceforth: MSZ], 3855, Chłapowski to Herriot, 12 August, 1932, 1–3; AAN, MPiH, 142, Zakłady Żyrardowskie. Uzupełnienie, 12 November 1935, 6.
22 In this section I use results from Jerzy Łazor, "'A Colony of Alien Capital.' French Investments, Polish Identity, and a Story of Murder in 1930s Warsaw," *Slavic Review* 81, no. 1 (Spring 2022) (2022): 122–41, https://doi.org/10.1017/slr.2022.79. Cf. Romuald Karaś, *Ostatni odruch* (Warszawa: Wydawnictwo Ministerstwa Obrony Narodowej, 1986).
23 Walder Michowicz ("Afera żyrardowska z 1934 r. Przyczynek do działalności kapitału francuskiego w Polsce," *Zeszyty Naukowe Uniwersytetu Łódzkiego. Seria I. Nauki Humanistyczne*, no. 21 (1961): 155–70) gives a good overview of Polish accusations against Boussac. Mihout-Natar ("L'intervention," 488–91) shows discrepancies in the company's balances.
24 AdC, CPC PL, 251, Laroche to Briand, 22 June 1926, 241–41v and 22 October 1926, 242–43v.
25 Julian Konar, "Strajk w Zakładach Żyrardowskich w 1926 r.," in *Z dziejów walk masowych klasy roborniczej w Polsce w latach 1918–1939* (Warszawa: Państwowe Wydawnictwo Naukowe, 1964), 47–114; Mihout, "L'intervention," 456–59.
26 AdC, CPC PL, 252, Laroche to Briand, 20 October 1928, 165.
27 Landau and Tomaszewski, *Sprawa*, 145; AdC, CPC PL, 400, [French Investors in Żyrardów to MAÉ], 1 December 1930, 1–3; AdC, CPC PL, 400, Boussac, Memorandum on the conflict in Żyrardów, 8 December 1931], 19–23; AdC, CPC PL, 400, FEW, Aide-memoire, 21 January 1931, 6–7.
28 AdC, CPC PL 400, Bressy to MAÉ, 26 April 1932, 30.
29 Mihout-Natar, "L'intervention," 574; Laforest, "La stratégie," 376.
30 Juliusz Kaden-Bandrowski, *Czarne skrzydła*, 2 vols. (Kraków: Wydawnictwo Literackie, 1975).
31 AdC, CPC PL, 252, Terver to Briand, 31 January 1928, 106.
32 AdC, CPC PL, 400, Bressy to MAÉ, 29 April 1932, 34.

33 *Ostatnie Wiadomości*, April 27, 1932, 2.
34 Czesław Miłosz, "Przeciwko nim. Z powodu procesu Blachowskiego, zabójcy Gastona Koehler-Badin," in *Wiersze*, vol. I (Kraków: Znak, 2004).
35 AdC, CPC PL, 400, Laroche to MAÉ, 10 May 1932, 67; AdC, CPC PL, 400, Laroche to [Berthelot], 10 May 1932, 68; AdC, CPC PL, 400, [Aupetit] to Laroche, 13 June 1932, 80–83; Laforest, "La stratégie," 394–95.
36 Landau and Tomaszewski, *Sprawa*, 152; AdC, CPC PL, 400, Laroche to Tardieu, 4 May 1932, 48–49v; AAN, MSZ, 3855, Szembek to MPiH, 2 May 1933, 12.
37 Łazor, "'A Colony"; Piotr Puchalski, *Poland in a Colonial World Order: Adjustments and Aspirations, 1918–1939* (London and New York: Routledge, 2022).
38 Jerzy Holzer, *Mozaika polityczna Drugiej Rzeczypospolitej* (Warszawa: Książka i Wiedza, 1974).
39 *ABC*, April 29, 1932; *Robotnik*, April 29, 1932, 2
40 *Ilustrowany Kuryer Codzienny*, May 2, 1932, 2.
41 *ABC*, May 6, 1932, 3.
42 *Wiadomości Literackie*, 5 June 1932, 1.
43 *Gazeta Polska*, 10 February 1932, 3 and 1 May 1932, 3; Cf. Tadeusz Włudyka, *"Trzecia droga" w myśli gospodarczej II Rzeczpospolitej: koncepcje Adama Doboszyńskiego a program obozu narodowego* (Kraków: Universitas, 1994); Howard J. Wiarda, *Corporatism and Comparative Politics: The Other Great "Ism,"* (Armonk: M.E. Sharpe, 1997), https://doi.org/10.4324/9781315481050.
44 *Robotnik*, 29 April 1932, 2; *Dobry Wieczór! Kurjer Czerwony*, 27 April 1932, 3.
45 *Express Poranny*, 18 May 1932, 3; *Dobry Wieczór! Kurjer Czerwony*, 28 April 1932, 3.
46 AdC, CPC PL, 400, Jochaud du Plessix to Laroche, 13 June 1932, 82–83.
47 Marek Arpad Kowalski, *Dyskurs kolonialny w Drugiej Rzeczypospolitej* (Warszawa: Wydawnictwo DiG, 2010); Lenny A. Ureña Valerio, *Colonial Fantasies, Imperial Realities: Race Science and the Making of Polishness on the Fringes of the German Empire, 1840–1920* (Athens, OH: Ohio University Press, 2019); Puchalski, *Poland.*
48 Kathryn Ciancia, *On Civilization's Edge. A Polish Borderland in the Interwar World* (Oxford: Oxford University Press, 2020), 16.
49 *Gazeta Polska*, 25 April 1933. Cf. *Wieczór Warszawski*, 27 April 1933 and 7 May 1933; *Kurjer Poranny*, 29 April 1933; Jan Kofman, "Koła wielkoprzemysłowe a kwestia kapitałów obcych w okresie 1920–1939," *Kwartalnik Historyczny* 82, no. 2 (1975): 303–20, 311–313.
50 AAN, MSZ, 3855, Szembek to MPiH, 2 May 1933, 12–13. Cf. AAN, MSZ, 3855, MSZ to MS, 25 January 1925, 64–66.
51 AAN, MSZ, 3855, Internal MSZ memo, 12 July 1933, 31–32.
52 AdC, CPC PL, 370, Lancial to Laval, 15 January 1934, k. 168–69; Zenon Szmidtke, *"Skarboferm" 1922–1939: związki polityki z gospodarką* (Opole: Państwowy Instytut Naukowy, 2005), 98.
53 Polish authorities had used the position of minority shareholders already in the 1920s: AdC, CPC PL, 252, Laroche to Briand, 20 October 1928, 165.
54 *Gazeta Polska*, 26 January 1934, 1; AdC, CPC PL, 400, Arvengas to Paul-Boncour, 24 January 1934, 138–38v.
55 AdC, CPC PL, 400, Extrait du discours du député Miedziński, reapporteur général du Budget en séance de la Commission de Finances de la Diète, 31 January 1934, 288; Mateusz Hübner, *"Pułkownicy": Rdzeń środowiska piłsudczyków w systemie polityczno-ustrojowym II Rzeczypospolitej* (Warszawa: Instytut Pamięci Narodowej, 2020), 8.
56 AdC, CPC PL, 400, Laroche to Barthou, 21 March 1934, 166–70v, quotation from page 167v; AdC, CPC PL, 400, Laroche to Barthou, 3 April 1934, 178–79.

57 AdC, CPC PL, 403, Jugement du Tribunal de commerce de la Seine (3ème Chambre), [10 April 1934], 225–27; AdC, CPC PL, 4001, Note, 6 July 1934, 81–83.
58 AdC, CPC PL, 401, Propositions d'arbitrage communiquées par M. Boussac à la Minorité, [1934], 36–45.
59 *Gazeta Polska*, 8 August 1934; AdC, CPC PL, 401, Laroche to Barthou, 8 August 1934, 115v; AdC, CPC PL, 401, Laroche to Barthou, 15 August 1934, 157.
60 AdC, CPC PL, 401, Laroche to Barthou, 8 August 1934, 115v.
61 AdC, CPC PL, 401, Laroche to MAÉ, 19 August 1934, 202–3.
62 Laforest, "La stratégie," 406–7; AdC, CPC PL, 401, Communiqué de l'agence Iskra concernant l'affaire de Żyrardów, 20 August 1934, 233.
63 Tomasz Głowiński, *Feliks Młynarski 1884–1972* (Wrocław: Gajt, 2012), 8, 475–81; Hübner, *Pułkownicy*, 8.
64 AdC, CPC PL, 401, Laroche to MAÉ, 11 August 1934, 134–35; AdC, CPC PL, 402, Communiqué de la minorité des actionnaires de Żyrardów, 9 August 1934, 25–26.
65 The National Archive, Kew, FO 371/17793, Internal FO comments to letter C5810/2849/55, 29 August 1934, 602.
66 AdC, CPC PL, 401, Laroche to MAÉ, 17 August 1934, 170–73.
67 AdC, CPC PL, 402, Laroche to Barthou, 5 September 1934, 43–45; Laroche to MAÉ, 6 September 1934, 58; and Bressy to Barthou, 27 September 1934, 125.
68 AdC, CPC PL, 401, Laroche to MAÉ, 19 August, 209–10.
69 AdC, CPC PL, 401, Barthou to Germain-Martin, 20 August 1934, 219–29.
70 AdC, CPC PL, 401, Léger to Laroche, 21 August 1934, 239; AAN, MSZ, 3855, Chłapowski to MSZ, 22 August 1934, 129–30.
71 AdC, CPC PL, 401, Laroche to Barthou, 22 August 1934, 254–56v and Laroche to MAÉ, 24 August 1934, 270; AAN, MSZ, 3855, Government Commissariat for Warsaw to MSZ, 20 August 1934, 112.
72 AdC, CPC PL, 401, MSZ to FEW, 29 August 1934, 305–7; AdC, CPC PL, 402, Barthou to MAÉ, 7 September 1934, 64.
73 "Polish textile Scandal. French case in Żyrardów Affair. M. Boussac's Charges against Authorities: 'Difficulties placed in company's way.' Price-Waterhouse Enquiry Plan Rejected," *Financial News*, 11 September 1934.
74 AdC, CPC PL, 402, Bressy to Barthou, 9 October 1934, 136–37.
75 AAN, MSZ, 3855, Chłapowski to MSZ, 24 November 1934, 234; Waldemar Michowicz, "Międzynarodowe tło tzw. afery żyrardowskiej 1934 r.," in *Żyrardów 1829–1945*, ed. Iwona Pietrzak-Pawłowska (Warszawa: Państwowe Wydawnictwo Naukowe, 1980), 241–56, 249.
76 AdC, CPC PL, 402, Bressy to MAÉ, 10 October 1934, 138.
77 AdC, CPC PL, 403, Laroche to MAÉ, 26 November 1934, 66–67.
78 AdC, CPC PL, 403, Bressy to Laval, 25 December 1934, 163.
79 AdC, CPC PL, 403, Laroche to Laval, 14 March 1935, 219–20.
80 AdC, CPC PL, 403, Note pour Monsieur Léger. Affair de Żyrardów, 29 May 1935, 233–34.
81 AdC, CPC PL, 403, Noël to MAÉ, 4 June 1935, 240–44.
82 AdC, CPC PL, 403, Noël to Laval, 14 November 1935, 279–80; AAN, MPiH, 142, Wniosek MPiH w porozumieniu z MS na Komitet Ekonomiczny Ministrów w sprawie zasad przejęcia przez kapitał krajowy "Zakładów Żyrardowskich," November 1935, 19–20; Michowicz, *Międzynarodowe tło*, 251.
83 AdC, CPC PL, 403, Noël to Laval, 7 August, 1935, 271–74; AAN, MSZ, 3856, Notatka z rozmowy p.p. Attaché Handlowego i Radcy Finansowego Ambasady RP w Paryżu z Panem Ambasadorem Noëlem, 30 January 1936, 4; AAN, MSZ, 3856, Wytyczne dla rokowań w sprawie wykupu akcyj większości "Zakładów Żyrardowskich," January 1936, 5–6; AdC, Fonds Nominatifs, Léon Noël, Noël to

MAÉ, 9 April 1936, np; AAN, MSZ, 3856, Sokołowski to mPiH, 23 June 1936, 36–36v.

84 AdC, Fonds Nominatifs, Léon Noël, Noël to MAÉ, 5 February 1936, n.p.

85 AdC, CPC PL, 403, Noël to Laval, 18 December 1935, 282.

86 Michowicz, *Międzynarodowe tło*, 250.

87 AAN, MSZ, 3856, Protokuł z konferencji odbytej w dniu 6 sierpnia 1936 r. w sprawie "Żyrardowa" u Pana Ministra Spraw Zagranicznych, 6 August 1936, 110–12; AdC, Fonds Nominatifs, Léon Noël, Boussac to Noël, 22 May 1936, n.p.; AAN, MSZ, 3856, FEW to MSZ, 9 July 1936, 42–45; Quotation from AAN, MSZ, 3856, Stebelski to Roman, 27 July 1936, 48.

88 AAN, MSZ, 3856, Protokuł konferencji pod przewodnictwem Pana Ministra Przemysłu i Handlu w dniu 21 sierpnia 1936 r. w sprawie "Żyrardowa," 21 August 1936, 89–90.

89 AAN, MSZ, 3856, Potocki to Roman, 23 October 1936, 121; AAN, MSZ, 3856, PEP to Roman, 29 October 1936, 122–24.

90 AAN, MSZ, 3856, Stebelski to Roman, 15 October 1936, 116–18.

91 AAN, MSZ, 3856, Łukasiewicz to [Beck], [11 November 1936], 139–42.

92 AAN, MSZ, 3856, Memorandum on the agreement on Żyrardów, 30 November 1936, 171.

93 AAN, MPiH, 142, Notatka w sprawie karnej Zakładów Żyrardowskich, 14 November 1935, 17–18.

94 AAN, MSZ, 3856, MSZ to FEW, 28 November 1936, 178; Michowicz, *Międzynarodowe tło*, 255.

95 Cf. "Une réponse de M. Boussac," *La Flèche*, 5 December 1936; AAN, MSZ, 3856, PEP to MSZ, 11 December 1936, 186; AAN, MSZ, 7148, PEP to Beck, 12 December 1936, 47.

96 Landau and Tomaszewski, *Sprawa*, 290; Laforest, "La stratégie," 415.

97 Michowicz, *Międzynarodowe tło*, 256.

Conclusions

Once Germany attacked Poland on 1 September 1939, with the Soviet Union joining from the east on 17 September, the writing was on the wall for French-owned companies in Poland. After Paris reluctantly declared war on Berlin, the 1,500 French citizens – "engineers, industrialists, traders and agents, professors, teachers, and governesses" – left Poland within a few days, and never returned.[1] Polish forces collapsed under the German and Soviet onslaught, and the country soon found itself divided between the two invaders.

The companies – some suffering serious loses during the September 1939 campaign – were left to fend for themselves. Their fate in the short-term depended on geography. The eastern part of Galicia was occupied by the Soviet Union until summer 1941. In the west, Łódź (as part of the Reichsgau Wartheland), Gdynia, and Upper Silesia together with most of the Dąbrowa Basin were annexed by the Reich. Between the two extremes, the General Government became Germany's puppet state, and included French holdings in Częstochowa, Warsaw, and, after August 1941, Eastern Galicia. Companies which operated in the General Government were able to continue their work, and some even reported profits. Others, faced with German takeovers, sold their shares to the new rulers or liquidated their firms. Others still were requisitioned by Germany, with compensation paid out.[2]

As the Germans were gradually displaced from occupied territories by the Red Army, companies once again faced a new reality. Some found themselves in the Soviet Union – and thus ended the majority of French holdings in Polish oil. The rest (excluding French investment in Cieszyn Silesia, which returned to Czechoslovakia) now became part of the new People's Poland, in which the communists gradually overcame resistance of all other political forces.

For French companies the regime change spelled disaster.[3] First, the authorities put many large companies under compulsory administration, which meant nationalization de facto, if not de jure. On 3 January 1946, the Poles adopted a new nationalization bill, which resulted in the formal takeover of the vast majority of French companies. Later, private banks – rather than undergo nationalization – were gradually liquidated.[4]

After the forced takeovers started, in November 1944 the French quickly prepared a list of companies with French interests.[5] Later, Ambassador Roger

DOI: 10.4324/9781003375586-8

Garreu warned the Polish Ministry of Foreign Affairs against forcing nationalization without due compensation. After the Poles pushed through with the bill, the French protested, and coordinated their efforts with their peers from other western countries. Ultimately, after long negotiations, on 19 March 1948 France and Poland signed an indemnization agreement. Paris, acting in the name of French citizens and firms, would receive 3.8 million tons of Polish coal as compensation for the nationalization of French economic interests in the country. Thus coal once again played a surprising role in mutual relations. In return, Poland would be free from any French claims, and would get additional credits from Paris.

With this agreement, the story of French investment in Poland, dating back to the 19th century, ended. The Poles and other nations of Central and Eastern Europe, now in the orbit of Moscow, would attempt a different solution to the problem of underdevelopment.

In this book I understood the global economy as a hierarchy, and development as improving a country's position in the global division of labour. This in turn entails moving it towards manufacturing each techno-industrial paradigm's leading products, and away from resources and industrial goods near the end of their product life cycle. In the interwar period, this meant investment in such capital- and technology-intensive branches as aviation or the automobile, although Poland could still profit from improving its basic infrastructure.

Studying the impact of French investment on Polish development paints a rather grim picture. It is a variation on the conflict between the core and the semi-periphery, broadly confirming the dangers of relying on foreign capital for development without a stringent industrial policy. The country predictably failed to profit from French investment in the interwar period due to two groups of factors. First, French companies were unlikely to invest in leading products in a semi-peripheral country. Second, the Poles mostly failed to implement policies which could have maximized the chances of such investment.

Despite the Franco–Polish alliance, Warsaw managed to get little money from Paris, and the vast majority of loans and credits it did get were earmarked for security-related expenses. From a developmental perspective, they were little more than a drain on the Polish budget and balance of payments. The structure of French FDI was likewise not conductive to development, with few greenfield investments, and most of the money in resource extraction and 19th-century industries, such as metallurgy and textiles. After all, investors are unlikely to move the manufacture of leading products to the periphery, unless government policy supports such actions. Moreover, even within these sectors, we see little modernization, particularly during the Great Depression, when French companies consistently underinvested, and – due to their interests in vulnerable industries – reported worse results than investors from other countries. With few exceptions, the French were more likely to transfer profits abroad, through window-dressing if needed.

When the Poles attempted to channel French money into specific developmental investments, such as infrastructure or high-tech sectors with military applications, they consistently ran into problems. In both areas, the political power held by the French allowed them to torpedo any foreign competition. In infrastructure, this made investment more expensive and sometimes delayed construction. Especially in the 1920s, as the stronger partner, Paris was able to force contracts which left little space for Polish developmental policy (such as the use of domestic contractors or resources). The situation was even worse in car production, where French-owned firms failed to properly cooperate with their Polish counterparts, or start manufacturing.

A lone success story highlights additional problems in this field. The Schneider-controlled Škoda was able to create a thriving greenfield factory in Warsaw based on a long-term government contract. However, the Czech producer continued to run into issues when cooperating with other companies in Poland, which lacked the necessary technology to provide Škoda with the materials it needed for production. Moreover, the Poles were seemingly unwilling to adapt new manufacturing processes, underlining the problem of technological bottlenecks, and the difficulty of transplanting a high-tech company into a new country if the latter lacks the necessary know-how. By the mid-1930s, the Polish government, which had initiated the project, decided to consolidate the state's control over the aviation sector and took over the factory.

At the heart of the Franco–Polish relationship was an inherent conflict, which we should expect in similar cases. The Poles – when their policy was dictated by economic, rather than purely defensive or financial considerations – hoped that their allies would help them scale a few rungs of the global economic ladder. This, however, made little sense to the French. They profited from contacts with Poland as a semi-peripheral state importing industrial products, where foreign investors could buy old factories and run them using cheap labour without further expenses. However, at the same time, for parts of the interwar period, the French relied on Poland as an ally – one whose usefulness depended on its military and economic strength.

Consequently, much of the investment in question was informed by politics. France supported engagement in Central and Eastern Europe primarily because of its security concerns – the idea of creating an Eastern Barrier against Germany, displacing German and Austrian capital in the region, or acquiring access to oil. However, as the Quai d'Orsay did not itself invest, its officials had to corral private companies, often leading to tensions between policymakers and firms. Capital owners were not always enamoured by the idea of placing capital in the region, which hindered Paris's designs. In some particularly important cases – such as the security-related infrastructural projects in Poland, or the mixed companies in Silesia – French authorities went beyond merely suggesting investment, but themselves sought investors, compelled them into forming consortiums, bullied into not working with German owners, or de facto picked winners from among various firms.

I have already alluded to the primary mechanisms which governed Franco–Polish relations. After 1918, Poland was ever the supplicant, asking the French for money and support. This dynamic allowed the continuous use of conditionality – the relentless interlinking of various, sometimes unconnected issues by the French in subsequent negotiations. As a result, Paris, which was objectively the stronger party, gained further power, and by controlling the flow of money, increased its influence over the Poles. This process was strengthened by direct connections between the two countries' militaries, and the activity of the French Military Mission.

If the French remained the stronger partner, consistently using conditionality to influence the Poles, Warsaw was left with less obvious strategies. Faced with unequal treaties, or powerful French diplomats, Warsaw would ignore particularly one-sided provisions, postpone answering certain letters, or implementing agreements. Once the authorities felt themselves stronger – as they did under Władysław Grabski in 1924, or after the coup of 1926, they also became more forceful, demanding rather than asking, or even reneging on certain agreements or concessions. By the 1930s, the Poles also made use of public opinion, using it as a shield against certain French demands. This was particularly visible in the Żyrardów conflict, although by 1936, the Polish government became hostage to the anti-French fervour it had fostered in the press. Generally, however, this suggests that even within an unequal relationship, the degree of asymmetry is not a given, and proper policy can help shield the weaker partner from the demands of the stronger one.

The Franco–Polish example showcases the difficult position of the semi-peripheries. Needing to import capital, Warsaw's actions were limited by the very relationship on which its representatives hoped to build their policies. Economic development is necessarily difficult, requiring good policies and a competent bureaucracy, yet relying on external help is not straightforward, as hierarchic logic precludes investment in leading products outside of the home country. Governments in developing state need to think twice before merely inviting foreigners in without proper safeguards.

Notes

1 Archives diplomatiques, Nantes [henceforth: AdN], Ambassade de France à Varsovie [henceforth: AFV], 9, Memo "Pologne," 25 June 1950, n,p.

2 Dariusz Jarosz and Maria Pasztor, *Conflits brûlants de la Guerre froide: les relations franco-polonaises de 1945 à 1954* (Panazol: Lavauzelle, 2005), 104–6; AdN, AFV, 7, November 1944 memos on: Société Anonyme de l'Industrie Textile; Établissements Ludwik Spiess i Syn; Société Électro-Gaz; Compagnie Gallicienne de Mines, n.p.

3 Jarosz and Pasztor, *Conflits*, 97–106.

4 Zbigniew Landau, "Czy w Polsce Ludowej dokonano nacjonalizacji banków?," *Przegląd Historyczny* 60, no. 4 (1969): 700–14.

5 AdN, AFV, 7, passim.

Bibliography

Archival documents

Archives départementales de Loire-Atlantique, Nantes
Fonds de la Compagnie des tramways de Nantes

Archives diplomatiques, La Courneuve
Correspondance politique et commercial, 1918–1940, Pologne
Papiers d'agents – Archives privées: Léon Noël, 1934–1940

Archives diplomatiques, Nantes
Consulat de France à Katowice
Ambassade de France à Varsovie

Archiwum Akt Nowych, Warszawa
Akta Wincentego i Władysława Choroszewskich
Ministerstwo Skarbu
Ministerstwo Spraw Zagranicznych
Ministerstwo Przemysłu i Handlu
Prokuratoria Generalna RP w Warszawie (1919–1939)

Archiwum Państwowe w Katowicach
Konwencja Węglowa w Katowicach
Polska Huta Skarbowa Ołowiu i Srebra w Strzybnicy
Skarboferm Spółka Dzierżawna
Towarzystwo Bezimienne Kopalń Węgla "Czeladź" w Czeladzi – Piaskach
Zakłady Hohenlohego SA Wełnowiec

Archiwum Państwowe w Łodzi
Francuska Spółka Akcyjna Generalna Kompania Przemysłu Przędzalniczego
Towarzystwo Anonimowe Zakładów Allart Rousseau i Spółka w Łodzi
Zakłady Przemysłu Włókienniczego "Polana" Spółka Akcyjna w Łodzi

Banque de France, Paris

Centralne Archiwum Wojskowe, Rembertów
I Oddział Sztabu Głównego
Biuro Administracji Armii Ministerstwa Spraw Wojskowych
Departament Sprawiedliwości Ministerstwa Spraw Wojskowych

Centre des archives économiques et financières, Savigny-le-Temple
Fonds Trésor. Relations financières internationales – Pologne 1919–1939
Pologne 1919–1939
Pologne 1924–1951

Family Archive of Bernard Bartet

Polish Institute and Sikorski Museum, London
Depositions concerning the Polish 1939 Campaign

The National Archives, Kew
Foreign Office

Press sources

ABC 1932
Dobry Wieczór! Kurjer Czerwony 1932
Express Poranny 1932
Financial News 1934
Gazeta Polska 1932, 1933, 1934
Gospodarka Narodowa 1934
Ilustrowany Kuryer Codzienny 1924, 1932
Kurjer Polski 1924
Kurjer Poranny 1924, 1933
Robotnik 1924, 1932
Ostatnie Wiadomości 1932
Wiadomości Literackie 1932

Statistical and legal publications

Dziennik Ustaw Rzeczypospolitej Poskiej 1922, 1923, 1924, 1931
Mały Rocznik Statystyczny 1939.
Rocznik Informacyjny o Spółkach Akcyjnych 1929, 1930.
Rocznik Polskiego Przemysłu i Handlu 1932, 1934, 1936, 1938.
Rocznik Statystyczny Rzeczypospolitej Polskiej 1930.
Sénat 1923.

Other primary sources

Bartoszewicz, Stefan. *Wspomnienia z przemysłu naftowego 1897–1930*. Lwów: Piller-Neumann, 1934.
Bielski, Zygmunt. "Rozwój techniki kopalnictwa naftowego za czasów polskich." *Nafta* 17, no. 4 (1938): 57–63.
Biliński, Leon. *Wspomnienia i Dokumenty. Tom II, 1915–1922*. Warszawa: Księgarnia F. Hoesicka, 1925.
Bóbr, Wacław. *Polski przemysł naftowy*. Warszawa: Przegląd Polityczny, 1928.

Dąbrowski, Marian, ed. *20-Lecie Komunikacja w Polsce Odrodzonej, 1918–1939.* Kraków: Koncern Prasowy "Ilustrowany Kuryer Codzienny", 1939.
Fryc, Jan. *Przedsiębiorstwa i kapitał w polskim przemyśle naftowym.* Warszawa: Polska Gospodarcza, 1930.
Gołębiowski, Jerzy, ed. *Kapitał państwowy w spółkach prawa handlowego u schyłku Drugiej Rzeczypospolitej. Szczegółowe sprawozdanie z działalności przedsiębiorstw o kapitale mieszanym za rok 1937 wzgl. 1937/1938.* Kraków: Wydawnictwo Naukowe Akademii Pedagogicznej, 2004.
Grabski, Władysław. *Dwa lata pracy u podstaw państwowości naszej: 1924–1925.* Warszawa: F. Hoesick, 1927.
Hilchen, Feliks. "Rola kapitału zagranicznego w Polsce." *Ekonomista*, no. 1 (1920).
Kaden-Bandrowski, Juliusz. *Czarne skrzydła.* 2 vols. Kraków: Wydawnictwo Literackie, 1975.
Kożuchowski, Józef. *Kapitał zagraniczny w przemyśle polskim.* Warszawa: Tygodnik "Przemysł i Handel," 1928.
Kożuchowski, Józef. *Przebudowa gospodarcza Polski.* Warszawa: Towarzystwo Pracy Społeczno-Gospodarczej, 1938.
Kruszewski, Stanisław. *Majątek Państwa Polskiego Według Stanu Na Dzień 1 Stycznia 1927 r.* Warszawa: Ministerstwo Skarbu, 1931.
Landau, Zbigniew, and Bronisława Skrzeszewska, eds. *Wojciech Korfanty przed Sądem Marszałkowskim: Dokumenty.* Katowice: Wydawnictwo "Śląsk," 1964.
Landau, Zbigniew, and Jerzy Tomaszewski. "Misja Prof. A. Benisa." *Teki Archiwalne* 6 (1959): 29–225.
Laroche, Jules. *La Pologne de Pilsudski: Souvenirs d'une ambassade 1926–1935.* Paris: Flammarion, 1953.
Litwiński, Léon. "Nafta małopolska i jej kulisy." *Kultura*, no. 11 (1960): 113–31.
Miłosz, Czesław. "Przeciwko nim. Z powodu procesu Blachowskiego, zabójcy Gastona Koehler-Badin." In *Wiersze*, Vol. I. Kraków: Znak, 2004.
Noël, Léon. *L'Agression allemande contre la Pologne: Une ambassade à Varsovie, 1935–1939.* Paris: Flammarion, 1946.
Polskie Kopalnie Skarbowe na Górnym Śląsku. Spółka Dzierżawna. Spółka Akcyjna w Katowicach. Société Fermière des Mines Fiscales de l'Etat Polonais en Haute-Silésie. Sociéte Anonyme à Katowice. Warszawa: Zakłady Graficzne B. Wierzbicki i Ska, 1929.
Pragier, Adam. *Czas przeszły dokonany.* Edited by Andrzej Friszke and Ewa Pejaś. Warszawa: Muzeum Historii Polski, 2018.
Rummel, Julian. "U kolebki Gdyni (fragment pamiętnika)." *Rocznik Gdyński*, 1977: 197–207.
Société Anonyme des Mines de Czeladz. Assemblée Générale Ordinaire du 31 Mai 1920. Paris: Imprimerie Devalois, 1920.
Wyszyński, Otto. "Francuskie kapitały w polskiej nafcie w świetle własnej oceny." *Nafta* 10, no. 10–11 (1931): 276–86.
Zawadzki, Władysław Marian. "Polityka finansowa w okresie 1931–1935." Edited by Zbigniew Landau and Jerzy Tomaszewski. *Kwartalnik Historyczny* 6, no. 1 (1965): 127–51.

Secondary sources

Aldcroft, Derek H. *Europe's Third World: The European Periphery in the Interwar Years.* Aldershot and Burlington: Ashgate Publishing, 2006.

Ambrochowicz-Gajownik, Anna. "Polsko–francuskie stosunki gospodarcze w okresie międzywojennym: nowe postulaty badawcze." *Przegląd Środkowo-Wschodni* 1(2016): 182–211. https://doi.org/10.32612/uw.2543618X.2016.pp.182-211

Ambrochowicz-Gajownik, Anna. "Koncert życzeń – żądania francuskie w negocjacjach gospodarczych z Polską w latach 1933–1935." *Studia z Historii Społeczno-Gospodarczej XIX i XX Wieku* 23 (December 30, 2020): 75–93. https://doi.org/10.18778/2080-8313.23.04

Arahoni, Yair. *The Foreign Investment Decision Process*. Boston: Harvard University, 1966.

Axenciuc, Victor. *Evoluția economică a României: cercetări statistico-istorice, 1859–1947. Vol. 1. Industria*. București: Editura Academiei Române, 1992.

Bairoch, Paul. *Economics and World History: Myths and Paradoxes*. Chicago: University of Chicago Press, 1995.

Banaszkiewicz, Aleksandra. *Bilans w polskiej perspektywie historycznej – wiek XIX i XX*. Toruń: Wydawnictwo Naukowe Uniwersytetu Mikołaja Kopernika, 2019.

Barjot, Dominique. "L'entreprise Hersent: ascension, prospérité et chute d'une famille d'entrepreneurs (1860–1982)." In *Le capitalisme familial. Logiques et trajectoires*, edited by Jean-Claude Daumas, 133–66. Besançon: Presses universitaires de Franche-Comté, 2003.

Barjot, Dominique. *La grande entreprise française de travaux publics (1883–1974)*. Paris: Economica, 2006.

Barjot, Dominique. "Public Utilities and Private Initiative: The French Concession Model in Historical Perspective." *Business History* 53, no. 5 (2011a): 782–800. https://doi.org/10.1080/00076791.2011.599590

Barjot, Dominique. "Une face méconnue du capitalisme français en Russie." In *La France et les Français en Russie*, edited by Annie Charon, Bruno Delmas, and Armelle Le Goff, 443–57. Paris: École nationale des Chartes, 2011b. https://doi.org/10.4000/books.enc.1306

Beaud, Claude. "Une multinationale française au lendemain de la Première Guerre mondiale: Schneider et l'Union Européenne Industrielle et Financière." *Histoire, économie et société* 2, no. 4 (1983): 625–45. https://doi.org/10.3406/hes.1983.1345

Beauvois, Yves. "Francja a rządy 'pułkowników' (wrzesień 1936 – wrzesień 1939)." *Dzieje Najnowsze* 31, no. 3 (1999): 127–37.

Bębnik, Grzegorz, Sebastian Rosenbaum, and Bartosz Węcki. *Wojciech Korfanty: 1873–1939*. 2nd ed. Warszawa, Instytut Pamięci Narodowej, 2023.

Berend, Iván T. *The Crisis Zone of Europe: An Interpretation of East-Central European History in the First Half of the Twentieth Century*. Trans. Adrienne Makkay-Chambers. Cambridge: Cambridge University Press, 1986.

Berend, Iván T. *History Derailed: Central and Eastern Europe in the Long Nineteenth Century*. Berkeley: University of California Press, 2003.

Bernadzikiewicz, Tadeusz. *Nowe prawo o bilansach: geneza – system – ocena*. Warszawa: Towarzystwo Wydawnicze Młodych Prawników i Ekonomistów, 1934.

Bernadzikiewicz, Tadeusz. *Koncern państwowy w Polsce*. Warszawa: Towarzystwo Wydawnicze Młodych Prawników i Ekonomistów, 1938a.

Bernadzikiewicz, Tadeusz. *Udział państwa w spółkach handlowych*. Warszawa: Towarzystwo Wydawnicze Młodych Prawników i Ekonomistów, 1938b.

Beyer, Christian. "Cartelization and Firm Performance in Upper Silesia 1880–1913." *European Review of Economic History*, 2021. https://doi.org/10.1093/ereh/heab006

Birdal, Murat. *The Political Economy of Ottoman Public Debt: Insolvency and European Financial Control in the Late Nineteenth Century*. London: I.B. Tauris, 2010.
Błahut, Karol Józef. *Polsko-niemieckie stosunki gospodarcze w latach 1919–1939*. Wrocław: Zakład Narodowy im. Ossolińskich, 1975.
Böhler, Jochen. *Civil War in Central Europe, 1918–1921. Reconstruction of Poland*. Oxford: Oxford University Press, 2018.
Boldizzoni, Francesco. *The Poverty of Clio: Resurrecting Economic History*. Princeton: Princeton University Press, 2011.
Bordo, Michael D., and Hugh Rockoff. "The Gold Standard as a 'Good Housekeeping Seal of Approval'." *The Journal of Economic History* 56, no. 2 (1996): 389–428.
Bouguen, Jean-Marie. *Le Pétrole En France. Genèse et Stratégies d'influence (1917–1924)*. Paris: Éditions L'Harmattan, 2013.
Bułhak, Henryk. *Polska – Francja: z dziejów sojuszu 1922–1939. Cz. 1, (1922–1932)*. Warszawa: Wydawnictwa Fundacji "Historia pro Futuro," 1993.
Bułhak, Henryk. *Polska – Francja: z dziejów sojuszu 1933–1936*. Warszawa: Wydawnictwo Neriton, 2000.
Bułhak, Henryk. "Polskie starania o francuską pożyczkę na cele obrony narodowej. Okres uzgadniania koncepcji i sposobów jej realizacji w latach 1929–1930." In *W kręgu idei, polityki i wojska. Studia ofiarowane profesorowi Januszowi Farysiowi w siedemdziesiątą rocznicę urodzin*, edited by Tomasz Sikorski, Henryk Walczak, and Adam Wątor, 361–72. Szczecin: Wydawnictwo Naukowe Uniwersytetu Szczecińskiego, 2009.
Burnel, Anne. *La société de construction des Batignolles de 1914 à 1939: histoire d'un déclin*. Genève: Droz, 1995.
Bussière, Éric. "La France et les affaires pétrolières au lendemain de la Première Guerre Mondiale: la politique des groupes financiers à travers celle de la banque de l'Union Parisienne." *Histoire, économie et société* 1, no. 2 (1982): 313–28, https://doi.org/10.3406/hes.1982.1294
Cain, Peter J., and Antony G. Hopkins. *British Imperialism, 1688–2015*. 3rd ed. London and New York: Routledge: 2016.
Cassis, Youssef. *Big Business: The European Experience in the Twentieth Century*. New York: Oxford University Press, 2004.
Chandler, Alfred. *Scale and Scope: The Dynamics of Industrial Capitalism*. Cambridge, MA: Harvard University Press, 1990.
Chang, Ha-Joon. *Kicking Away the Ladder: Development Strategy in Historical Perspective*. London: Anthem Press, 2002.
Chang, Ha-Joon. *Bad Samaritans: The Myth of Free Trade and the Secret History of Capitalism*. New York: Bloomsbury Press, 2008.
Chirot, Daniel. *Social Change in a Peripheral Society: The Creation of a Balkan Colony*. New York: Academic Press, 1976.
Ciałowicz, Jan. *Polsko-francuski sojusz wojskowy: 1921–1939*. Warszawa: Państwowe Wydawnictwo Naukowe, 1971.
Ciancia, Kathryn. *On Civilization's Edge. A Polish Borderland in the Interwar World*. Oxford: Oxford University Press, 2020.
Cienciała, Anna Maria, and Titus Komarnicki. *From Versailles to Locarno: Keys to Polish Foreign Policy, 1919–25*. Lawrence: Kansas University Press, 1984.
Crockett, Jameson W. "The Polish Blitz, More than a Mere Footnote to History: Poland and Preventive War with Germany, 1933." *Diplomacy & Statecraft* 20, no. 4 (2009): 561–79. https://doi.org/10.1080/09592290903455667

Cywiński, Bohdan. *Przemysł polski i nasze położenie gospodarcze. Uwagi na tle bilansów przemysłowych spółek akcyjnych z lat 1928–1933*. Warszawa: Skład Główny w Domu Książki Polskiej, 1934.

Czaja, Stanisław, and Bogusław Fiedor. *Oblicza polskiego etatyzmu gospodarczego: spór o miejsce państwa w gospodarce w okresie międzywojennym, powojennym i po 1990 roku: liberalizm versus etatyzm*. Wrocław: Wydawnictwo Uniwersytetu Ekonomicznego we Wrocławiu, 2021.

D'Angio, Agnès. *Schneider & Cie et les travaux publics, 1895–1949*. Paris: École nationale des Chartes, 1995.

D'Angio, Agnès. "Schneider et Cie face aux risques géopolitiques en Europe centrale et orientale (1918–1939)." *Les cahiers Irice* 2, no. 6 (2010): 35–59. https://doi.org/10.3917/lci.006.0035

Daheur, Jawad. "Productive or Extractive Periphery? Russian Poland and Timber Exports to Germany in the Late Nineteenth and Early Twentieth Centuries." *Global Environment* 15, no. 1 (February 1, 2022): 107–47. https://doi.org/10.3197/ge.2022.150105

David, Thomas. *Nationalisme économique et industrialisation: l'expérience des pays d'Europe de l'Est (1789–1939)*. Genève: Librairie Droz, 2009.

Debeir, Jean-Claude. "Le problème des exportations de capitaux français de 1919 á 1930. Subsitutions et concurrences." *Relations internationales* 6 (1976): 171–82.

Duroselle, Jean Baptiste. *Politique étrangère de la France: la décadence, 1932–1939*. II. Paris: Éditions du Seuil, 1983.

Eloranta, Jari, Stefan Nikolić, and Flóra Macher. "Between Disintegration and Convergence, 1918–1939: Flows of Capital, Goods, and Labor." In *The Economic History of Central, East, and South-Eastern Europe: 1800 to the Present*, edited by Matthias Morys, 216–42. London and New York: Routledge, 2021.

Evans, Peter B. *Embedded Autonomy: States and Industrial Transformation*. Princeton Paperbacks. Princeton: Princeton University Press, 1995.

Feinstein, Charles H., and Katherine Watson. "Private International Capital Flows in Europe in the Inter-War Period." In *Banking, Currency, and Finance in Europe Between the Wars*, edited by Charles H. Feinstein, 94–130. Oxford University Press, 1995. https://doi.org/10.1093/0198288034.003.0004

Franaszek, Piotr. "Kapitał francuski w procesie centralizacji kapitału w polskim przemyśle naftowym 1920–1939 (koncern naftowy 'Dąbrowa' i grupa 'Małopolska')." *Studia Historyczne* 29, no. 2 (1986): 229–43.

Franaszek, Piotr. "Galicyjski przemysł naftowy do 1914 r. w świetle najnowszych badań." *Rocznik Naukowo Dydaktyczny WSP w Krakowie. Prace Historyczne* 3, no. 126 (1992): 113–35.

Frank, Alison Fleig. *Oil Empire: Visions of Prosperity in Austrian Galicia*. Cambridge, MA: Harvard University Press, 2005.

Freeman, Chris, and Francisco Louçã. *As Time Goes by: From the Industrial Revolutions to the Information Revolution*. Oxford: Oxford University Press, 2001.

Frieden, Jeffry A. "International Investment and Colonial Control: A New Interpretation." *International Organization* 48, no. 4 (1994): 559–93. https://doi.org/10.1017/S0020818300028319

Garlicki, Andrzej. *Józef Piłsudski: 1867–1935*. 3rd ed. Warszawa: Czytelnik, 1990.

Gatejel, Luminița, and Jerzy Kochanowski. "Transport, Infrastructure and Communication." In *The Routledge History Handbook of Central and Eastern Europe in the Twentieth Century: Challenges of Modernity*, edited by Stanislav Holubec,

Władysław Borodziej, and Joachim von Puttkamer, 129–82. London–New York: Routledge, 2020.

Gerschenkron, Alexander. *Economic Backwardness in Historical Perspective: A Book of Essays*. Cambridge, MA: Harvard University, 1962.

Girault, René. *Emprunts russes et investissements francais en Russie, 1887–1914: recherches sur l'investissement international*. Paris: A. Colin, 1973.

Głowiński, Tomasz. *Feliks Młynarski 1884–1972*. Wrocław: Gajt, 2012.

Gołębiowski, Jerzy. *Sektor państwowy w gospodarce Polski międzywojennej*. Warszawa–Kraków: Państwowe Wydawnictwo Naukowe, 1985.

Gołębiowski, Jerzy. *Przemysł wojenny w Polsce 1918–1939*. Kraków: Wydawnictwo Naukowe WSP, 1990.

Górnicki, Leonard. "Kodeks Handlowy." In *Prawo handlowe i gospodarcze II Rzeczypospolitej*, edited by Robert Jastrzębski, 53–120. Warszawa: Wolters Kluwer Polska, 2019.

Grabowski, Tadeusz. *Inwestycje zbrojeniowe w gospodarce Polski międzywojennej*. Warszawa: Wydawnictwo Ministerstwa Obrony Narodowej, 1963.

Grabowski, Tadeusz. *Rola państwa w gospodarce Polski (1918–1928)*. Warszawa: Państwowe Wydawnictwo Ekonomiczne, 1967.

Granovetter, Mark S. *Society and Economy: Framework and Principles*. Cambridge, MA and London: The Belknap Press of Harvard University Press, 2017.

Grant, Jonathan A. *Between Depression and Disarmament: The International Armaments Business, 1919–1939*. Cambridge: Cambridge University Press, 2018. https://doi.org/10.1017/9781108552721

Grzegorz, Piątek. *Miasto, modernizm, modernizacja 1920–1939*. Warszawa: Wydawnictwo WAB, 2022.

Grzyb, Mieczysław. *Narodowościowo-polityczne aspekty przemian stosunków własnościowych i kadrowych w górnośląskim przemyśle w latach 1922–1939*. Katowice: Uniwersytet Śląski, 1978.

Hinkkanen-Lievonen, Merja-Liisa. "Exploited by Britain? The Problems of British Financial Presence in the Baltic States after the First World War." *Journal of Baltic Studies* 14, no. 4 (1983): 328–39. https://doi.org/10.1080/01629778300000341

Hobson, John A. *Imperialism: A Study*. New York: James Pott & Company, 1902.

Holzer, Jerzy. *Mozaika polityczna Drugiej Rzeczypospolitej*. Warszawa: Książka i Wiedza, 1974.

Hovi, Kalervo. *Cordon Sanitaire or Barrière de l'est?: The Emergence of the New French Eastern European Alliance Policy, 1917–1919*. Translated by Sirkka Battarbee and Keith Battarbee. Turku: Turun yliopisto, 1975.

Hovi, Kalervo. *Alliance de Revers: Stabilization of France's Alliance Policies in East Central Europe 1919–1921*. Translated by Kaija London and Gary London. Turku: Turun yliopisto, 1984.

Hübner, Mateusz. *"Pułkownicy": Rdzeń środowiska piłsudczyków w systemie polityczno-ustrojowym II Rzeczypospolitej*. Warszawa: Instytut Pamięci Narodowej, 2020.

James, Harold. *The End of Globalization: Lessons from the Great Depression*. Cambridge, MA and London: Harvard University Press, 2002.

Janus, Piotr. *W nurcie polskiego etatyzmu. Stefan Starzyński i Pierwsza Brygada Gospodarcza 1926–1932*. Kraków: Wydawnictwo Avalon, 2009.

Jaros, Jerzy. *Historia górnictwa węglowego w Zagłębiu Górnośląskim w latach 1914–1945*. Katowice—Kraków: Państwowe Wydawnictwo Naukowe, 1969.

Jasiński, Leszek Jerzy. *Bliżej centrum czy na peryferiach? Polskie kontakty gospodarcze z zagranicą w XX wieku*. Warszawa: Centrum Europejskie Natolin, Wydawnictwo Trio, 2011.

Jastrzębski, Robert. "Prawo handlowe i gospodarcze." In *Prawo handlowe i gospodarcze II Rzeczypospolitej*, edited by Robert Jastrzębski, 21–52. Warszawa: Wolters Kluwer Polska, 2019.

Jedlicki, Jerzy. *Nieudana próba kapitalistycznej industralizacji: analiza państwowego gospodarstwa przemysłowego w Królestwie Polskim XIX w*. Warszawa: Książka i Wiedza, 1964.

Jílek, Lubor. "Impasses d'une «politique Nationale» d'approvisionnement: Capitaux Français Dans Les Pétroles de Galicie 1918–1926." *Relations Internationales* 43 (1985): 323–41.

Jones, Geoffrey. "The end of nationality? Global Firms and 'Borderless Worlds'." *Zeitschrift für Unternehmensgeschichte* 51, no 2 (2006): 149–65. https://doi.org/10.1515/zug-2006-0203

Judson, Pieter M., "Seeing the Habsburg Monarchy as a Global Empire in an Age of Self-Styled Nation-States," *Geschichte Und Region / Storia e Regione* 30, no. 1 (2021): 223–29.

Kaliński, Janusz. "State Entrepreneurship in Interwar Poland." *Studia Historiae Oeconomicae* 41, no. 1 (2023): 43–78. https://doi.org/10.14746/sho.2023.41.1.003

Karaś, Romuald. *Ostatni odruch*. Warszawa: Wydawnictwo Ministerstwa Obrony Narodowej, 1986.

Kasprowicz, Bolesław. "Problemy ekonomiczne budowy i eksploatacji portu w Gdyni w latach 1920–1939." *Zapiski Historyczne* XXII, no. 1–3 (1956): 119–74.

Kawalla, Iwona. "Działalność Polskiego Eksportu Naftowego w latach 1933–1939." In *Kresy Wschodnie. Gospodarcze i społeczne znaczenie polityki kresów*, edited by Tomasz Głowiński. Wrocław: Gajt, 2015.

Kecskés, D. Gusztáv. "East-Central European Nationalities and French Foreign Policy during the First World War." In *Nationalisms in Action: The Great War and Its Aftermath in East-Central Europe*, edited by László Szarka and Attila Pók, translated by Péter Barta, 41–61. Komárom: J. Selye University – Faculty of Education, 2023.

Kecskés, D. Gusztáv. "The Anatomy of an Attempt to Create a Sphere of Influence: French Policy towards Central and Eastern Europe in the 1920s." In *Wars and Betweenness: Big Powers and Middle Europe, 1918-1945*, edited by Aliaksandr Piahanau and Bojan Aleksov, 27–40. Budapest: Central European University Press, 2020.

Keller, Dawid. "Regulator, właściciel czy…? Dyskusje o roli państwa wobec kolei w okresie międzywojennym – wprowadzenie do zagadnienia." In *Państwo wobec kolei żelaznych w Polsce*, edited by Michał Kapias and Dawid Keller. Rybnik: Muzeum w Rybniku, 2017.

Kicinger, Anna. "Polityka migracyjna Polski 1918–2003." PhD, Warsaw University, 2011.

Knakiewicz, Zenobia. *Deflacja polska 1930–1935*. Warszawa: Państwowe Wydawnictwo Ekonomiczne, 1967.

Kofman, Jan. *Economic Nationalism and Development: Central and Eastern Europe between the Two World Wars*. London and New York: Routledge, 2018.

Kofman, Jan. "Koła wielkoprzemysłowe a kwestia kapitałów obcych w okresie 1920–1939." *Kwartalnik Historyczny* 82, no. 2 (1975): 303–20.

Kofman, Jan. "How to Define Economic Nationalism? A Critical Review of Some Old and New Standpoints." In *Economic Nationalism in East Central Europe and South America, 1918–1939*, edited by Henryk Szlajfer. Genève: Librairie Droz, 1990.

Konar, Julian. "Spór o Żyrardów." *Sprawy Międzynarodowe* 16, no. 2 (1963): 76–85.

Konar, Julian. "Strajk w Zakładach Żyrardowskich w 1926 r." In *Z dziejów walk masowych klasy roborniczej w Polsce w latach 1918–1939*, 47–114. Warszawa: Państwowe Wydawnictwo Naukowe, 1964.

Konderski, Wacław. *Z działalności banków polskich w latach 1928-1935: Wspomnienia*. Warszawa: Książka i Wiedza, 1962.

Kotlarz, Grzegorz, Henryk Dąbrowski, and Edward Wieczorek. *Magistrala węglowa: najciekawsze linie kolejowe Polski*. 2nd ed. Rybnik: Eurosprinter, 2017.

Kowalski, Marek Arpad. *Dyskurs kolonialny w Drugiej Rzeczypospolitej*. Warszawa: Wydawnictwo DiG, 2010.

Kuisel, Richard F. *Capitalism and the State in Modern France: Renovation and Economic Management in the Twentieth Century*. Cambridge: Cambridge University Press, 1981.

Kukułka, Józef. *Francja a Polska po Traktacie Wersalskim: 1919–1922*. Warszawa: Książka i Wiedza, 1970.

Kulka, Grzegorz. "Sprawy honorowe gen. Włodzimierza Ostoi-Zagórskiego w latach 1923–1928." *Dzieje Najnowsze* 48, no. 3 (2016): 107. https://doi.org/10.12775/DN.2016.3.06

Laforest, Christophe. "Kulisy zrzeczenia się przez Polskę czwartej raty pożyczki francuskiej w 1925 r." Translated by Maria Pasztor. *Dzieje Najnowsze* 31, no. 3 (1999): 91–99.

Laforest, Christophe. "La Stratégie Française et La Pologne (1919–1939). Aspects Économiques et Implications Politiques." PhD, Université Paris 1 Panthéon-Sorbonne, 2001.

Laforest, Christophe. "La stratégie française et la Pologne (1919–1939). Aspects économiques et implications politiques." *Histoire, économie et société* 22, no. 3 (2003): 395–411. https://doi.org/10.3406/hes.2003.2328

Lamm, Patrick. *Enquête sur l'affaire Boussac*. Paris: Éditions Robert Laffront, 1985.

Lampe John R., and Marvin R. Jackson, *Balkan Economic History, 1550–1950: From Imperial Borderlands to Developing Nations*. Bloomington: Indiana University Press, 1982.

Landau, Zbigniew. *Polskie zagraniczne pożyczki państwowe 1918–1926*. Warszawa: Książka i Wiedza, 1961.

Landau, Zbigniew. "Stosunek rządów pomajowych do napływu kapitałów zagranicznych do Polski." *Śląski Kwartalnik Historyczny Sobótka*, no. 3–4 (1962): 408–25.

Landau, Zbigniew. *Plan Stabilizacyjny 1927–1930. Geneza, Założenia, Wyniki*. Warszawa: Książka i Wiedza, 1963.

Landau, Zbigniew. "Oligarchia finansowa Drugiej Rzeczypospolitej." *Przegląd Historyczny* 62, no. 1 (1971): 75–92.

Landau, Zbigniew. "The Inflow of Foreign Capital into Poland after the Coup d'etat of May 1926." *Acta Poloniae Historica* 46 (1982): 159–77.

Landau, Zbigniew. "Foreign Capital in Poland 1918–1939." *Acta Poloniae Historica* 59 (1989): 55–94.

Landau, Zbigniew. *Bank Gospodarstwa Krajowego*. Warszawa: Oficyna Wydawnicza SGH, 1998.

Landau, Zbigniew, and Jerzy Tomaszewski. *Kapitały obce w Polsce 1918–1939: materiały i dokumenty*. Warszawa: Książka i Wiedza, 1964.

Landau, Zbigniew, and Jerzy Tomaszewski. *Gospodarka Polski miedzywojennej 1918–1939. Vol. 1: W dobie inflacji 1918–1923*. Warszawa: Książka i Wiedza, 1967.

Landau, Zbigniew, and Jerzy Tomaszewski. *Anonimowi władcy: z dziejów kapitału obcego w Polsce: 1918–1939*. Warszawa: Wiedza Powszechna, 1968.

Landau, Zbigniew, and Jerzy Tomaszewski. *Gospodarka Polski miedzywojennej 1918-1939. Vol 3: Wielki kryzys 1930–1935*. Warszawa: Książka i Wiedza, 1982.

Landau, Zbigniew, and Jerzy Tomaszewski. *Sprawa żyrardowska. Przyczynek do dziejów kapitałów obcych w Polsce międzywojennej*. Warszawa: Książka i Wiedza, 1983.

Łaptos, Józef, and Mariusz W. Majewski. "Francuska pomoc w wyposażeniu armii polskiej (1919–1939)." *Annales Universitatis Paedagogicae Cracoviensis. Studia Historica* 14 (2013): 102–16.

Łazor, Jerzy. "Kapitał francuski w Polsce międzywojennej. Stan badań i postulaty badawcze." *UR Journal of Humanities and Social Sciences* 4, no. 1(10) (2019): 29–52. https://doi.org/10.15584/johass.2019.1.3

Łazor, Jerzy. "'Broń dyplomatyczna pierwszej rangi?' Powstanie polsko-francuskiego Banku Śląskiego SA po I wojnie światowej." *Roczniki Dziejów Społecznych i Gospodarczych* 81 (2020a): 289–320. http://doi.org/10.12775/RDSG.2020.10

Łazor, Jerzy. "Wpływ kapitału francuskiego na modernizację Polski międzywojennej." In *Przemiany modernizacyjne w Drugiej Rzeczypospolitej*, edited by Paweł Grata, 195–209. Rzeszów: Wydawnictwo Uniwersytetu Rzeszowskiego, 2020b.

Łazor, Jerzy. "Pierwsza francusko–polska koncesja kolejowa z 1924 r. Przyczynek do relacji finansowo-gospodarczych Polski i Francji po pierwszej wojnie światowej." *Kwartalnik Historyczny* 128, no. 3 (2021): 785–812. http://doi.org/10.12775/KH.2021.128.3.03

Łazor, Jerzy. "'A Colony of Alien Capital.' French Investments, Polish Identity, and a Story of Murder in 1930s Warsaw." *Slavic Review* 81, no. 1 (2022a): 122–41. https://doi.org/10.1017/slr.2022.79

Łazor, Jerzy. "Kto ma budować Gdynię? Wpływ władz w Paryżu na kształt konsorcjum francusko–polskiego." *Dzieje Najnowsze* 54, no. 3 (2022b): 5–26. https://doi.org/10.12775/DN.2022.3.01

Łazor, Jerzy. "French Capital, Gdynia, and the Position of Polish Coal on International Markets in the Interwar Period." In *Fueling the World Economy: Seaports, Coal, and Oil Markets during the Early Globalization*, edited by Daniel Castillo Hidalgo and Cézar Honorato, 99–121. Cham: Palgrave Macmillan, 2023. https://doi.org/10.1007/978-3-031-32565-6_6

Łazor, Jerzy. "Francuskie inwestycje w polskim sektorze naftowym w okresie międzywojennym." In *Pieniądz, historia, polityka. Studia ofiarowane prof. dr. hab. Wojciechowi Morawskiemu w 70. rocznicę urodzin*. edited by Łukasz Dwilewicz and Jerzy Łazor. Warszawa: Oficyna Wydawnicza SGH, 2024.

Łazor, Jerzy, and Bogdan Murgescu. "Economic Development." In *The Routledge History Handbook of Central and Eastern Europe in the Twentieth Century: Challenges of Modernity*, edited by Stanislav Holubec, Władysław Borodziej, and Joachim von Puttkamer, 313–84. London–New York: Routledge, 2020.

Leszczyńska, Cecylia. *Polska polityka pieniężna i walutowa w latach 1924–1936: w systemie Gold Exchange Standard*. Warszawa: Wydawnictwo Uniwersytetu Warszawskiego, 2013.

Leszczyńska, Cecylia. "Level of Living of Polish Citizens in the Interwar Period, and Its Diversification." *Roczniki Dziejów Społecznych i Gospodarczych* 76 (December 1, 2016): 93. https://doi.org/10.12775/RDSG.2016.04

Leszczyński, Adam. *Leap into Modernity: Political Economy of Growth on the Periphery, 1943–1980*. Frankfurt am Main: Peter Lang Edition, 2017.

Lethbridge, Eric. "National Income and Product." In *The Economic History of Eastern Europe 1919–1975, v. I. Economic Structure and Performance Between the Two Wars*, edited by Michael Charles Kaser and E.A. Radice, 532–97. Oxford: Clarendon Press, 1985.

Lipson, Charles. *Standing Guard: Protecting Foreign Capital in the Nineteenth and Twentieth Centuries*. Berkeley: University of California Press, 1985.

Luszniewicz, Jacek. "Etatism of the Economy of the Second Polish Republic in the Period of Parliamentary Democracy: Conditions, Stages, Evaluation (Part 2: 1923–1926)." *Studia i Prace KES* 9 4, no. (36) (2018a): 65–84.

Luszniewicz, Jacek. "Etatism of the Economy of the Second Polish Republic in the Period of Parliamentary Democracy: Conditions, Stages, Evaluation (Part 1: 1918–1923)." *Studia i Prace KES* 9 3 no. (35) (2018b): 35–60.

Madajczyk, Czesław. "Spory wokół sprawy elektryfikacji Polski (1926–1930)." *Najnowsze Dzieje Polski: materiały i studia z okresu 1914–1939* 5 (1962): 153–220.

Maddison Project Database, version 2020. Jutta Bolt, and Jan Luiten van Zanden, "Maddison Style Estimates of the Evolution of the World Economy. A New 2020 Update." *Maddison-Project Working Paper* WP-15, 2020.

Majcher-Ociesa, Edyta. *Interwencjonizm państwowy w przemyśle Drugiej Rzeczypospolitej w latach 1930–1939*. Kielce: Kieleckie Towarzystwo Naukowe, 2019.

Majewski, Mariusz W. "Początki produkcji silników lotniczych w II Rzeczypospolitej (1921–1926)." *Annales Universitatis Paedagogicae Cracoviensis. Studia Historica* 2, no. 17 (2003): 201–21.

Majewski, Mariusz W. "Druga próba uruchomienia produkcji silników lotniczych Polskie Zakłady Škody (1926–1935)." *Annales Universitatis Paedagogicae Cracoviensis. Studia Historica* 4, no. 28 (2005): 148–65.

Majewski, Mariusz W. "Poszukiwania złóż ropy naftowej i gazu w Polsce (1919–1939)." *Annales Universitatis Paedagogicae Cracoviensis. Studia Historica* 8 (2009): 129–54.

Majewski, Mariusz W. "Rozwój motoryzacji w Polsce w latach 1919–1930." *Annales Universitatis Paedagogicae Cracoviensis. Studia Historica* 9, no. 78 (2010): 56–77.

Majewski, Mariusz W. "Eksploatacja licencji motoryzacyjnych w Państwowych Zakładach Inżynierii (1930–1936)." *Annales Universitatis Paedagogicae Cracoviensis. Studia Historica* 10, no. 95 (2011): 82–98. https://doi.org/10.24917/2918

Marguerat, Philippe. "Les investissements français dans le Bassin danubien durant l'entre-deux-guerres: pour une nouvelle interprétation." *Revue historique* 39, no. 1 (2004): 121–62. https://doi.org/10.3917/rhis.041.0121

Masyk, Roman. "Zagadnienie czystych producentów ropy w II Rzeczypospolitej." In *Pieniądz, historia, polityka. Studia ofiarowane prof. dr. hab. Wojciechowi Morawskiemu w 70. rocznicę urodzin*, edited by Łukasz Dwilewicz and Jerzy Łazor (Warszawa: Oficyna Wydawnicza SGH, 2024, forthcoming).

Mazur, Wojciech. *Pod wiatr. Francja i lotnictwo wojskowe II Rzeczypospolitej (1921–1938)*. Kraków: Ksiegarnia Akademicka Publishing, 2015. https://doi.org/10.12797/9788376386577

Mclean, David. "Finance and 'Informal Empire' before the First World War." *The Economic History Review* 29, no. 2 (1976): 291–305.

Mędrzecki, Włodzimierz. *Kresowy kalejdoskop: wędrówki przez ziemie wschodnie Drugiej Rzeczypospolitej 1918-1939*. Kraków: Wydawnictwo Literackie, 2018.

Meyer, Richard Hemmig. *Bankers' Diplomacy; Monetary Stabilization in the Twenties*. New York: Columbia University Press, 1970.

Michowicz, Waldemar. "Afera żyrardowska z 1934 r. Przyczynek do działalności kapitału francuskiego w Polsce." *Zeszyty Naukowe Uniwersytetu Łódzkiego. Seria I. Nauki Humanistyczne* 21 (1961): 155–70.

Michowicz, Waldemar. "Międzynarodowe tło tzw. afery żyrardowskiej 1934 r." In *Żyrardów 1829–1945*, edited by Iwona Pietrzak-Pawłowska, 241–56. Warszawa: Państwowe Wydawnictwo Naukowe, 1980.

Mielczarek, Ryszard. *Budowa portu handlowego w Gdyni w latach 1924–1939*. Gdańsk: Instytut Kaszubski, 2001.

Mihout-Natar, Mylène. "L'intervention Des Capitaux Français Dans La Pologne de La Seconde République (1918–1939): Contribution à l'histoire de l'impérialisme Économique Français En Europe Centrale." PhD, Université Charles de Gaulle – Lille III, 2002.

Mitchell, Brian R. *International historical statistics: Europe 1750–1993*. Basingstoke: Macmillan Press, 1998.

Morawski, Wojciech. *Słownik historyczny bankowości polskiej do 1939 roku*. Warszawa: Muza SA, 1998.

Morawski, Wojciech. *Od marki do złotego. Historia finansów Drugiej Rzeczypospolitej*. Warszawa: Wydawnictwo Naukowe PWN, 2008.

Morawski, Wojciech. "Galicyjskie zagłębia naftowe." In *Problemy energetyczne Polski. Część I: Surowce*, edited by Anna Jarosz-Nojszewska and Wojciech Morawski, 33–50. Warszawa: Oficyna Wydawnicza SGH, 2016.

Murgescu, Bogdan. "Anything but Simple: The Case of the Romanian Oil Industry." In *History and Culture of Economic Nationalism in East Central Europe*, edited by Helga Schultz and Eduard Kubů, 231–50. Berlin: Berliner Wissenschafts-Verlag, 2006.

Murgescu, Bogdan. "Economic Revival in East Central Europe after the Great War." In *A New Europe, 1918–1923: Instability, Innovation, Recovery*, edited by Bartosz Dziewanowski-Stefańczyk and Jay M. Winter, 69–81. London and New York: Routledge, 2022.

Nayberg, Roberto. "La politique française du pétrole à l'issue de la première guerre mondiale: perspectives et solutions." *Guerres mondiales et conflits contemporains* 4, no. 224 (2006): 111–33.

Nolan, Peter, Jin Zhang, and Chunhang Liu. "The Global Business Revolution, the Cascade Effect, and the Challenge for Firms from Developing Countries." *Cambridge Journal of Economics* 32, no. 1 (2007): 29–47. https://doi.org/10.1093/cje/bem016

Nötel, Rudolf. "International Capital Movements and Finance in Eastern Europe 1919–1949." *VSWG: Vierteljahrschrift Für Sozial – Und Wirtschaftsgeschichte* 61, no. 1 (1974): 65–112.

Nötel, Rudolf. "International Credit and Finance." In *The Economic History of Eastern Europe 1919–1975, v. II. Interwar Policy, The War, and Reconstruction*, edited by Michael Charles Kaser and E.A. Radice, 170–295. Oxford: Clarendon Press, 1986.

Nowicki, Józef. *Teoria ekonomii II Rzeczypospolitej*. Warszawa: Książka i Wiedza, 1988.

Pasztor, Maria. "Główne elementy obrazu Polaka w oczach francuskich elit politycznych w okresie międzywojennym." *Dzieje Najnowsze* 31, no. 3 (1999a): 113–26.

Pasztor, Maria. *Polska w oczach francuskich kół rządowych w latach 1924–1939*. Warszawa: Wydawnictwo Akademickie Dialog, 1999b.

Patelski, Mariusz. "Henry Le Rond – generał (prawie) nieznany." *Indeks* 9–10 (2004/2003): 57–60.

Perez, Carlota. *Technological Revolutions and Financial Capital: The Dynamics of Bubbles and Golden Ages*. Cheltenham: Edward Elgar, 2002.
Piątek, Grzegorz. *Sanator. Kariera Stefana Starzyńskiego*. Warszawa: W.A.B., 2016.
Pietrzak-Pawłowska, Irena. "Zagłębie Dąbrowskie i Okręg Loary: penetracja kapitałów francuskich po 1870 r." *Kwartalnik Historyczny* 72, no. 4 (1965): 785–809.
Pietrzak-Pawłowska, Irena. "Les investissements français en Pologne." In *La position internationale de la France: aspects économiques et financiers, XIXe–XXe siècles*, edited by Maurice Lévy-Leboyer, 319–24. Paris: Éditions de l'École des hautes études en sciences sociales, 1977.
Pochna, Marie-France. *Bonjour, monsieur Boussac*. Paris: R. Laffont Opera mundi, 1980.
Porter-Szűcs, Brian. *Poland in the Modern World: Beyond Martyrdom*. Chichester: Wiley-Blackwell, 2014.
Prados de la Escosura, Leandro "World Human Development: 1870–2007," *Review of Income and Wealth* 61, no. 2 (2015): 220–47. https://doi.org/10.1111/roiw.12104
Przegiętka, Marcin. *Komunikacja i polityka: Transport kolejowy i drogowy w stosunkach polsko-niemieckich w latach 1918–1939*. Warszawa: Instytut Pamięci Narodowej, 2015.
Przemysław, Dąbrowski, "'Panama żyrardowska' w okresie dwudziestolecia międzywojennego." *Studia Iuridica Lublinensia* 21(2014): 11–31.
Przewłocki, Jan. *Wojciech Korfanty: polityka, wzloty i niepowodzenia*. Kielce: Szumacher, 1993.
Puchalski, Piotr. *Poland in a Colonial World Order: Adjustments and Aspirations, 1918–1939*. London and New York: Routledge, 2022.
Puś, Wiesław. *Przemysł Królestwa Polskiego w latach 1870–1914. Problemy struktury i koncentracji*. Łódź: Uniwersytet Łódzki, 1984.
Putnam, Robert D. "Diplomacy and Domestic Politics: The Logic of Two-Level Games." *International Organization* 42, no. 3 (1988): 427–60.
Reckendrees, Alfred, Boris Gehlen, and Christian Marx. "International Business, Multinational Enterprises and Nationality of the Company: A Constructive Review of Literature." *Business History* 64, no. 9 (2022): 1567–99. https://doi.org/10.1080/00076791.2022.2118718
Reinert, Erik S. *How Rich Countries Got Rich – and Why Poor Countries Stay Poor*. London: Constable, 2007.
Relich, Mariusz. "Załamanie motoryzacji w Polsce na skutek tzw. demotoryzacji kraju w latach 1931–1935 i próby jej odbudowy w drugiej połowie lat 30. XX wieku." In *Na lądzie, w wodzie i w powietrzu…Z dziejów transportu i komunikacji na ziemiach polskich na przestrzeni wieków*, edited by Tomasz Głowiński and Robert Klementowski, 201–12. Wrocław: Gajt, 2014.
Rigó, Máté. *Capitalism in Chaos: How the Business Elites of Europe Prospered in the Era of the Great War*. Ithaca and London: Cornell University Press, 2022.
Rosenberg, Emily S. and Norman L. Rosenberg. "From Colonialism to Professionalism: The Public-Private Dynamic in United States Foreign Financial Advising, 1898–1929." *The Journal of American History* 74, no. 1 (1987): 59–82.
Roszkowski, Wojciech. "The Growth of the State Sector in the Polish Economy in the Years 1918–1926." *Journal of European Economic History* 18, no. 1 (1989): 105–26.
Roszkowski, Wojciech. *Land Reforms in East Central Europe after World War One*. Warsaw: Institute of Political Studies, Polish Academy of Sciences, 1995.
Ryszka, Franciszek. "Przywileje kapitału zagranicznego w Polsce burżuazyjno-obszarniczej." *Czasopismo Prawno-Historyczne* 6, no. 1 (1954): 302–48.

Schramm, Tomasz. *Francuskie misje wojskowe w państwach Europy Środkowej: 1919–1939*. Poznań: Uniwersytet Adama Mickiewicza, 1987.
Seidler, Roman. "Bilans płatniczy polski za rok 1928." *Kwartalnik Statystyczny* 7, no. 4 (1930): 1469–1541.
Skiba, Jakub. "Polska polityka finansowa wobec zbrojeń w latach 1935–1939." In *Pieniądz, historia, polityka. Studia ofiarowane prof. dr. hab. Wojciechowi Morawskiemu w 70. rocznicę urodzin*, edited by Łukasz Dwilewicz and Jerzy Łazor. Warszawa: Oficyna Wydawnicza SGH, forthcoming in 2024.
Smerek, Mieczysław. "Bilans płatniczy Polski za rok 1929." *Kwartalnik Statystyczny* 8, no. 1 (1930): 169–329.
Smerek, Mieczysław. "Bilans płatniczy Polski za rok 1930." *Statystyka Polski*, Seria B 17 (1933): 1–87.
Sosnowska, Anna. *Explaining Economic Backwardness: Post-1945 Polish Historians on Eastern Europe*. Translated by Jasper Tilbury and Anna Sosnowska. Budapest: Central European University Press, 2019.
Soutou, Georges-Henri. "La politique économique de la France en Pologne (1920–1924)." *Revue Historique* 251, no. 1 (1974): 85–116.
Soutou, Georges-Henri. "L'impérialisme du pauvre: la politique économique du gouvernement français en Europe Centrale et Orientale de 1918 à 1929. Essai d'interprétation." *Relations internationales* 3, no. 7 (1976): 219–39.
Soutou, Georges-Henri. "L'Alliance franco-polonaise (1925–1933): ou Comment s'en débarrasser." *Revue d'Histoire Diplomatique* 95, nos. 2–4 (1981): 295–348.
Spaulding, Robert Mark. *Osthandel and Ostpolitik: German Foreign Trade Policies in Eastern Europe from Bismarck to Adenauer*. Providence, RI: Berghahn Books, 1997.
Staphe, Christian. *Ma vie avec Boussac le "Vosgien"*. Haroué: Gérard Louis, 2017.
Stawecki, Piotr. "Pożyczka francuska z 1936 roku." *Kwartalnik Historyczny*, no. 1 (1967): 49–68.
Stevenson, David. "France at the Paris Peace Conference. Addressing the Dilemmas of Security." In *French Foreign and Defence Policy, 1918–40: The Decline and Fall of a Great Power*, edited by Robert Boyce, 10–29. London and New York: Routledge, 1998.
Stiglitz, Joseph E., and Bruce C. Greenwald. *Creating a Learning Society: A New Paradigm for Development and Social Progress*. New York: Columbia University Press, 2014. https://doi.org/10.7312/stig15214
Stone, Daniel. "The Giesche Company: Anaconda Copper's Subsidiary in Interwar Poland." *Slavic Review* 56, no. 4 (1997): 679–97. https://doi.org/10.2307/2502117
Szlajfer, Henryk. "Economic Nationalism of the Peripheries as a Research Problem." In *Economic Nationalism in East Central Europe and South America, 1918–1939*, edited by Henryk Szlajfer, 55–130. Genève: Librairie Droz, 1990a.
Szlajfer, Henryk. "Editor's Introduction." In *Economic Nationalism in East Central Europe and South America, 1918-1939*, edited by Henryk Szlajfer. Genève: Librairie Droz, 1990b.
Szmidtke, Zenon. *"Skarboferm" 1922–1939: związki polityki z gospodarką*. Opole: Państwowy Instytut Naukowy, 2005.
Teichova, Alice. *An Economic Background to Munich: International Business and Czechoslovakia 1918–1938*. London: Cambridge University Press, 1974.
Teichova, Alice. "Industry." In *The Economic History of Eastern Europe 1919–1975, t. I. Economic Structure and Performance*, edited by Michael Charles Kaser and E.A. Radice, 222–322. Oxford: Clarendon Press, 1986.

Thomas, Martin. "French Empire Elites and the Politics of Economic Obligation in the Interwar Years." *The Historical Journal 52*, no. 4 (December 2009): 989–1016. https://doi.org/10.1017/S0018246X09990379

Todd, David. *A Velvet Empire: French Informal Imperialism in the Nineteenth Century*. Princeton: Princeton University Press, 1978.

Tomaszewski, Jerzy. "Economic Differentiation and the National Question in Poland in the Twentieth Century." In *Economic Change and the National Question in Twentieth-Century Europe*, edited by Alice Teichova, Herbert Matis, and Jaroslav Pátek, 338–56. Cambridge, U.K.; New York: Cambridge University Press, 2000.

Tooley, T. Hunt. *National Identity and Weimar Germany: Upper Silesia and the Eastern Border, 1918–1922*. Lincoln: University of Nebraska Press, 1997.

Toye, John, and Richard Toye. "The Origins and Interpretation of the Prebisch-Singer Thesis." *History of Political Economy* 35, no. 3 (2003): 437–67. https://doi.org/10.1215/00182702-35-3-437

Trachtenberg, Marc. *Reparation in World Politics: France and European Economic Diplomacy, 1916–1923*. New York: Columbia University Press, 1980.

Valerio, Lenny A. Ureña. *Colonial Fantasies, Imperial Realities: Race Science and the Making of Polishness on the Fringes of the German Empire, 1840–1920*. Athens, OH: Ohio University Press, 2019.

Vernon, Raymond. "International Investment and International Trade in the Product Cycle." *The Quarterly Journal of Economics* 80, no. 2 (1966): 190–207. https://doi.org/10.2307/1880689

Wallerstein, Immanuel. *World-Systems Analysis. An Introduction*. Durham and London: Duke University Press, 2004.

Wandycz, Piotr Stefan. *France and Her Eastern Allies 1919–1925: French-Czechoslovak-Polish Relations from the Paris Peace Conference to Locarno*. Minneapolis: The University of Minnesota Press, 1962.

Wandycz, Piotr Stefan. *The Twilight of French Eastern Alliances, 1926–1936: French-Czechoslovak-Polish Relations from Locarno to the Remilitarization of the Rhineland*. Princeton: Princeton University Press, 1988.

Wellisz, Leopold. *Foreign Capital in Poland*. London: George Allen & Unwin, 1938.

Wiarda, Howard J. *Corporatism and Comparative Politics: The Other Great "Ism"*. Armonk: M.E. Sharpe, 1997. https://doi.org/10.4324/9781315481050

Wilkins, Mira. *The Maturing of Multinational Enterprise: American Business Abroad from 1914 to 1970*. Cambridge, MA: Harvard University Press, 1974.

Włudyka, Tadeusz. *"Trzecia droga" w myśli gospodarczej II Rzeczpospolitej: koncepcje Adama Doboszyńskiego a program obozu narodowego*. Kraków: Universitas, 1994.

Wójcik, Teodor. "Centralne Warsztaty Samochodowe w Warszawie w latach 1918–1928: Przyczynek do genezy polskiej motoryzacji." *Przegląd Historyczno-Wojskowy* 14, no. 65, no. 2 (2013): 187–95.

Wolf, Nikolaus. "Should I Stay or Should I Go? Understanding Poland's Adherence to Gold, 1928–1936." *Historical Social Research* 32, no. 4 (2007): 351–68.

Wolff, Larry. *Inventing Eastern Europe: The Map of Civilization on the Mind of the Enlightenment*. Stanford: Stanford University Press, 1994.

Yergin, Daniel. *The Prize: The Epic Quest for Oil, Money, and Power*. New York: Simon & Schuster, 1991.

Żarnowski, Janusz. *Polska 1918–1939: praca, technika, społeczeństwo*. 2nd ed. Warszawa: Książka i Wiedza, 1999.

Zarycki, Tomasz. *Ideologies of Eastness in Central and Eastern Europe*. London and New York: Routledge, 2014.

Index

Pages in **bold** refer to tables and pages followed by "n" refer to notes.

www.ingramcontent.com/pod-product-compliance
Ingram Content Group UK Ltd.
Pitfield, Milton Keynes, MK11 3LW, UK
UKHW020004200926
475702UK00015B/2463
* 9 7 8 1 0 3 2 4 5 1 4 3 5 *